Prospective Theory

**Appreciative Inquiry: Toward a
Methodology for Understanding and
Enhancing Organizational Innovation**

Prospective Theory

Appreciative Inquiry: Toward a Methodology for Understanding and Enhancing Organizational Innovation

David L. Cooperrider

Dissertation Abstract *Appreciative Inquiry: Toward a Methodology for Understanding and Enhancing Organizational Innovation* by David Loy Cooperrider was first published August 19, 1985.

ISBN 13: 978-1-7348450-1-3

Publisher's Acknowledgements:
Book and cover design by Debbi Stocco
Book editing by Janet Musick
Cover photo by *Alma Thomas

*Alma Woodsey Thomas was an African-American artist and is now recognized as a major American painter of the 20th century. Thomas is best known for the "exuberant", colorful, abstract, and expressionist paintings such as the one on our cover called "Eclipse." We chose the cover and the metaphor of eclipse because it represents the paramount aim in prospective theory building. As a form of engaged scholarship the call to prospective theory is to use the power of ideas, grounded research, and our future-forming theoretical imagination and mind to conceptually *establish-the-new* and *eclipse-the-old*, seeking to open the future to new and better possibilities, for enlivenment, and for building a better world toward full-spectrum flourishing.

Printed in the United States

Preface

With an Expanded Contemporary Introduction on Prospective Theory

IT'S BEEN NEARLY 40 YEARS since my PhD research was launched in 1980 at the world-renowned Cleveland Clinic, today a leading 21st century health system that's one of the most advanced medical centers technologically, scientifically, and organizationally in terms of *relationship-centered care* ever created. It totals more than 8 million patient visits annually and has more than 67,500 employees, a figure that includes more than 17,000 registered nurses and advanced practice providers, and more than 4,520 physicians and scientists in 140 specialties. Among a myriad of distinctive accolades, the Cleveland Clinic is now celebrated as the #1 heart center in the world and it became, as a direct extension our work, the first healthcare provider in the United States to become a signatory to the United Nations Global Compact.

When the dissertation *Appreciative Inquiry: Toward a Methodology for Understanding and Enhancing Organizational Innovation* was defended in 1985, no one suspected that decades later an online search of the term "Appreciative Inquiry" would return nearly 8 million "hits" or that the Cleveland Clinic in terms of size as well as its medical breakthroughs would experience exponential 10x growth. Later, I will share Dr. William Kiser's recent words about the deep impact of appreciative inquiry. Dr. Bill Kiser was the CEO and Chairman of the Board of Governors and years later he spoke at our university. He described how appreciative inquiry peered into the soul of the organization while creating a compelling logic and language for the "egalitarian group practice." The multi-year research project set up a deeply developmental organizational stage, he remarked, for one of "the institution's eras of greatest growth."

My overarching aim with the dissertation was to propose the vision and conceptual logic of Appreciative Inquiry ("AI") as a research methodology whereupon the knowledge interest was not intervention but a new form of future-forming or prospective theory. The theory building's primary task would be one of anticipation and projecting possibilities for betterment. AI was intended as an approach to "a humanly significant science" that could, in a rigorous and multi-methodological way bridge the realms of the sacred and secular, aesthetics and empiricism, and eclipse the human science theory or practice divide, not by emphasizing more action but by arguing for magnitudes more, not less, of a focus on theory-building itself. For many, the idea of more theory for more relevance, was paradoxical. For others, especially practitioners, it was a complete contradiction. But for me it was about, as Alfred North Whitehead once wrote, "the adventure of ideas."[1]

Early on in the dissertation I wrote:[2]

"Virtually unexamined...are the diverse and intricate ways in which theory is creative of the social-organizational future and hence, how science can play a more collaborative role in the conscious evolution of culture...as a vehicle for human development and social-organizational transformation (p. ii.)."

Later the dissertation, the heart of it, began to define appreciative inquiry:

---

1. Whitehead, A. N. (1967). *Adventure of Ideas*. New York: The Free Press.

2. Cooperrider, D. (1986). *Appreciative Inquiry: Toward a Methodology for Understanding and Enhancing Organizational Innovation.* See pages ii, 5, and 47 in the original dissertation.

"Appreciative inquiry is presented here as a mode of action-research that meets the criteria of science as spelled out in generative-theoretical terms. Going beyond questions of epistemology, appreciative inquiry has as its basis a metaphysical concern: it posits that social existence as such is a miracle that can never be fully comprehended... Serious consideration and reflection on the ultimate mystery of being engenders a reverence for life that draws the researcher to inquire beyond superficial appearances to deeper levels of the life-generating essentials and potentials of social existence (p. 5)."

"In contrast to a type of research that is lived without a sense of mystery, the appreciative mode awakens the desire to create and discover new social possibilities that can enrich our existence and give it meaning. In this sense, appreciative inquiry seeks an imaginative and fresh perception of organizations as 'ordinary magic,' as if seen for the first time...an inquiry that takes nothing for granted, searching to apprehend the basis of organizational life and working to articulate those possibilities giving witness to a better existence (p. 47)."

Did you notice the focus in each of these passages? Firstly, it is quite clear that there is the spotlight on theory and research. Secondly, there is the conspicuous absence of virtually any mention of organization development (OD) practice. Yet, to this day, even amidst AI's astonishing spread and growth, the paramount secret of appreciative inquiry was and still is this: that Appreciative Inquiry was not intended as a tool for doing the work of organization development and human systems change.[3] Likewise, if there is a slight bit of unease or disappointment, it is that very few of the thousands of applications today, admittedly even my own, go to the radical depth of knowledge creation exemplified in the original writing. The key

---

3. Frank Barrett shares the important story of "the lost minor detail" about the original dissertation intention. He overcomes the seeming paradox of the focus on theory *or* practice by creatively calling me "a theoretical activist." See Barrett, F. (2017) "David L. Cooperrider: The Articulator of Appreciative Inquiry" in Szabla, D. & Pasmore, et. al. (Eds.), *The Palgrave Handbook of Organizational Change Thinkers.* New York: Palgrave Macmillan.
https://link.springer.com/referenceworkentry/10.1007%2F978-3-319-49820-1_36-2

concept of AI as a theory-building method for the collaborative construction of a better future has for too long been glossed over in the rush to take the gift of AI into the applied world of practice. The dissertation directly, not incidentally, focused on appreciative inquiry as a research method: "as a mode of conducting action-research that meets the criteria of science as spelled out in generative-theoretical terms." But now one caveat is required. My goal here in shedding light on this lost "minor detail" is not at all to depreciate the practice view of AI whose message and methods have spread around the world. The global reception and reach of AI, in its applied practice form, has been wonderfully humbling and heartening. Consider observations and remarks like these, drawn from a wide array of scholars, executives, and world leaders:

"I would like to commend you for your methodology of Appreciative Inquiry and to thank you for introducing it to the United Nations. Without this, it would have been very difficult, perhaps even impossible, to constructively engage so many leaders of business, civil society, and government."

> – United Nations Secretary General and Nobel Laureate Kofi Annan, (in his letter to David Cooperrider)

"Appreciative Inquiry is revolutionizing the field of organization development and change."

> – Professor Robert Quinn, University of Michigan in *Change the World: How Ordinary People Can Accomplish Extraordinary Things*

"The invention of Appreciative Inquiry aligns seamlessly with the science of positive emotions and positive psychology and is an exemplary means to leverage the fruits of this science for the greater good."

> – Barbara L. Frederickson, Kenan Professor, University of North Carolina and Tang Prize Laureate for Highest Achievement in Field of Psychology

"Appreciative Inquiry, as I'm learning it, supports our altruistic nature, our compassion for others, including more secure and positive states where people express more tolerance and greater willingness to help one another... it diminishes our destructive emotions; the moment you think of others, your mind widens."

> – His Holiness the Dalai Lama,
>   The United Religions Initiative Interfaith Summit in Jerusalem

"Appreciative Inquiry is the best large group method in the world today."

> – Rodrigo Loures, CEO Nutrimental Foods and Former Chair of the Brazil President's Council for National Industrial Competitiveness

"AI re-balances the polarity between deficit and strength-based approaches to transformational change, between love and fear as motivating forces for learning and growth. This is much needed in our world today. It has been the easiest innovation to be adopted by my McKinsey colleagues globally...Generations to come will benefit from this legacy."

> – Johanne Lavoie, Partner, McKinsey and Company

Observations like these on the applied practice of AI are not atypical.[4] Quite the contrary. Today AI's approach to life—inspired instead of problematizing and technocratic change, is being practiced everywhere: the corporate world, the world of public service, of economics, of education, of faith, of philanthropy, and social science scholarship—it affects them all. In his New York Times best-selling leadership book, Marcus

---

4. On the practice side, Bob Stiller, the CEO of Green Mountain Coffee Roasters, used appreciative inquiry to advance sustainable enterprise—going green and leveraging business as a force for societal good—and for building everything from corporate strategy to a high purpose culture. When Bob started using appreciative inquiry, the company was little known and relatively small; it had $150 million in sales. A little over a decade later, it was valued as a $24 billion dollar company. Bob's life was touched by appreciative inquiry and the company was named most ethical corporation in the world repeatedly. Bob decided appreciative inquiry should be made available to all young business students, entrepreneurs, and future leaders so he gave a transformative gift to Champlain College, establishing the *David L. Cooperrider for Appreciative Inquiry* at the Stiller School of Business. Here are some of the quotes and experiences leaders have shared related to Appreciative Inquiry: see https://www.champlain.edu/ai-home/what-is-appreciative-inquiry/praise-for-appreciative-inquiry.

Buckingham concluded that AI, in a three-legged stool image, was one crucial leg of the three most important catalysts for "the strengths revolution" in management. Beyond what he called the seminal work of appreciative inquiry, the other critical sources of the strengths revolution included Peter Drucker's classic, *The Effective Executive,* and Martin Seligman's human science call for a field of "positive psychology" in 2000. Together, appreciative inquiry, Drucker's management theory, and positive psychology were synergistically generative and they propelled vast new vistas for a society-wide, positive-strengths movement, as Buckingham declared: "because it works."[5]

Today, for the practitioner, there are more than 290 books that touch on and speak to the practices of AI in and across many domains in organization development and the field of change management. There are books for families and teachers; for leadership development and executive coaching; for advances in applied positive psychology; for evaluation studies; for second generation forms of action research; for enriching design thinking; for building corporate strategy and deeply developmental organizations; for advancing sustainable economic development; for working with whole cities and entire industries; for advancing democratic practices and participatory rural development; for helping to create the field of positive peacebuilding and advancing interfaith dialogue; for enriching experiential learning methods; for designing flourishing enterprise and positive institutions; for advancing social constructionist practices and narrative therapy; and for helping to build the domain of large group methods and "whole systems" change. And again, celebrating the applied practice side of the equation, Kenneth Gergen writes:

---

5. Buckingham, M. (2006). *Go Put Your Strengths to Work*. New York, NY: Free Press. On pages 1-2 Buckingham writes: "It's hard to trace the source of the strengths movement. Some will identify Peter Drucker, citing his seminal 1966 book, *The Effective Executive*, in which he wrote: 'The effective executive builds on strengths—their own strengths, the strengths of superiors, colleagues, subordinates; and on the strengths of the situation...' Some will cite a 1987 article that launched a new discipline called *Appreciative Inquiry*, whose basic premise, according to its founder, David Cooperrider, was 'to build organizations around what works rather than fix what doesn't.' Some will make reference to Dr. Martin Seligman's 1999 speech after becoming president of the American Psychological Association."

"The growth and application of Appreciative Inquiry over the past two decades has been nothing short of phenomenal. It is arguably the most powerful process of positive organizational change ever devised."[6]

Enter the 2020s and the Call to Reclaim AI's Superpower: Toward Prospective Theory

For reasons that are a mystery to me, here we are in the early months of the 2020s and I've never, in one year, received more requests for copies of the original work—the dissertation itself. One hypothesis is that a very recent and popular blog post, "Appreciative Inquiry in a Broken World," seems to have touched a chord. It received more than 7,000 likes in a matter of days, and I soon published it in a refereed journal with my great colleague Ron Fry in the Journal of Applied Behavioral Science (Cooperrider and Fry, 2020.)[7] One citation in that article made reference to the early dissertation while also making it available as a dusty download. And people did.

Soon I was receiving emails. It's important to note that tremendous turbulence of the moment was one of unprecedented dislodgement. Like dials on a seismograph, the opening scenes of the 2020s arrived, as we all experienced it, as disruptive prelude: megafires and cries for climate action in January, a global pandemic in March, an economic crash in April, and worldwide protests for racial justice and systemic change in June. Soon leaders at Fortune 500 companies such as Progressive Insurance, Intel, and Parker and at hospitals such as University of Texas Medical Branch and the world-renowned Cleveland Clinic "rediscovered" appreciative inquiry. I met, for example, with Dr. Bud Isaacson, the executive dean of the Cleveland Clinic Lerner College of Medicine (the place where appreciative

---

6. Whitney, D. K., Trosten-Bloom, A., & Rader, K. (2010). *Appreciative Leadership: Focus on What Works to Drive Winning Performance and Build a Thriving Organization.* New York: McGraw-Hill. See the the book's preface for Ken Gergen's full quote and commentary on Appreciative Inquiry.

7. Cooperrider, D. & Fry, R. (2020). Appreciative Inquiry in a Pandemic: An Improbable Pairing. *Journal of Applied Behavioral Science 56*(3), 266-271.

inquiry was born) and he remarked, "Too many of your dissertation ideas have been oversimplified over the years and I wish everyone interested in AI would read the early work." He spoke about how appreciative inquiry, in his experience, might just reach its highest potential for impact for organizations in the midst of a pandemic, in times where corporate cultures are almost totally tested and forged in the crucible of crises, during the most challenging times of external adaptation and internal integration.

Another long-respected professional in the field of change leadership, Gary Hubbell, e-mailed and remarked, "My recent re-reading your dissertation (from decades ago) could not have come at a better time…never doubt for a moment how you and how your work is an inspiration and compass for so many of us." My response back? I said, "Wow Gary, you took the time to read an academic dissertation from decades ago?" He immediately wrote back, explaining the multiple fronts covered in the dissertation that deserve deeper reading. He said: "I believe that publishing the dissertation as a book would be a great contribution." Likewise, and presaging this by just a month or two earlier, I was approached by Dr. Jean Pages and Jean-Christophe Barralis at the *Institut Français d'Appreciative Inquiry* in France, and was urged to consider the same thing. They wanted to explore publishing the dissertation in French, making it easily and digitally available (where now it's so difficult to find and translate) with a short contemporary commentary. All of this was beginning to appear as a classic synchronicity.

In addition to these, someone named Jane Day (I did not even know her) sent me a lengthy and thoughtful correspondence emphasizing her joy, hope, and her inspiring experience of "the adventure of ideas" in "going back to the beginnings:"

> "Your discovery and framing of Appreciative Inquiry, originally put forth in your dissertation, is creating for me today a paradigmatic shift at a foundational level that is causing me to see and therefore operate differently in every area of my life: my research; my management consulting; my work to help people, and most importantly

in my parenting and in my marriage with my husband…Your PhD adventure and the way you framed it, aligns with the greatest of my own adventures and, above all, I want to express my overwhelming gratitude to you for your courageous and insightful work which empowers all of us to look to our positive core to generate magnificent possibilities for ourselves and for those whom we serve."

Shortly after that note of gratitude, Jane Day applied to Case Western Reserve University. With her strong credentials, she was accepted into our doctoral (DM—practitioner-scholar) program. In that email, she quoted from an early section in the dissertation where I reflected on the experience as "the high point moment in my life." She wondered: how could a PhD dissertation project possibly be a thrill, an adventure, and a peak experience? The idea of "research alive" spoke to her, especially (and here I'm supposing) in contrast with widely read books with graphically telling titles such as *Surviving Your Dissertation* (2014)[8] by Kjell Eric Rudestam and Rae Newton.

Reading Jane's letter, from a young and inspired scholar in the making, was the moment that I decided to say "yes" to afford the dissertation as a book, and thereby make it more available to everyone wishing to understand the arc of appreciative inquiry's growth and writings. Moved by her letter and also motivated by our passionate doctoral students (perennially seeking out the dissertation as a model), the primary purpose of this volume became clear:

> *To speak to a younger generation of thinkers and to invite them, through the dissertation example and others, to follow their hearts, to courageously dare in scholarship and ask the big question in relation to the call of our times, and to open wide new vistas and directions for appreciative inquiry and to especially explore the power of the second word in the "Appreciative" and "Inquiry" duet. Appreciation is about valuing the "life-giving" in ways that serve to inspire our collaboratively constructed future. Inquiry is*

8. Rudestam, Kjell & Newton, Rae (2014). *Surviving Your Dissertation* (4th ed). Sage Publications.

the experience of mystery, moving beyond the edge of the known to the unknown, which then changes our lives. Taken together, where appreciation and inquiry are wonderfully entangled, we experience knowledge that's not inert but alive, as well as an ever-expansive inauguration of our world to new possibilities.

With a Contemporary Lens or Overlay From My PhD Research Course on Theory Building

This volume, then, shares the earliest AI writing exactly as it was in the dissertation, including its errors as well as my acknowledgements to so many others.[9] And, as an important addition in the remainder of this preface, I offer up this new introduction on "prospective theory" as an expanded and contemporary advance. As the passage of time has enabled me to look more closely at what was written, I feel both a deep satisfaction with the original vision and scholarly logic offered for Appreciative Inquiry, as well as its enormous impact, growing community of writers and co-creators, and continuing reverberation. Following the tradition of authors such as Carl Rogers (1995)[10] who have re-issued their favorite works to help with a return to the deeper core while also adding brief reflections on key points of emphasis, contemporary advances, or editorial commentary, I want to zero in here, in the remainder of this introduction, on reclaiming and renewing elements of that lost "minor detail" of AI's original purpose. While

9. This volume shares the earliest AI articulation and theory, exactly as it was, including its errors, as well as my gratitude to so many others. I hope you pause on the acknowledgements, as it honors nearly 40 people who helped bring appreciative inquiry into our world, especially my PhD mentors Suresh Srivastva and Ronald Fry, and great colleagues Frank Barrett and John Carter. In addition to those honored in the earliest stages, there are many significant others helping to inspire AI's prospective theory focus: Ken and Mary Gergen; Lindsey Godwin; James Ludema; Danielle Zandee; Jane Dutton; Gervase Bushe; Nadya Zhexembayeva; Ante Glavas; Sara Lawrence Lightfoot; Jacqueline Stavros; Kim Cameron; J. W. Otte; Pamela Robinson; Tojo Thatchenkery; Michelle McQuaid; Martin Seligman; Harlow Cohen; Hallie Preskill; Michel Avital; Peter Sorenson; Chris Laszlo; Ignacio Pavez; Veronnica Hopper; Diana Bilimoria; Robert Quinn; Diana Whitney; Cathy Royal; Charleyse Pratt; Eileen Wasserman; Sandra Waddock; Peter Senge; Raj Sisodia; Jane Watkins; Estelle Archibald, Linda Robson; and every one of the scholars referenced in this introduction chapter. Thank you to one and all and every one of the passionate doctoral students I have had and will have the privilege to learn from.

10. Rogers, C.R. (1995). *On Becoming a Person: A Therapist's View on Psychotherapy*. Boston: Houghton Mifflin.

geared to a more specialized and smaller audience—for example, doctoral students and researchers in the human sciences—I do hope this work speaks to and elevates the potentials for scholarly practitioners and the organization development field at large. Theory building can raise the efficacy and impact of every appreciative inquiry project, perhaps in a more productive way than any other set of interventions. Yet it is rarely taught, except as a footnote, even in the most in-depth practitioner certificate programs, executive education offerings, or even masters programs in organization development and change.

The reclaimed, refreshed and renewed elements of AI emerge from a PhD research methods course that I currently teach as a direct outgrowth of the dissertation as its root. So now I want to shift this narrative and turn for a moment to an overview of that course. For those wanting more, I will provide, in Appendix C in this book, the complete syllabus for the seminar, including an extensive research methods readings list, the developmental learning assignments, and the ways the dissertation (via this book) might be brought into any human science research practicum. You, the reader, might even want to review the detailed course overview, again in Appendix C, before starting to read this volume. In many ways, the dissertation is and was a prolepsis, a preview, a foreshadowing of AI's theory-building potential. The current PhD methods course I teach is called: *Seminar on Prospective Theory: Appreciative Inquiry as World Making.*

Let me now turn to and share the spirit and then the methodological advances proposed in the course, including how I use the dissertation in it, along with other exceptional readings such as Sarah Lawrence-Lightfoot's *The Art and Science of Portraiture*, and Mary and Ken Gergen's *Playing with Purpose: Adventures in Performative Social Science,* and many more.[11]

---

11. Lawrence-Lightfoot, S. (1983). *The Good High School: Portraits of Character and Culture.* New York: Basic Books. Also see: Lawrence-Lightfoot, S. & Davis, J. H. (1997). *The Art and Science of Portraiture.* San Francisco: Jossey-Bass. Also see: Gergen, M. M. & Gergen, K. J. (2016). *Playing With Purpose: Adventures in Performative Social Science.* Routledge.

How Might We Enrich and Empower the Generative Potential of Human Science Theory?

Here below is an excerpt from the course syllabus (read more in Appendix C.)

The spirit flowing through our doctoral seminar on human science inquiry is this: …that qualitative research and theory building in the social sciences is one of the greatest adventures and significant vocations life can present.

The impact of good theory, no matter how tiny or vast, can instantly move across our intimate planet and affect every human and living system in this interconnected, relationally alive, and reverberating universe. Ideas change the world. They assert that the truth of human freedom must count, and count affirmatively in the ways we understand ourselves and our worlds. Ideas can be about life and they can be life-giving in the sense that they can inspire, and open us to new horizons and new depths. A new idea, especially the idea whose time has come in a prospective and betterment sense, does more than inform: it transforms. We've all experienced it. A single new understanding can change us deeply.

Through thrilling, creative human science inquiry, we are lured into life's compelling mysteries and with that special "spirit of inquiry" we are often gifted when least expected, with fresh questions that startle, interrupt, evoke. And, for those that allow themselves to "dare in scholarship," there always seem to be changes—transformed conceptions of life's potentials, surprising turns in relationships, decisive shifts in perspective, and articulations of generative knowledge in the service of building a better world. But the true gift of theory, indeed any good methodology of inquiry, is that it can tap into the adventure of ideas, empirical discovery, and the moral imagination to build better together.

The course—building upon and advancing the quest established in my own PhD dissertation—is about the craft of grounded and future-forming theory construction. It's a way of doing research in the human sciences that exists, in William James' contrast, "not as a dull habit but as an acute fever." It is about what leading scholars, some of them directly inspired by appreciative inquiry, are now calling research-method alive (see Carlsen and Dutton, 2011; Dutton, 2003.)[12]

The subtitle for this seminar on "Appreciative Inquiry as World Making" grows out of a fusion of three exciting movements sweeping the social sciences. The first is constructionism's social epistemology, especially a second-generation collaborative constructionism that is creating an era of radically new possibilities for dialogue across previously polarized paradigms, for example, the bringing together of qualitative and quantitative methods, dialogues between objectivist and interpretive practices, inquiries that are human-focused and ecologically attuned, and honoring the significant dialogues between frontiers in science and understandings from aesthetic, contemplative, indigenous, pragmatist, and spiritual traditions. In the sessions to follow, much will be said about constructionism's unique relational and polyphonic capacity—its profound respect for multiple voices—to bring out and connect the best across diverse paradigms. But, for present purposes, here right now, there is a need to mention one contribution of even more significant dimension.

In a word, it is the idea of "generative theory"—something that the prolific Kenneth Gergen proposed and first articulated in a classic article in 1978 in the *Journal of Personality* and *Social Psychology*, and which has subsequently been enriched in many writings, most notably, in a major work, *Toward Transformation in Social Knowledge* (Gergen, 2006) and *Realities and Relationships* (Gergen, 1997), published as a true landmark by Harvard University Press. Generative theory unites and eclipses, perhaps in the most articulate way ever, the artificial dualism separating theory from practice, something that heretofore has weakened the human sciences, keeping it from its full potential in terms of relevance, and on the periphery of society's greatest upheavals and most imaginative opportunities.

---

12. Carlsen, Arne & Dutton, Jane (2011). *Research Alive: Exploring Generative Moments in Doing Qualitative Research.* Sweden: Liber AB. Also see: Dutton, Jane (2003). "Breathing Life into Organizational Studies" *Journal of Management Inquiry, 12* (1), 5-19.

What is the advance? In my view, it is the complete re-working of
the concept of what it means to do good theory. Historically, the
invitation to generative theory will be marked as a call that paves
the way for elevating the craft of theory construction beyond the
margins to the core of human science work. Hopefully, it will be
recognized, not as a threat, but as an inspiring challenge toward
more daring, purposeful, multi-paradigmatic and speculative writing. Hopefully, it will lead to methods courses that value, elevate,
and nourish each student's unique voice and their imagination and
mind. Generative theory, as many are now realizing, has the broad
potential to be an antidote to the inert, the secure, and the trivial in
our fields. Good theory, in this view, is not just backward-looking,
trying to standardize and simplify life or yesterday's patterns by
stressing conformity to what we find. Instead, it is increasingly
being viewed across the academy as a rich cultural resource for
creating, elevating, and shaping the world in a future-forming way
to our most imaginative ideals and purposes. It takes the idea of
interconnection and relatedness to heart in a serious, epistemological way. Instead of "cogito ergo sum," there is the invitation to
"communicamus ergo sum: "I communicate therefore I am." It
is a way of saying, in a resounding way, that there is no longer
room for excluding voices from our theory-building/world-making
tasks. In the beginning, argued Martin Buber, is the relationship.
Likewise, we are all theorists. And, when judged against the call of
our times, we need to draw on the entire universe of our collaborative and imaginative strengths. Especially for those intrigued with
"engaged scholarship" (see Andrew H. Van de Ven, 2007), they are
invited to transfer their conception of the individual as the center
of human knowledge, to an understanding that centralizes social
relationships carried out in language, dialogue, and participatory
discovery.[13]

The generative theory perspective, as we shall see, is releasing
extraordinary benefits and creative advances in scholarship and
practice. The key, especially for future scholars, will be in coming to grips with all the implications, opportunities, and the new

---

13. Van de Ven, Andrew (2007). *Engaged Scholarship: A Guide for Organizational and Social Research.*
New York: Oxford University Press.

horizons of a decisive shift from a "correspondence theory" of truth to an entirely new standard that aims even higher. Good theory (see Gergen, 2014), if it is to really matter, is that which should be judged not by its mirroring capacity but by its overall anticipatory, expressive, and generative capacity: "Generative theory is that which has capacity to challenge the guiding assumption of the culture, to raise fundamental questions regarding contemporary social life, to foster reconsideration of that which is "taken for granted" and thereby furnish new alternatives for social actions."[14]

The emerging story of generative theory from a philosophical point of view is neither simple nor is it complete. The "intelligibility nuclei" or its cross-paradigmatic stance deserves, in many places throughout this seminar, greater explanation than time allows. To be sure, the overarching purpose of this course is, in fact, more methodological; it is about the practices for constructing theory as future-forming and world-making.

The major mixed methods strategy that we shall put forward for furthering the construction of generative theory emerges from a merger of two other stand-out approaches to knowledge, Glaser and Strauss's Grounded Theory method, and appreciative ways of knowing that are best articulated in our own expansive work on appreciative inquiry. What emerges from the synthesis of each is the pragmatic core of our approach. This bringing together and interweaving—of appreciative ways of knowing, grounded theory method, and generative theory—is, as we shall see, long overdue. If we succeed in bringing these together in a practical way, this alone will comprise the largest value of this seminar.

From Grounded Buildup to Generative Breakthrough

The course—built around this book/dissertation—is designed as a methodological practicum in future-forming theory. The process of good theory construction is portrayed as the discovery of theory from data in the real world of life (the grounded experience in human systems), resulting

14. Gergen, K. J. (2014). *Toward Transformation in Social Knowledge* (2nd ed). Springer.

in the co-construction meaning, vision, strengthened relationships via co-inquiry, and knowledge of consequence.

The course asserts, in Lewinian fashion, that "there is nothing so practical as good theory"—it then focuses on the methods, personal disciplines, and empirical, aesthetic and imaginative perspectives needed to bring this dictum alive in what I am now calling Prospective Theory...theory that is future-forming, anticipatory, a resource for world-makers, and built on the idea of homo-prospectus. We are anticipatory beings (see Cooperrider, 1990.)[15] Whereas homo sapiens defines human beings as "wise," what humans do especially uniquely is to prospect the future. We are, as Marty Seligman and colleagues (2016) have academically explored, *Homo Prospectus*. The focus on prospection is now one of the hottest domains in cognitive psychology, sociology, neuroscience, and now, theory-building. It's a view whose basic theorem is that mental anticipation now pulls the future into the present and reverses the direction of causality. It's not just the past that causes human action, nor the current environment, but the ever-moving anticipatory ways we project the future ahead of us. Prospection conditions every action, moment of meaning making, our perceptions, our collective imaginations, learning, experiencing of emotions, relational patterns, and all sense possibility. We survive or thrive by considering our prospects (Seligman, Railton, Baumeister and Sripada, 2016).

Prospective theory, as I define it through an appreciative and enlivenment paradigm, is:

1. Theory inspired by life and designed to apprehend the best in all of life's fullest and best future possibilities while being grounded in the midst of the *extraordinary*, the *ordinary*, as well as the *tragic*;

2. Has the enlivenment and generative capacity to challenge the

---

15. Cooperrider, David (1990). "Positive Image, Positive Action: The Affirmative Basis of Organizing". In S. Srivastva & David Cooperrider (Eds.) *Appreciative Management and Leadership*, San Francisco, CA: Jossey-Bass. Also see: Seligman, M., Railton, P., Baumeister, R., & Sripada, C. (2016). *Homo Prospectus*. New York, NY: Oxford University Press.

status quo *and open the world to new better possibilities* for life and living;

3. Articulates a future story of prospective possibility. It involves a proleptic merging of the ideal conditioned in the texture of the actual—e.g., vivid utopias that are right there in front of us—informing our future story for establishing the new and eclipsing the old. And all of this in the service of *advancing of a world of full-spectrum flourishing*…a world where human organizations can excel, all people can thrive, and our living biosphere can flourish, now and across the generations.

In *Figure One,* I provide a framework of prospective theory concepts and heuristics and it is offered below. Building on the circular emergence metaphor made popular by Jim Collins (2009)[16] in his research *Good to Great*, the future-forming "prospective theory" model below illustrates the research journey's core components moving from *appreciative inquiry* and the *grounded portraiture* buildup all the way to the *generative* breakthrough. What the circle or flywheel means is that, no matter how dramatic the end results or generative breakthroughs, these never happen in one fell swoop. In building up from grounded research, often through weeks and months in the field and reams of data, emergent themes, early codes, memo writing, and generating theoretical distinctions, there is no single defining action, no solitary lucky break, or miracle moment. Rather, the grounded and then aesthetic theory-building process, being totally circular and iterative, resembles pushing a giant flywheel, relentlessly turn upon turn, at first strenuous and then building up to a momentum until patterns of precious insight and prescient breakthrough emerge. Edison famously said, "Genius is one percent inspiration, ninety-nine percent perspiration" and so too is theory-building: theoretical articulations are the result of hard work, disciplined imagination and rigorous methods, as well as embodied passion, participatory voice, and poetic inspiration.

---

16. Collins, J. C. (2009). *Good to Great.* New York, NY: Random House.

Figure I-1: Model for Prospective Theory Building

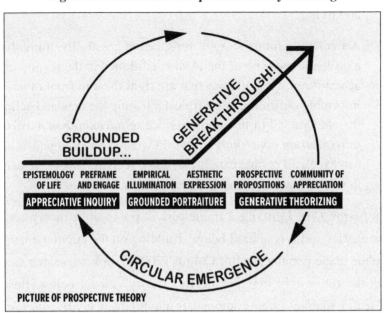

So, with the build-up in the circular emergence in mind, let us consider six elements or constituents for prospective theory-building moving through three interdependent phases. As the reader will see, all of these components of theory construction are evidenced, foreshadowed and illustrated in the dissertation. The elements, all combined, resonate with our central quest:

> "How might we enliven, enrich, and elevate the empirical and imaginative processes for building prospective or future-forming theory with {life-giving and life-bettering} generative potential?"

Let me summarize the six interdependent constituents:

1. *It Starts With an Epistemology of Life: The Appreciable World is Larger than Our Appreciative Eye.* Ever since Gareth Morgan's (1980) "Paradigms, Metaphors, and Puzzle Solving in Organizational Theory," the organizational sciences have come to understand the power of metaphor in shaping research method and theory.[17] All theories are based on implicit

---

17. Morgan, G. (1980). "Paradigms, Metaphors, and Puzzle Solving in Organization Theory." *Administrative Science Quarterly*, 25(4), 605-622.

images or metaphors that lead us to see, understand, and do research in distinctive ways. The use of metaphor implies a way of thinking and a way of seeing that pervades how we understand our world generally. For example, the enlightenment and soon-to-come industrial age, built heavily upon the metaphor of "clockwork universe" and human "organizations as machines." So ingrained are images such as these that sometimes it's difficult so see how pervasive they've become in our mechanistic theories of "bureaucracy," as well as deficit-based "problem-focused" methods of management focused on "breakdowns of the parts;" "prediction and control;" "loss of efficiencies;" "gap analysis;" "replaceable parts;" "standardizing and objectivizing analytics;" "resistance and inefficiencies;" and "organizational diagnosis preceding problem intervention."

When we say all theory is conditioned by metaphor, the consequences are far-reaching. What appreciative inquiry did, in its earliest writing, was to ask this essential question: if our goal is to develop the generative potential of theory—to harness inquiry to help our systems aim higher and better, open up fresh opportunities for better living, and to even think beyond the possible like designers, artists, visionaries, and our most generative scientists—then what are the metaphors or images of enlivenment that could set in motion or elevate our collective capacities for generativity?

What *Appreciative Inquiry: Toward a Methodology for Understanding and Enhancing Organizational Innovation* did then, was to propose a radical shift.[18] It began to look at the lives of generative thinkers and scientists such as Albert Einstein. It began to look at generative theory artist-academics such as Sarah Lawrence-Lightfoot. It began to explore the works of people with moral imagination and humanly significant impact, such as Albert Schweitzer. Here is just a sampling of their words, just to get a feel for the life-centric, living systems approach that's invited by the appreciative search and stance:

Albert Einstein spoke about awe and the methodological power of this

---

18. See many of these quotes in Cooperrider (1986) and on pp. 109–113 in this volume.

embodied state of feeling, embracing the idea of the miracle and mystery of life when he spoke about the spirit of inquiry:

> "The most beautiful thing we can experience is the mysterious. It is the source of all true art and science. He to whom the emotion is a stranger, who can no longer pause to wonder and stand wrapped in awe, is as good as dead—his eyes are closed." – Albert Einstein

Sarah Lawrence-Lightfoot, the acclaimed Harvard sociologist who created the grounded theory advance called "portraiture," speaks eloquently to the need for empathy, respect, knowing from the inside—what she and Jerome Bruner call an embodied kind of "life writing"—and to presume the reality of life-giving "goodness" in order to discover it, extend it, and give it a more prominent place in our lives: She writes:

> "Portraiture is a method of qualitative research that blurs the boundaries of aesthetics and empiricism in an effort to capture the complexity, dynamics, and subtlety of human experience and organizational life...to illuminate the dimensions of goodness."

Likewise, it's precisely this kind of stance—this ethical affirmation of life—that pragmatically elevates our perception beyond the world of ordinary objects, igniting the appreciative capacity that Albert Schweitzer called "the reverence for life."

> "In all respects the universe remains mysterious to humankind... As soon as the human being does not take existence for granted, but beholds it as something unfathomably mysterious, thought begins. This phenomenon has been repeated time and time again in the history of the human race. Ethical affirmation of life is the intellectual act by which humankind ceases simply to live at random...[Such] thought has a dual task to accomplish: to lead us out of a naive and into a profounder affirmation of life and the universe; and to help us progress from ethical impulses to a rational system of ethics."

Today these words, "ethical affirmation of life" or "the experience of mystery as the source of all true art and science," or the portraitist's call to illuminate the true, the good, the better, and the possible suggests a stance toward what's being called in biology and across the sciences the emerging new "age of enlivenment"—a focus on life, auto-poetic living systems, and what appreciative inquiry is inviting us to consider as the metaphor for our times. Instead of the metaphor of the world as a lifeless machine or an entropically breaking down "problem to be solved," the appreciative approach proposes that it's time for the human sciences to elevate and embrace "the miracle and mystery of life on this planet" as its starting point.

That's when the word "appreciation" begins to take on depth and meaning in a generative theory-building sense. To appreciate means to value. It means to value those things of value that give life, inspire life, elevate life—and thereby help us see, in the texture of the actual, those "intimations of something more." To inquire indicates curiosity, rigorous search, and the desire for penetrating understanding because of the overarching reverence for life, the mystery of emergence, and one overarching truth: the appreciable world—that is, the world of value worth valuing from the microcosm of the human brain and its 100 billion neurons, to the 100 billion galaxies in the universe—is larger than any set of appreciative eyes.

Recall how the use of metaphor implies a way of thinking and a way of seeing that pervades how we understand our world generally. As we know, a miracle is something that is beyond all possible verification, yet is experienced as real. As a symbol, the word "miracle" represents a unification of the sacred and secular into a realm of totality that is at once terrifying and beautiful, inspiring and threatening. Quinney (1982) has suggested, with respect to the rejuvenation of human science theory, that such a unified viewpoint is altogether necessary; that it can have a powerful impact on human science precisely because in a world that is at once a sacred gift and a secular co-construction of meanings, there is no place, knowledge, or phenomenon that is without mystery.[19] The "miracle," then, is prag-

---

19. Quinney, Richard (1982). *Social Existence*. Beverly Hills, CA: Sage Publications.

matic in its effect when sincerely apprehended by a mind that has chosen not to become "tranquilized in the trivial." In this sense, the metaphor of organizational and all of "life as a mystery and miracle" is not so much an idea as it is—or can be—a central feature of experience enveloping (1) our perceptual consciousness; (2) our way of relating to others, the world; and (3) our way of knowing. It's about a re-enchantment of our world as a methodological vehicle and imperative for our theoretical work. When we fuse the word "inquiry"—that is, *the experience of mystery that takes us beyond the known to the unknown and changes our lives*—with the word "appreciation," we are talking about things like awe, inspiration, veneration, delight, wonderment, humility, curiosity, and valuing.

The Greeks used the word *thaumazein*, an experience that lies on the borderline between wonderment and admiration. Appreciation not only draws our eye toward life, but stirs our feelings, excites our curiosity, and provides inspiration to the envisioning mind. In this sense, the ultimate generative power for the construction of new values and images is the apprehension of that which has value. Life appreciation, I contend, is creative rather than conservative precisely because it allows itself to be energized and inspired by the voice of mystery. As an active process of valuing the factors that give rise to the life-enhancing organization, appreciation has room for the vital uncertainty, the indeterminacy that is the trademark of something alive. Appreciative Inquiry, at a paradigm level, is part of today's emerging "enlivenment" and "relational being" paradigms (Weber, 2008; Gergen, 2014)[20] and represents the capacity to rediscover in life and organizations what Jerome Bruner refers to as the "immensity of the commonplace," or what James Joyce terms the "epiphanies of the ordinary" (in Cooperrider, 1990). What needs to be stressed here is that

---

20. Weber, Andreas (2008). *Enlivenment: Toward a Poetics for the Anthropocene.* Cambridge Mass: MIT Press. Also see: Gergen, K. (2009). *Relational Being: Beyond Self and Community.* New York: Oxford University Press. Also see: Cooperrider, David (1990). "Positive Image, Positive Action: The Affirmative Basis of Organizing." In S. Srivastva & David Cooperrider (Eds.) *Appreciative Management and Leadership.* San Francisco, CA: Jossey-Bass.

this kind of appreciative stance and associated ways of knowing involving wonder, awe, humility, and entering into the unknowing experience of mystery is more than an attitude: it is a matter of both attitude *and* method. Even though it is conspicuously neglected in research methods books and courses, wonderment as receptive appreciation, as well as its contribution to the desire and depth of exploration, underpins all key processes in all inquiry. For Einstein, this kind of appreciation of life's thrilling complexity plays a leading role in discovery and nurturing hunches, because it is a mobilizing driver of imagination. In many ways, I've begun to question today whether there can even be inquiry where there is no appreciation, valuing, or amazement. Can we really know anything about organizations and living systems—or indeed know anything about anything—without wondering about it first? [21] "There are only two ways to live your life," proposed Einstein. "One is as though nothing is a miracle. The other is as though everything is a miracle."[22]

2. It Builds Generative Momentum Via Social Process as Method: First the Pre-Frame...and the Engaging of a Wide Spectrum of Stakeholder Voices. At the center of prospective theory—much as the design-thinking profession has repeatedly learned in its quest to make breakthrough innovation happen better and more often—is the recognition that the generative

---

21. Carlsen, A. & Sandelands, L. (2014). *First Passion: Wonder in Organizational Inquiry. Management Learning*, pp. 1-8. Sage Publications. https://journals.sagepub.com/doi/pdf/10.1177/1350507614533756. The authors raise a powerful question for every research methods course: "The first question of organizational studies is the one we rarely think to ask, namely, how should we come to our subject? Indeed, they write: "Wonder is the first passion in all inquiry and our reason to know, yet a phenomenon that is largely neglected in organizational research."

22. In these days, most scientists and scholars view it as an insult if they are accused of being drawn toward mysticism and a reuniting of the sacred and secular, especially if they are making the argument that the experience of the mystical or life as a mystery is a legitimate knowledge *method*, that is, it is something that can consciously be harnessed in the service of creating knowledge of consequence. I still cannot help but puzzle over how far we've drifted from amazement and enchanted experience of our world. We do not come close to teaching the importance of this in our research methods courses. In her Cambridge University book, *Intellectual Shamans: Management Academics Making a Difference,* Sandra Waddock (2015) spotlights the work of 26 scholars and shows how the spirit of appreciative inquiry and something of an enlivenment paradigm is associated, in almost every instance, with generative scholarship that makes a high purpose difference in the field and for the greater good. I was honored to be featured in the volume, especially pages 246-278, and it is a volume that's now being brought into many research seminars.

potential of inquiry is not enriched as a solo act (lone genius) but as a symphony of strengths (the power of collective intelligence). True innovation happens when strong multi-disciplinary groups come together, build a collaborative and appreciative interchange, and explore the intersection of their different perspectives, experiences, and inquiry capacities into "what's best or what gives life?" and "what's possible and what's even beyond the seemingly possible?"

This, of course, raises many questions. For example, who will be involved in sense-making and sense-giving, what are our values and purposes, and how might we frame the inquiry in the most elevated, curiously interesting, or promising way possible? Viewed as a kind of inseparable double helix, the inquiry is actually launched as stakeholders and participants, as co-inquirers, are thoughtfully identified. They are identified with the recognition that such a constellation of intellectual and engaged resources depends also on the preliminary framing of the topic or research opportunity and vice-a-versa. The first step in prospective methodology is aligning the what of the inquiry with the who—and ultimately, the why, where, and when.

who | what

Proleptic theory's aim is to create new knowledge that makes an enduring difference and opens the world to new possibilities, causes it to move toward a conception of a simultaneous *knowing and undergoing* that embraces a worldview of our fundamental interrelatedness. In appreciative inquiry, we call this the "principle of simultaneity," with the recognition that the studying of a phenomenon actually changes it, even from the moment of the first observations or questions deployed. Moreover, the human sciences are scarcely alone in this. In the early 1920s, renowned physicist Werner von Heisenberg articulated this principle for the physical world. The "Heisenberg observer effect" tells us that the smallest entities in the physical world do not behave at all like larger scale objects. Until an instrument or act of observation registers them, the quanta have neither a unique location nor a unique state. It's only when we observe its state that a quantum particle is essentially forced to choose one probability, and that's the state we observe. Here we might say that inquiry-and-change are intrinsically and perhaps wonderfully entangled. We cannot step out of relationship. Even the simple act of inserting a thermometer into a glass of water to determine the water's temperature will change the temperature. Meg Wheatley sums it up in relational terms: "In the quantum world, relationships are not just interesting; to many physicists, they are all there is to reality." Then she continues, "Several years ago I read that elementary particles were 'bundles of potentiality'."[23]

That's a metaphor for what we are involved with when we study human systems though a future-forming theory lens. It involves a conception of inquiry-and-change as a powerfully entangled simultaneity, one that places human relationships at the center. It posits that it is in relationships that we discover and determine what is valuable, good, worthwhile, meaningful, desired, better, plausible, pragmatic, and possible. Moreover, it would not be extreme to say that the life and death of generative theorizing—discovering and mobilizing those "bundles of potentiality"—depends powerfully on the kind of generative collective intelligence that's greater than the sum of the parts. Knowledge, especially knowledge of consequence, happens the moment we begin to profoundly inquire together, speak together, trust together, raise innovative and even heretical questions together, mutually listen together, include and give full voice to each other, share stories of generative life and promising potential, combine our vast universe of strengths together, and discover, dream and design together. Indeed, it may seem like common sense, especially in the context of organizations, but we

---

23. Meg Wheatley, as quoted in Cooperrider, D. (2017) *The Gift of New Eyes: Personal Reflections After 30 Years of Appreciative Inquiry in Organizational Life.* In Shani, A., et. al. (Eds.) *Research in Organizational Change and Development*, Vol. 25, Bingley UK: Emerald Publishing.

need to underscore it: the relational *process* of knowing is just as important as the *content* and, in this view, the higher the quality of the connections, the higher generative potential of knowing (Dutton and Heaphy, 2003.)[24]

Through what we call *social process as method*, the participants and the researcher become synergistic; we can think of human science theory, especially future-forming theory, as an invitation to a dance into new and more promising forms of life. So where does it start? It starts with a pre-sumption and preliminary framing or question:

"If human systems become or tend to grow into the direction of what they/we most deeply, powerfully, and rigorously study, then the question is: what kind of world do we want to help to create through the scientific construction of reality?"

And in a more context sensitive way:

"If human systems, including ours, tend to grow into the direction of what they/we most deeply, powerfully, frequently, and rigorously study, then what is it that they/we want to learn and grow our way into, to become, and to empower and enable?"

With the assumption that one productive sign of generative research is that the seed topic, never rigid, gets enriched and elevated as the grounded research cycles emerge, we recognize that even the earliest pre-framing can be fateful. As we know, starting points can be seismic. In complexity theory, the phenomenon is known as "sensitive dependence on initial conditions." In much the same way that a snowball can turn into an avalanche, or a tiny seed can grow into a giant redwood, topic choice and pre-frames can certainly reverberate.

In the language of Positive Organizational Scholarship (see Cameron, et al., 2003) it involves a values-choice and a research focus—a positive bias—seeking fresh understanding of dynamics described by words like

---

24. Dutton, J. & Heaphy, E. (2003). *The Power of High-Quality Connections at Work.* In Cameron, K., Dutton, J., & Quinn, R. E. (Eds.) *Positive Organizational Scholarship* (pp. 263-278). San Francisco, CA: Berrett-Koehler Publishers.

excellence, thriving, abundance, resilience, or exceptional.[25] Yet there is one caveat: it is not about positive or negative per se as frozen binaries, but about "the positive," not as an answer, but as an open question. What transcends the polarity is enlivenment, that is, the search for what gives life, once again, in virtually all settings: in the midst of the extraordinary, in the midst of the ordinary, and in the midst of tragedy.

The picture below shows us a ladder as one elevationary technique that prospective theory uses to step from lower to higher in the pre-frame (where "pre" stands for positive re-framing.)

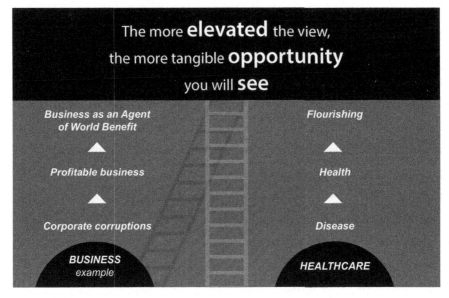

For example, decades ago, the healthcare field framed its topic largely as "the absence of disease" and thereby emphasized diagnostics into the root causes of the illness. Some years later, moving up the ladder, more and more studies began to define the concept of health itself and began, at larger population levels, to track its averages and norms. And then, more recently, some of the most exciting and thrilling work in the field has elevated the

25. Cameron, K. S., Dutton, J. E., & Quinn, R. E. (2003). *Foundations of Positive Organizational Scholarship*. San Francisco, CA: Berrett-Koehler Publishers. Also see, Cameron, K. & Spreitzer, G., (2011). *Oxford Handbook of Positive Organizational Scholarship*. Oxford: Oxford University Press.

topic focus, discovering concepts such as "flourishing" or "thriving" or quest to study "super-immunity."

The same thing is occurring in our own field of organizational science. Of course, there are studies in business research of corporate corruption. Up the ladder a bit is the topic of profitable business. But today, one of the largest and most promising prospective theory studies in the world involves a data-bank with 8,000 interviews into "business as an agent of world benefit" not as an assertion, but a question: what does it look like? Where is it happening? What are the enablers? What about business as a force for peace in high conflict zones? What about business as a force for enabling a massive transition to a bright green economy of 100% clean, abundant, renewable energy? Or high purpose business as a home for dignified work, economic empowerment and eradication of extreme poverty?[26]

Finally, there are two other moves that we've found especially useful in the topic pre-framing. The first is personal. It's a question that asks researchers to reflect upon themselves: what is the emerging topic that's going to light you up? Howard Thurman once said: "Don't ask what the world needs. Ask what makes you come alive, and go do it. Because what the world needs is people who have come alive." To be sure, it makes so much sense: won't we tend to bring more of everything—research resources, motivation, passion, rigor, desire to make a difference—if the topic itself brings us to life?

And the second topic-framing move is about the world, not the world as it is, but the world that we sense is wanting to emerge. Professor Otto Sharmer at MIT calls the reflective process involved one of "presencing."[27] It's about inquiring into or framing up topics related to questions emerging from the future and for the future: "What's the future that is wanting to be born?" Think about that question and listen deeply to your answer.

26. See www.aim2flourish.com and the Fowler Center for Business as an Agent of World Benefit at https://weatherhead.case.edu/centers/fowler/

27. Sharmer, Otto (2013). *Leading From the Emerging Future: From Ego-System to Eco-System Economies.* San Francisco, CA: Berrett-Koehler Publishers.

Perhaps it's a world of "full-spectrum flourishing"? So what exactly is full-spectrum flourishing, and where might it be emerging? Or perhaps one future that you sense is wanting to happen concerns the next stage in democracy where nature, the biosphere, and future generations are part of democracy's fuller voice and the consent of the many—including voices of the more-than-human world? Or is your passion focused on economies that are regenerative, renewing, and reviving—where the Hippocratic oath of "do no harm" becomes an authentic economic ethic, and a shared reality in the making? In other words, a powerful topic choice can be a response to the voice of future, a future we sense is wanting to happen, one that requires us to tap into a deeper level of our humanity, of who we really are and who we want to be or become as a society, an organization, an earth system, or world. This kind of *prospecting* involves a future we can sense, feel, and actualize by shifting the inner place from which we operate. It is a future that, in today's moments of unprecedented disruption, begins to presence itself through us.

Prospective theory, we contend, depends on prospectively rich topic frames. As the earliest writings on appreciative inquiry proposed (see p. 224 in this volume), we live in worlds our questions create. Could it be that it is through our topic framing and subsequent choice of research questions, that we largely create the world we later discover? In Letters to a Young Poet, Rainer Maria Rilke wrote:

Be patient...try to love the questions themselves...
Live the questions now.
Perhaps you will then gradually, without noticing it,
Live along some distant day into the answer.

3. *From An Appreciative Stance to Empirical Illumination.* Our demarcation of the phase of "grounded portraiture" is inspired by a union of two landmark contributions to the field of research methodology. The first is *The Discovery of Grounded Theory* (Glaser and Strauss, 1967) and the second

is *The Art and Science of Portraiture* (Lawrence-Lightfoot, 1993). In both, the first step is grounded illumination and experiential surfacing, literally gathering data from the ground up through deeply intimate listening to the voices, experiences, actions, and meanings of people in the real world. When the book *The Discovery of Grounded Theory* burst on the scene, it launched a Kuhnian paradigm shift, upending social scientific approaches to the kinds of grand theorizing via deductive propositions to be verified through reductionist research. Doctoral students, for example, would rarely see themselves as grand theorists—such as Parsons, Marx, and Durkheim—but would instead seek to take a smaller proposition from some grand theory and set out to verify the validity. But the call to grounded theory challenged all of this and asserted, first of all, that we can all be original theorists, and that theory developed inductively from the real world, with real voices, and in real settings, could not only create more relevance in theory, but also invite more original and creative theorizing. Discovery of theory, especially in relationship to under-studied phenomenon, or fresh new domains, is just as important to a significant human science as verifying someone else's theory and perhaps even more important than ever in a world where everything is in flux. Think, for example, of the Greek philosopher Heraclitus who posited "the only constant in life is change" and that a human being "cannot step into the same river twice." In such a world, like ours, where change is never ever again going to slow down, the discovery mindset could become even more valuable over time than the verification mindset. The grounded theory strengths, in terms of discovery, involve many things: its exquisite sensitivity to context; its openness to methodological bricolage and triangulation; it's iterative circular emergence requiring a steady movement between data and emerging concepts, between emerging concepts and their relationships, between emerging theory and the sudden formulation of new questions that often invite more theoretically sensitive sampling; and its focus more on vivification (living proof or vivid illustration) more than abstract verification. The ultimate prize: it's the construction of vivid and vivifying theory, one with originality, high resolution and relevance, fresh conceptual language, and an illuminating storyline ready to grow into something prescient, future-forming, and generative.

4. *From Empirical Illumination to Aesthetic Expression*. In appreciative inquiry, there is movement from "the best of what is" to the ideals of "what might be" to the "consent of what should be" to the activation of collective innovation and the "experiencing of what can be." (See this volume on pp. 107–108). In many ways, this follows the double dictionary definition of appreciation. The first description of appreciation is appreciation as valuing those things worth valuing. The second dictionary definition is appreciation as an increase in value, as in, "our home has appreciated in value." Today, this shift from "grounded theory's" empirical illumination to aesthetic expression is best known as the Art and Science of Portraiture. Brought into prominence in qualitative research by Sara Lawrence-Lightfoot, the acclaimed sociologist from Harvard, whose theory-building work has been recognized via many awards such as the MacArthur Fellowship, Harvard's George Ledlie Prize for research that makes the "most valuable contribution to science," the Candace Award from the National Coalition of 100 Black Women; and a featured PBS television documentary "African American Lives." She is the first African American woman in Harvard's history to have an endowed professorship named in her honor.

Beyond this introduction, a brief mention of the story of portraiture is important. At the age of eight, Sara Lawrence-Lightfoot's mother gave her a gift. The gift was an actual experience of being the subject of an intimate charcoal drawing. Sara recounts the embodied way of knowing and the skilled hands of the artist:

"Her well-worn, strong, and knowing hands moved quickly and confidently across the paper. She seemed totally relaxed and unself-conscious; her fingers a smooth extension of the charcoal. Her deep calm soothed me and made me feel relaxed. But what I remember most clearly was the wonderful, glowing sensation I got from being so fully attended to. There were no distractions. I was the only one in her gaze. My image filled her eyes, and the sound of the chalk stroking the paper was palpable. The audible senses translated to tactile ones. After the warmth of this human encounter, the artistic product...not like looking in the mirror at my reflection. Instead, they seemed to capture my "essence"; qualities of character and history, some of which I was unaware, some of which I resisted mightily, some of which felt deeply familiar. But the translation of image was anything but literal. It was probing, layered, and interpretive. In addition to portraying my image, the piece expressed the perspective of the artist and was shaped by the evolving relationship between the artist and me. I also recognized that in searching for the essence, in moving beyond the surface image, the artist was both generous and tough, skeptical and receptive. I was never treated or seen as object but always as a person of myriad dimensions."

Years later, Lawrence-Lightfoot created a sociology of organizations, especially educational systems, and felt the echoes of being on the other side of the artist's palette. She wanted to develop an organizational analysis, a text, that came as close as possible to painting with words. She wanted the people and organizations to reveal their deeper essence and to feel "seen"—fully attended to, recognized, appreciated, respected as she as a child had been attended to—and she wanted them to feel both the discovery and generosity of the process as well as the penetrating and careful inquiry.

The human systems portraiture process is shaped as a dialogue between the portraitist and the human system, each one shaping a discourse rich in meaning, resonance, narrative, and image. It's a genre of inquiry that seeks to join science and art, vigilance to empirical description and aesthetic expression, and provide witness to potentials. Always seeking all the voices and experiences in real-life situations, the person of the researcher is more evident and more visible than in any other research form. So, the balancing of personal predisposition lies in uniting, in a paradoxical way, the theoretical imagination and mind of the researcher (analytic rigor and poetic inspiration and license) with community building (acts of intimacy, connection, caring, and co-inquiry). The goal: a kind of knowledge of this world equal to the power of our minds, hearts, and full voices to imagine a better one—a kind of "people's scholarship." Completely sensitive to context, the portraitist searches for the central story, tracing and interpreting an authentic narrative into an aesthetic whole "which often feels like weaving a tapestry or piecing together a quilt." The shaping hand of the researcher—and generative imagination and touch to follow—is counterbalanced by penetrating search that is the signature of good research.

The Art and Science of Portraiture, via its appreciative stance toward life, its expanding sense of possibility, and its search for betterment transports the grounded theory build-up into the future. The search for what gives life when the living system is most alive ignites the imagination moving us from the strong mast—the best of "what is"—to the sail of the imaginary of "what might be."

5. *Prospective Propositions as Appreciative Abduction.* We are beginning to understand that theories are often more generative in their impact when data is more evocative than definitive and when theories paint vivid images, often through vignettes, of possible and better futures. What do we mean by theory? Simply put:

> Theory, especially future-forming theory, involves concepts and
> their interrelationships that prospectively propose how and/or why a
> phenomenon might occur or could be made possible in cognitively
> compelling, emotionally expressive, and relationally life-elevating
> ways.

Taking inspiration and logic from searching for the life-giving in today's and yesterday's worlds, generative thinkers often think beyond the possible while seizing people by the imagination and transporting them from their current world to another world. While deductive methods start with abstract principles and move toward concrete reality, and while inductive method starts with concrete reality and builds in a sense-making way

37

toward abstract principles, it is now time for abductive reasoning (a seismic little phrase coined by pragmatist philosopher Charles Sanders Peirce) that calls for a kind of sense-giving leap of imagination and visualization. The abductive process can be creative, intuitive, even revolutionary. It's the logic of what could be, a speculative gesture that can come to us in a seeming flash. Often it emerges, after lots of work, as a new "connecting of the dots" involving an "aha" or disruptive, game-changing synthesis.[28]

The appreciative inquiry method tutors us in how to move from emergent themes to the development of possibility propositions, intended to be provocative and prescient, logically compelling, and prospectively aspirational (see this volume p. 114). The vision here is a science not of probabilities but of possibilities. Here it is considered axiomatic that every living system is, in fact, an open-ended indeterminate system and, in the human organizational domain, every system is capable of becoming other than it is, that is, capable of:

> (1) becoming more than it is at any given moment, and (2) learning how to actively take part in guiding its own evolution. Hence, appreciative knowledge of what is (in terms of "peak" social innovations in organizing) is suggestive of what might be and such knowledge can be used to generate images of realistic developmental opportunities that can be experimented with on a wider scale. In this sense, appreciative inquiry can be both pragmatic and visionary. It becomes provocative to the extent that the abstracted findings of a study take on normative value for members of an organization, and this can happen only through their own critical deliberation and choice ("We feel that this particular finding is [or not] important for us to envision as an ideal to be striving for in practice on a wider scale"). It is in this way then, that appreciative inquiry allows us to put intuitive, visionary logic on a firm empirical footing and to use systematic research to help invite an organization's members to shape the social world according to their own imaginative and moral purposes (see this volume, p. 108).

---

28. Martin, R. (2009). *The Design of Business: Why Design Thinking is the Next Competitive Advantage.* Boston, MA: Harvard Business Press.

When Einstein said, "Imagination is more important than knowledge," he was speaking to precisely the abductive leap and the need to celebrate speculation as research method. Karl Weick gave it a perfect name: "disciplined imagination."[29]

In portraiture terms, too, it is about elevating aesthetic expression, and an articulation of the best possible futures, not in thinly thought-out utopian terms, but in theoretically thick as well as in richly grounded ways. Appreciation, we need to underscore here, not only draws our eye toward life, but stirs our feelings, excites our curiosity, and provides inspiration to the envisioning mind. In this sense, the ultimate generative power for the construction of new values and images is the apprehension of that which has value. Nietzsche once asked of appreciation, "Does it not praise? Does it not glorify? Does it not select? Does it not bring 'that which is appreciated' to prominence? In all this, does it not strengthen or weaken certain valuations?" (Rader, 1973, p. 12). No one has expressed this more effectively than the artist Vincent van Gogh, who, in a letter to his brother (in Rader, 1973, p. 10), spelled out what could actually be an entire theory-building course on the relationship between appreciation and the emergence of new values. He describes something akin to the three phases in our circular emergence wheel (see p. 32):

> I should like to paint a portrait of an artist friend, a man who dreams great dreams, who works as the nightingale sings, because it is in his nature. He'll be a fine man. I want to put into my picture of appreciation, the love I have for him. So, I paint him as he is, as faithfully as I can. But the picture is not finished yet. To finish it, I am now the arbitrary colorist. I exaggerate the fairness of the hair; I come even to use orange tones, chromes, and pale lemon-yellow. Behind the head, instead of painting the ordinary wall of the mean room, I paint infinity, a plain background of the richest, intense blue that I can contrive—and, by this simple combination of the bright

---

29. Weick, K.E. (1989). "Theory Construction as Disciplined Imagination." *The Academy of Management Review, 14* (4), 516.

head against the rich blue background, I get a mysterious effect, like a star in the depths of an azure sky.

Like appreciative inquiry and Sara Lawrence-Lightfoot's social science portraiture, van Gogh begins with the gift of new eyes and appreciative cognition—"so I paint him as he is, as faithfully as I can." He viewed his friend through what some have called "the cognitive power of love" and focused on those qualities that excited his preference and kindled his imagination—"but the picture is not finished yet." The key point is that van Gogh did not merely articulate admiration for his friend: He created new values and new ways of helping us see the world through the very act of valuing—i.e., aesthetic illumination.

If this sounds too ethereal, then the volume to come may come across as too concrete. As mentioned at the outset today the Cleveland Clinic, the birthplace of appreciative inquiry, is a leading 21st century health system that's one of the most advanced medical centers technologically, scientifically, and organizationally in terms of *relationship-centered care* ever created. Dr. William Kiser was the CEO and chair of the Board of Governors and years later talked about how appreciative inquiry helped them see into the soul of the organization while creating a logic and language for the "egalitarian group practice." It helped set the stage, he remarked, for one of the institution's eras of greatest growth. When he was nearing 90 years old, he spoke at our university and surprised me with a gift. It was decades after our research. And he brought to the occasion the first draft of one of the chapters in the dissertation (see this volume, p.197). He said: "I kept it safe in my files." He then showed students and others of us his handwritten notes scribbled on every page and throughout the margins. He reflected on the meaning of it all. There was moisture in his eyes. For him the remembering was joyful:

"Those were magical years for me and our group...the appreciative analysis literally peered into our soul and helped us see into the profound and institutionally meaningful possibilities. Our exceptional growth, experienced across the next decade thereafter, was far beyond what even I could have imagined. We were seen in ways we could not have seen ourselves. The momentum we experienced would not have happened without the shared visions and discoveries that poured out of not simply the pages of the research, but everyone's minds and hearts as we worked with and expanded and extended the theory's emergent themes with our 8,000 people. The inquiry brought us together in open dialogues over and over. It helped us understand and appreciate our group practice as an institutional breakthrough, while enabling us to better innovate and lead the way in new frontiers in medicine, strengthen our culture of patient care around our collaborative DNA, and grow dramatically."

When the theory-building started, the organization had around 8,000 people. Today the Cleveland Clinic has more than 67,500 employees, a figure that includes more than 17,000 registered nurses and advanced practice providers and more than 4,520 physicians and scientists in 140 specialties. In its world class service, it has more than 8 million patient visits annually. Among its many distinctive accolades, the Cleveland Clinic is now celebrated as the #1 heart center in the world and it became, as a direct extension our work, the first healthcare provider in the United States to become a signatory to the United Nations Global Compact (which also leveraged appreciative inquiry in its early and most powerful growth stage.)

It might be useful for you, the reader, to quickly revisit van Gogh's letter above, because what transpired at the Cleveland Clinic was akin to what was inside van Gogh's "methodological" letter to his brother. The appreciations expressed by artist and theorist alike are not separate from their mode of expression. Today we say "appreciation *appreciates*"—or as Nietzsche (in Rader, 1973, p. 12) so powerfully elaborated in his theory of aesthetics:[30] "Valuing is creating: hear it, ye creating ones! Valuation is itself the treasure and jewel of valued things."

---

30. Rader, M. (1973). *A Modern Book of Esthetics: An Anthology*. New York: Holt, Rinehart and Winston.

6. *An Ongoing Community of Appreciation*: Obviously, this is not theory as usually understood. Theory is generally concerned with "What is the case?" and is essentially "downstream theory" where we stand on a bridge looking at the waters that have already passed beneath. We live now in a world in which "upstream theory" capacity is essential, where attention to a future-forming stance is increasingly required for in all of our systems and institutions if they are to succeed and innovate. What is required then, as Gergen suggests, is preparation for increasing the vast, and often untapped, participation potential in the generative processes of co-creation. For this we need increased "double loop" theory-building capacity for the ongoing creation of new ideas and new and better forms of life.

We call these ever-strengthening co-inquiry cultures "communities of appreciation." It's about activating the reflexive step where we move from "knowing what" to getting better together at "knowing how" together, thereby enriching the potentials of social process as method. Scholarship by Frank Barrett has shown that *doing* inquiry is also an *undergoing* in the midst of inquiry, and often leaves behind four kinds of competence:[31]

1. *Appreciative Competence*: the human capacity to appreciate positive possibilities by selectively focusing on current and past strengths, successes and potentials;

2. *Expansive Competence:* the ability to challenge habits and conventional practices, provoking members to experiment in the margins;

3. *Generative Competence:* the community of inquiry constructs integrative systems that track "progress moments" to study results, contributions, and instill in the system grounded hope and empowerment.

4. *Collaborative Competence:* the community of inquiry creates

---

31. Barrett, F. (1995). "Creating Appreciative Learning Cultures." *Organizational Dynamics, 24* (2), 36-47.

forums for dialogue and the inclusive exchange of diverse perspectives to transform systems. Collaborative systems that allow for dialogue promote the articulation of multiple perspectives and encourage continuous, active debate and increase the participation potential for subsequent inquiries.

All of this is a way of saying that every proleptic theory-building process can collaterally and directly result in a system's increased capacity for making future-forming theory-building into an upward spiral. In education, it is called "learning to learn" better together. It's about developing cultures of co-inquiry and curiosity more than advocacy and answers. Instead of frozen ideals, we find open minds and growing ideals. One useful distinction is the difference we see between the word "affirmation" and the word "appreciation," where an affirmation is often an answer (holding some positive thought or belief in a *firm* way) instead of appreciation-*as-inquiry*.

In contrast to the affirmative projection that seeks certainty and control over events, the appreciative eye actually seeks uncertainty as it is thrown into the elusive and emergent nature of organizational life itself. Appreciation is creative rather than conservative precisely because it allows itself to be energized and inspired by the voice of mystery. Over and over it asks: "what gives life to this living system when it is most alive across life's full spectrum of experience—in times of the extraordinary, the ordinary, and moments of potentially magnified meaning-making we call the tragic (think here of the generative theory of Victor Frankl while in the horrifying Nazi concentration camps.) As an active process of noticing and valuing the factors that give rise to the life-enhancing organization or system, appreciation has room for the vital uncertainty, the indeterminacy, that is the trademark of something alive. In this sense, too, it differs from affirmation in that it is not as directly instrumental. It does not have the capability of shaping the world closer to preexisting wants or ideals because it tends, in the end, to transform those wants and ideals into something very different from that which was originally affirmed. One of the great paradoxes of human systems development is that high values, affirmations, and ideals can be a human system's best friend, but they can also be a community's largest barrier to betterment. While our ideals are the best we have, sometimes we hold on to them so firmly that they become our biggest obstacle. Theorist Henry Nelson Wieman (1926, p. 286) gave a clear description of the paradox involved here in his comparative analysis of *Religious Experience and Scientific Method*:

> "We are very sure that the greatest obstacle in the way of individual growth and social progress is the ideal [affirmative projection] which dominates the individual or group. The greatest instrument of achievement and improvement is the ideal, and therefore our constant failures, miseries, and wickedness are precisely due to the inadequacy of our highest ideals. Our ideals have in them all the error, all the impracticability, all the perversity and confusion that human beings that themselves erring, impractical, perverse and confused, can put into them. Our ideals are no doubt the best we have in the way of our constructions. But the best we have is pitifully inadequate. Our hope and full assurances...[are] that we can improve our ideals. If we could not be saved from our ideals, we would be lost indeed."[32]

A community of appreciation "learns to learn" whereby a system's best affirmations or ideals are held perpetually in play—regenerating, renewing and replenishing—because life, almost by definition, is always busting out all over. AI's future-forming and prospective capacity lies precisely in its "inquiry inspired by life" and in its ultimate search, not in current ideals (certainties), but in the future-forming lure of unexplored possibilities (those intimations of something more) where possibility and positive potential abound. Perhaps this is where the secular and the spiritual pragmatically unite (see p. 109 in this volume). Secular pragmatism finds wonder in the endless possibilities of life in which ever-provisional truths are inseparable from contexts of use and possibilities for action (James,

---

32. Wieman, Henry (1926). *Religious Experience and Scientific Method.* NY: Macmillan.

1907) while spiritual literacy (see Brussat and Brussat, 1996) is often spoken about as the "capacity for finding sacred meaning in all aspects of life." This reunion, in research terms, represents an inexhaustible source of generative potential:

In a world that is conceived at once as sacred gift and a secular co-construction of meanings, there is no place, knowledge, or phenomenon that is without mystery.

Inquiry is the experience of mystery which takes us beyond the known to the unknown and thereby changes our lives—and often our worlds.

We are infants when it comes to our understanding of appreciative processes of knowing and collaborative construction of future-forming theory with longer-term generative impact. Yet we are beginning to see that the power of appreciation rests with its mutually upbuilding and relationally generative capacity development. Through appreciation of organizational life, members of an organization learn to value not only the life-enhancing organization but also learn, in the midst of co-inquiry into the true, the good, the better and the possible, to appreciate themselves together, as a community of inquiry. Inquiry can be intensely relational. Hearing stories of "high point moments" in life and listening to one another's aspirations and dreams show us we are not alone.

Human relationships come alive where there is an appreciative eye, where people see and lift up the deepest and best in one another's life-giving experiences. As new potentials for inquiry are revealed and experienced within the community of co-inquiry, new insights are made available and shared with others in the system and beyond. As sharing occurs, the inquiry becomes increasingly a joint process of knowing—others are invited to explore and question their own ideals or images of emerging potential into an ever-expanding domain of relatedness. Through this kind of heart-circulating and ever-widening dialogue, new knowledge and new images of possibility are constantly being made articulate. And, while such knowledge is frequently felt as an interruption and provocative stretch beyond the status quo, it is valued and turned into a future-forming project because it represents something of a precious birth, a new co-creation and vital coherence, especially in the elevation of *our* shared belief in betterment *together*.

David L. Cooperrider, PhD
Case Western Reserve University
April 10, 2021

APPRECIATIVE INQUIRY: TOWARD A METHODOLOGY
FOR UNDERSTANDING AND ENHANCING
ORGANIZATIONAL INNOVATION

by
DAVID LOY COOPERRIDER

Submitted in partial fulfilllment of the requirements
for the Degree of Doctor of Philosophy

Thesis Advisor: Suresh Srivastva

Department of Organizational Behavior
CASE WESTERN RESERVE UNIVERSITY
August 19, 1985

CASE WESTERN RESERVE UNIVERSITY

GRADUATE STUDIES

We hereby approve the thesis of

___David Loy Cooperrider_____.

candidate for the_____Ph.D._____

degree.*

Signed: _____
                    (Chairman)

_____

_____

_____

_____

Date ___August 19, 1985_____

*We also certify that written approval has

been obtained for any proprietary material

contained therein.

Dissertation Abstract

by
David L. Cooperrider

THE AIM OF THIS DISSERTATION is to explore, describe, and propose an action-oriented approach to organizational inquiry that is uniquely intended for the study and enhancement of organizational innovation. Such a viewpoint requires that we elevate the status of theory and begin developing new understandings of the subtle yet complex Lewinian proposition that there is nothing so practical as good theory. Virtually unexamined by the social-administrative sciences in general—and action-research in particular—are the diverse and intricate ways in which theory is creative of the social-organizational future and how science can play a more collaborative role in the conscious evolution of culture.

First, the dissertation argues for an enriched, multi-dimensional view of action research that seeks to be theoretically generative. In its uni-dimensional problem-solving form, action-research has largely failed as an instrument for advancing social knowledge with consequence and has not, therefore, achieved its potential as a vehicle for human development and social-organizational transformation. It is contended that a primary barrier circumventing the potential of action-research has been its romance with action at the expense of theory. An appeal is made to define the scientific aims of action-research in ways that re-unite the dynamic interrelation of theory and practice. Building on a socio-rationalist view of science, ways are explored to increase the generative potential of action-research.

Appreciative inquiry is then presented as a mode of action-research that meets the criteria of science as spelled out in generative-theoretical terms. It is illustrated through a five-year study of a major social innovation in the healthcare industry. Through an appreciative process of theorizing about the emergence of an egalitarian organization, the dissertation traces two cases that show how inquiry itself can be used to create a more egalitarian organizational future. An analysis of field data suggests that the potential of egalitarian systems is coterminously affected by: (1) organizational ideology; (2) structures of work and political interaction; and (3) predominant social paradigms of organizational thought and action.

The dissertation concludes with five major propositions concerning the appreciative mode of inquiry and makes a call to the field to experiment with a humanly significant process of social-organizational inquiry, an inquiry based on co-appreciative modes of questioning, valuing, knowing, choosing and enacting.

Acknowledgements

IN AN ALMOST LITERAL SENSE, this dissertation has exhibited a life of its own since its inception in 1981. Its character—right from the start—was expansive and exploratory, always providing a compelling lure to venture into areas lying beyond the reach of my current competencies. There were many times, too many to count, when I hesitated to accept its challenges. I remember those moments with remorse. There were other times, however, when I embraced the challenges. Indeed, I remember a mixture of emotions as I followed the thesis down the path of a number of rocky and unmarked trails. During some of those times, I remember only fear and anxiety. But mostly, when I glance in retrospect over the entire process of social-organizational inquiry, I experienced adventure.

The thrill of adventure was made possible because of the inspiration, love, care, and encouragement of a special "community of competence." To be sure, this study is a product of the human group; the ideas and systems of meaning reported here would not have been possible without the cooperation and sharing that took place between the author and a number of close friends, colleagues, relatives, companions, and teachers. While the activities of thinking and writing are solitary ones, they are activities that cannot be done alone.

It is with great pleasure that I acknowledge the immeasurable contribution of members of my dissertation committee. Dr. Eric Neilsen was especially important as a model in the complex and intellectually demanding area of theory building. He was also impactful as a friend and colleague; it was through his encouragement and assistance that I was able to present the ideas in the dissertation, for the first time, to fellow professionals in the field at a National Academy of Management meeting. Through this public sharing, the ideas in the thesis were, of course, refined. But, more important, the experience will always be remembered as a significant stepping stone in my entry into the profession.

Dr. Ronald Fry helped bring focus, clarity, and coherence to the dissertation. Through his insightful analysis, Dr. Fry helped me to see beyond the trees to the essential forest of the study. Early on, I had ideas for an even *more* expansive dissertation. It was his insistence that "appreciative inquiry" was the essential contribution that really allowed me to sit down and accomplish the task of writing. As a colleague, Dr. Fry has always been an important source of ideas and experience. And, as a teacher, he has been a splendid model on how to synthesize thought and action, theory and practice.

I am also grateful to Dr. Paul Salipante, who joined my committee from outside the department. He was especially instrumental in helping refine earlier drafts of the egalitarian theory. Also, it was Dr. Salipante who introduced me to Dr. Rene Bouwen of the University of Leuven in Belgium. Dr. Bouwen provided a number of useful insights and is now experimenting with processes of appreciative inquiry in his research on organizational innovation in Europe.

I am particularly thankful to the chairman of my committee, Dr. Suresh Srivastva. The conceptual seed for the entire study was planted by Dr. Srivastva. It has survived and flourished largely because of his unbounded commitment and patience; and also because of the fertile atmosphere of thinking, questioning, learning and valuing that is uniquely generated wherever he goes. Dr. Srivastva is an exceptional human being. He embodies the spirit of inquiry and concern for social existence that is being argued for in the dissertation. His example has given me courage. Instead of becoming "tranquilized in the trivial," I was able to entertain and embrace questions for which there are few, if any, final answers. There are no words to describe what his mentorship and friendship has meant to me. He makes people happen. No student could ask for more than what Suresh has given me.

A number of good friends and colleagues deserve my deepest thanks as well. There have been many fruitful dialogues over the past six years. In particular, I am indebted to classmates Dennis O'Connor, Harlow Cohen, Constance Savage, Allan Plath, Toni Denton, and Irene Devine. There were also many important discussions with Jeff Petee, Al Jensen, Hand Jonas, V. Nilakant, Marty Kaplan, Frank Barrett, Carole Parker, Rich Rosen, Veronica Hopper, M.V.H. Rao, Jean Neumann, Barry Morris, and Karen Locke. Much appreciation also goes to a number of other faculty colleagues here at CWRU, in particular Drs. William Pasmore, David Kolb, and Mitchell McCorcle. The typing of the manuscript was handled magnificently by Retta Holdorf. Without her caring support, friendship, and expert advice, the dissertation would never have reached its final form. And perhaps most important, I owe a debt of gratitude to Dr. William Kiser, chairman of the Board of Governors, and to all the members of the Cleveland Clinic Foundation who shared in the study both in terms of much time and energy and in terms of financial support.

Finally, I would like to thank my family. First, my appreciation goes to my parents, Loy and Fran Cooperrider, who taught me to think, to question, and to value the world of people, ideas and nature. Secondly, I am thankful to my wife and partner, Nancy. I have never met anyone who lives the appreciative ideal more than Nancy. Her artistic approach to living has lifted me beyond the depths of despair and has taught me how to begin seeing the beauty inherent in ordinary life. Also, it was because of her steadfast support that I was able to bypass expediency for integrity as it related to this academic pursuit.

This work is dedicated to Daniel Paul Cooperrider, my ten-month-old son whose birth taught me the profound meaning of the word *miracle*. It was only after witnessing his delivery that I was able to put words to the central theme of the study. Indeed, the fact that students of organizational life can even begin inquiring into the potentials of social existence is, in and of itself, a miracle that can never be fully comprehended.

Table of Contents

List of Tables

List of Figures

I

Introduction

If I were to wish for anything, I should not wish for wealth and power, but for the passionate sense of the potential, for the eye which, ever young and ardent, sees the possible. Pleasure disappoints, possibility never. And what wine is so foaming, what so fragrant, what so intoxicating, as possibility!

– Søren Kierkegaard

AS IS GENERALLY UNDERSTOOD, THE scientist is ideally an impartial bystander, objectively recording the world of things and people, careful not to participate in or contaminate the world he or she hopes to understand. In this view of science, the world exists "out there" just waiting to be recorded; so, too, the scientist is but a recording instrument, waiting to assemble data from that which is given to the senses. Knowledge, it is contended, is merely interpretive, not creative. And, just as the present is given, the future also is largely determined by laws and forces that guide the history and nature of man. In such a world, the concepts of freedom and responsibility and love and will have little place. Mind is separate from body and theory is divorced from practice.

So pervasive has been this viewpoint that only now are we beginning to see the integral unity of theory and practice, and only now are we beginning to scratch the surface of the incredibly complex Lewinian proposition that there is nothing so practical as good theory. Virtually unexamined by the social-administrative sciences in general—and action-research in particular—are the complex and subtle ways in which theory is creative of the social-organizational future and hence how science can play a more collaborative role in the conscious evolution of culture.

This dissertation is best understood as a conceptual case study whose aim is to explore, describe, and propose an action-oriented approach to organizational inquiry that is uniquely intended for the study and enhancement of *social innovation*. As a conceptual itinerary, the dissertation proposes a broad refiguration of action-research. It seeks to advance a position that goes beyond the conventional problem-solving frame to include an appreciative dimension of inquiry whereby social existence is experienced and embraced as a mystery that can never be fully understood. As a descriptive analysis, however, the study does more than simply make a conceptual proposal; it describes, in detail, a five-year research process founded on the appreciative mode. Through the presentation of multiple sources of data, it illustrates the power of appreciative theorizing, not only as a means for understanding organizational practice, but also as a formative agent in the process of social-organizational innovation itself.

This dissertation argues for an enriched, multi-dimensional view of action-research that seeks to be theoretically generative.[1] It begins with the observation that action-research has become increasingly rationalized and enculturated to the point where it risks becoming little more than a crude empiricism imprisoned in a deficiency mode of thought. In its conventional *unidimensional* form, action-research has largely failed as an instrument for advancing social knowledge of consequence and has not, therefore, achieved its potential as a vehicle for human development and social-organizational transformation. While the literature consistently signals its worth as a managerial tool for problem-solving (first-order incremental change), it is conspicuously quiet concerning reports of discontinuous change of

---

1. While I draw most of my examples from the Organization Development (OD) school of action-research, the argument presented here should be relevant to other applications as well. As noted by Peters and Robinson (1984), the discipline of action-research has been prevalent in the literature of community action, education and educational system change, and organizational change, as well as discussions of the social sciences in general.

the "second order," where organizational paradigms, norms, ideologies, or values are transformed in fundamental ways (Watzlawick, et al., 1974).

In the course of the dissertation, a number of broad, yet interrelated, concerns are touched upon—scientific, metaphysical, normative, and pragmatic. Linking these streams is an underlying conviction that action-research has the potential to be to the post-industrial era what "scientific management" was to the industrial. That is, just as scientific management provided the philosophical and methodological legitimacy required to support the bureaucratic, organization form (Clegg and Dunkerly, 1980; Braverman, 1974), action-research might well provide the intellectual rationale and reflexive methodology required to support the emergence of a more egalitarian "post-bureaucratic" form of organization. The essential distinction, however, is that, unlike scientific management that provided the means for a *techno-rational* science of administration, action-research holds unique and essential promise in the *socio-rational* realm of human affairs: It has the potential to become the paradigmatic basis of a truly significant—a humanly significant—applied science of administration.

It is contended that a primary barrier circumventing the potential of action research has been its romance with "action" at the expense of "theory." This, unfortunately, has led many in the discipline to seriously underestimate the power of theory as a means for social-organizational reconstruction. Drawing largely on the pioneering and synthesizing work of Kenneth Gergen (1978; 1982), a re-examination of the character of theoretical knowledge and its role in social transformation is presented. Then an appeal is made to define the scientific aim of action-research in ways that reunite the dynamic interpenetration of theory and practice. The aim of science, in this point of view, is not the detached discovery and verification of social laws allowing for technocratic prediction and control. Instead, an alternative is highlighted that defines good science by its "generative capacity," that is:

...the capacity to challenge the guiding assumptions of the culture, to raise fundamental questions regarding contemporary social life, to foster reconsideration of that which is "taken for granted" and thereby furnish new alternatives for social actions (Gergen, 1978, p. 1346).

Obviously, the foundation for such a view has been developing for some time. The last decade, for example, has witnessed an enormous confluence of thinking concerning the paradigmatic refiguration of social thought. As Geertz (1980) notes, there has been a "blurring of genres" as many social scientists have abandoned—without apology—the misdirected quest to mimic the "more mature" physical sciences. Turning away from a Newtonian laws-and-instance type explanation rooted in logical empiricist philosophy, many social theorists have instead opted for an interpretive form of inquiry that connects organized action to its contextually embedded set of meanings:

...looking less for the sort of things that connect planets and pendulums and more for the sort that connects chrysanthemums and swords (Geertz, 1980, p. 165).

Indeed, prominent members from throughout the field have publicly given up on the logical positivist idea of "certainty through science" and are embarking on approaches to research that grant pre-eminence to the historically situated (ever-changing) "interpretive schemes" used by members of a given group to give life and meaning to their actions and decisions (Bartunek, 1984). Indicative of the shift away from the logical positivist frame, researchers are converging around what has been termed the "socio-rationalist" metatheory of science (Gergen, 1982). Recognizing the symbolic nature of the human universe, one now finds a flurry of innovative work supporting the theme that there is little about human development or organizational behavior that is "pre-programmed" or stimulus-bound in any direct physical or biological way. In this sense, the social universe is generally understood to be open to indefinite revision, change, and self-propelled development. This recognition is a crucial one because, to the extent to which social existence *is* situated in a symbolic realm, beyond deterministic forces, then the logical positivist foundation of social science is negated and its concept of knowledge is rendered illusionary.

Nowhere is this better evidenced than in the variety of works concerned with organizational paradigms (Brown, 1978; McHugh, 1970); beliefs and master scripts (Sproull, 1981; Beyer, 1981); idea management and executive mind (Srivastva, 1983; 1985); theories of action and presumptions of logic (Argyris and Schon, 1978; Weick, 1983); consciousness and awareness (Faucheux, 1985; Harrison, 1982; Lukes, 1974); and, of course, an array of work associated with the concept of organizational or corporate culture (Ouchi, 1978; Schein, 1983; Van Maanen, 1982; Deal and Kennedy, 1982; Sathe, 1983; and Hoffstede, 1980). As Ellwood prophetically suggested almost half a century ago, "This is the cultural view of human society that is revolutionizing the social sciences" (Ellwood, 1938, p. 561).

The development of this focus on the symbolic realm—on the power of ideas—by such independent sources with such diversity in objectives is responsive to the reality of organized life in the modern world. However reluctantly, it seems even the most traditional social thinkers are now recognizing the distinctiveness of the post-industrial world for what it truly is: *an unfolding drama of human interaction whose potential seems limited or enhanced primarily by our symbolic capacities of mind and our social capacity for constructing meaningful agreements allowing for the committed enactment of collective life.*

Never in the history of humankind have ideas, information, beliefs, *or* theory been so central in the formulation of reality itself. Social existence, of course, has always depended on some kind of idea system for its meaningful sustenance. The difference now, however, is that what was once background has become foreground. In today's world, the very survival of society continues to be experienced less as a mechanical extension of machines, and even less as a gift of fateful nature, and more and more as a social construction of interacting minds, "as a game between persons" (Bell, 1973). And, under these conditions (i.e., a structural-developmental changeover from an agrarian society to a goods-producing society and then to an information society), ideas and meaning systems take on a whole new life and character: Ideas are thrust center stage as the prime unit of relational exchange governing the creation or obliteration of social existence.

Implications for Action-Research

This line of argument applies no less potently to current conceptions of social science. *That is, to the extent that the primary product of science is systematically refined idea systems (theory), it, too, must be recognized as a powerful agent in the enhancement or destruction of human life.* And, while this presents an unresolvable dilemma for a logical empiricist conception of science, it spells real opportunity (and responsibility) for an administrative science that wishes to be of vital significance to organizations and society. Put most simply, the theoretical contributions of science may be among the most powerful resources human beings have for contributing to change and development in the groups and organizations in which they live. This, it will be argued, is precisely the meaning of Kurt Lewin's early view of action science when he proposed: "There is nothing so practical as good theory" (1952, p. 169).

Ironically, the discipline of action-research continues to insist on a sharp separation of theory and practice, and continues to underrate the role of theory in social reconstruction. The irony is that it does so precisely at a time when the cultural view of organizing is reaching toward paradigmatic status. The sad and perhaps tragic commentary on action-research is that it is becoming less consequential as its opportunity to contribute is rising (Argyris, 1983).

Observers such as Rappaport (1970) and Bartunek (1983) have lamented the fact that action researchers have come to subordinate research aims to action interests. Levison (1972) has gone even further by branding the discipline as "atheoretical." And Friedlander and Brown (1974) have noted that, in the very definition of action-research in classic texts (i.e., French and Bell), there is virtually no mention of theory building as an integral and necessary component of the research/diagnostic process or the process of organizational change. When theory is mentioned, it is most always referred to as a springboard for research or diagnosis, not the other way around. Bartunek concludes that:

> ...even the most recent papers that describe action-research strate-
> gies tend to focus primarily on the process of action-research and
> only secondarily on the specific theoretical contributions of the
> outcomes of such research (1983, pp. 3-4) [e.g., Frohman, Sashkin
> and Kavanaugh, 1976; Shani and Pasmore, 1982; Susman and
> Evered, 1978; see Pasmore and Friedlander, 1982 for an exception].

According to Argyris (1983), the lack of useful theorizing is attributable to a couple of key sources. The first is that practice-oriented scholars tend to become so client-centered that they fail to question clients' own definition of problems and thereby ignore building testable propositions and theories embedded in everyday life. Academics, on the other hand, who are trained to be more scientific in their bent, also constrain the development of useful theory by their very criteria of "normal" science, which defines good research by its detachment, rigor, unilateral control, and operational precision. In a word, creative theorizing has literally been assaulted on all fronts by practitioners and academic scientists alike. It can be noted also that implicit, even in the critique by Argyris (1983) and others like it (e.g., Friedlander and Brown, 1974), there is an underlying assumption that action-research has *natural* conflicts built into it that are likely to lead to "action" (consulting) or to "research" (diagnosis or the development of organizational theory), but not to both. The situation is summed up by Friedlander and Brown (1974) in their comprehensive review of the field, in which they conclude:

> We believe that research will either play a far more crucial role in

the advancement of this field or become an increasingly irrelevant appendage to it...We have generally failed to produce a theory of change which emerges from the change process itself. We need a way of enriching our understanding and action synergistically rather than at one or the other's expense—to become science in which knowledge-getting and knowledge-giving are an integrated process, and one that is valuable to all parties involved (p. 319).

The authors conclude the review with a plea for a metatheoretical revision of science that integrates theory and practice. But in another review more than a decade later, Friedlander (1984) observes (at a recent symposium on the topic) little progress coming from top scholars in the discipline. He then puts words to a mounting frustration over what appears as a recurring problem:

> They pointed to the shortcomings of traditional research and called for emancipation from it; but they did not indicate a destination. There is as yet no new paradigm that integrates research and practice, or even optimizes useful knowledge for organizations... I'm impatient. Let's get on with it. Let's not talk it, write it, analyze it, conceptualize it, research it. Instead, let's actively engage and experiment with new designs for producing knowledge that is, in fact, used by organizations (p. 647).

Overview and Plan of the Dissertation

As the end of the 20th Century nears, thinkers in organizational behavior are beginning to see, without hesitation, why an administrative science based on a physical science model is simply not adequate as a means for understanding or contributing in relevant ways to the workings of complex, organized human systems (see, for example, Susman and Evered, 1978; Beyer and Trice, 1982). Kurt Lewin had understood this almost half a century earlier but his progressive vision of an action science fell short of offering a clear, metatheoretical alternative to conventional conceptions of science (Peters and Robinson, 1984; Lewin, 1977). Indeed, the epistemological ambiguity inherent in Lewin's writing has been cited as a major shortcoming of his work. And yet, with hindsight, it can be argued that the ambiguity was intentional and was perhaps part of Lewin's social sensitivity and genius. The metatheoretical confusion might very well have been a protective measure, an attempt by Lewin to shield his fresh vision of an action science from the fully dominant logical-positivist temper of his time. In any event, whether planned or not, Lewin walked a tightrope between two fundamentally opposed views of science and never did make it clear exactly how it was that theory could be used as both an interpretive and creative element. This achievement, as we might guess, would have to wait for a change in the intellectual ethos of social science.

Increasingly, the literature signals disenchantment with theories of science that grant priority to the external world in the generation of human knowledge. Instead there is growing movement toward a viewpoint that grants pre-eminence to the cognitive processes of mind and symbolic processes of social construction. In his recent work, *Toward Transformation in Social Knowledge*, Gergen (1982) synthesizes the essential whole of this movement and takes it one important step beyond disenchantment to a bold, yet workable, conception of science that firmly unites theory with practice. From a historical perspective, there is no question that this is a major achievement; it is an advance that puts mature completion to Lewin's work, which was brought to a halt by his untimely death. But it is more than that. What Gergen offers, albeit indirectly, is a desperately needed clue of how to revitalize an action-research discipline that has never reached its potential.

In Chapter II, the socio-rationalist foundation of social science is reviewed and used as a platform from which to construct a process of organizational inquiry that re-unites theory and practice—and thereby elevates the role of theory in its work with organizations. The chapter contrasts socio-rationalist assumptions with those of logical empiricism and then seeks to examine in detail the claim that social theory and practice are, indeed, part of a synthetic whole. After examining just why and how theory attains its power to effect cultural practice, then a more troublesome question is addressed: Assuming that *generative* theory is a legitimate output of good scientific work—and that it is, in fact, capable of provoking debate, stimulating normative dialogue, and furnishing conceptual alternatives needed for social transformation, then why has action-research downplayed creative theorizing in its work with organizations?

It is here that the conceptual heart of the chapter is developed. Basically, it argues that the generative weakness of contemporary action-research rests with the discipline's unquestioned commitment to a secularized problem-oriented view of the world—and thus to the subsequent loss of our capacity as researchers and participants to marvel and thereby embrace the miracle and mystery of social organization. If we acknowledge Maslow's (1968) admonition that true science begins and ends in wonder, then we immediately shed light on why action-research has failed to produce innovative theory capable of inspiring the imagination, commitment, and passionate dialogue required for the consensual re-ordering of social conduct.

Appreciative inquiry is then presented as a mode of conducting action-research that meets the criteria of science as spelled out in generative-theoretical terms. Going beyond questions of epistemology, appreciative inquiry has as its basis a *metaphysical* concern that posits that *social existence* is, indeed, a miracle that can never be fully comprehended (Quinney, 1982; Marcel 1963). It is at this level of understanding that the uniqueness of the appreciative mode is explored. More than a method or technique, the appreciative mode of inquiry is described as a way of living with, being with, and directly participating in the varieties of organizations we are compelled to study. Growing out of serious consideration and reflection of the ultimate mystery of being, it is argued that a reverence for life is engendered that draws the researcher to inquiry beyond superficial appearances to deeper levels of the life-generating essentials and potentials of social existence. That is, the action-researcher is drawn to affirm and thereby illuminate the factors and forces of organizing that serve to nourish the human spirit.

Thus, this chapter seeks to enrich our conception of an applied administrative science by introducing a "second dimension" of action-research going beyond a secularized problem-solving frame.

Chapter III takes the proposal and describes the processes of observation used in a study of a major social innovation in the health-care industry. As one of the largest tertiary care medical group practices in the world, the Cleveland Clinic (CC) provided a prototype post-industrial setting for studying egalitarian processes of organizing that are shown to depart from the conventional bureaucratic ideal-type. Key features of the five-year study are summarized into a general model of appreciative knowing and learning that consists of: (1) topic choice as an appreciative act of valuing; (2) articulation of normative theory; (3) consensual validation and development of normative theory; (4) experimentation with normative theory; and (5) revisitation of normative theory. The aim throughout the study was to bring generative-theoretical understanding to the "emerging" egalitarian organization and to use the *process* of theorizing as a springboard for normative dialogue and experimentation, i.e., "What kind of organizational world do we want to construct together?" "Does the egalitarian theory represent an ideal we feel the organization ought to be living up to and be evolving toward?"

Chapter IV describes how the emerging theory was further refined through an interactive process of joint inquiry. Here it was felt that the generative potential of the theory would be enhanced by direct engagement whereby organizational participants would (1) consensually validate and then refine the theory as their own normative ideal, and (2) use the emerging theory as a starting point for collective experimentation for moving closer to the ideal. A quantitative and qualitative description of this process indicates not only the power of theory as a means for organizational transformation but, *more importantly, highlights how essential the consensual and experimental processes are for adding to the generative potential of knowledge.* In this sense, the content and process of knowing are inseparable. Social knowledge or theory is a product of the human group.

The dissertation concludes with a detailed articulation of the theory of the egalitarian organization. As an offspring of the co-appreciative learning process with members of the Cleveland Clinic, the theory presents a propositional logic for a form of organizing that is yet to be fully realized. Going beyond the bureaucratic frame, the egalitarian theory of organizing is premised on the emergence of an *interhuman* administrative rationality that transcends rather than replaces instrumental rationality as a basis for collective action.

In a very real sense, the concluding chapter is not a conclusion. Consistent with socio-rationalist principles of knowing, the propositions in Chapter V are best understood as a series of questions, challenges and possibilities. They are intended to expand the realm of that which is considered possible. Finally, the chapter ends with a short epilogue that comments on yet another phase in which members of the CC are now taking the theory. Summary principles are then articulated about the appreciative mode itself, without which the egalitarian theory would not have been possible.

II

Toward Appreciation in Action-Research

We are some time truly to see our life as positive, not negative, as made up of continuous willing, not of constraints and prohibition.

– Mary Parker Follett

We are steadily forgetting how to dream; in historical terms, the mathematicist and technicist dimensions of Platonism have conquered the poetical, mythical, and rhetorical context of analysis. We are forgetting how to be reasonable in non-mathematical dialects.

– Stanley Rosen

THIS CHAPTER PRESENTS A CONCEPTUAL refiguration of action-research, arguing for a multi-dimensional view that is theoretically generative and progressive in a broad human sense. In short, the position taken here argues that, for action-research to reach its potential as a vehicle for social-organizational innovation, it needs to begin advancing theoretical knowledge of consequence. Recognizing that good theory may be one of the most powerful means human beings have for producing change in a post-industrial world, this chapter seeks to explore and propose ways to elevate the status of theory and to ignite the spirit of imagination required for catalytic theorizing.

The position unfolds in the following way. First, an overview is presented of an emerging social science paradigm that grants pre-eminence to cognitive processes of mind and symbolic processes of social construction in the generation of human knowledge and meaning. Here, socio-rationalist metatheory is contrasted to logical positivism along ten dimensions. The purpose of the comparison is to highlight that the socio-rationalist assumption base represents an epistemological point of view that firmly unites theory and practice and hence is uniquely suited as a philosophical foundation for action-research. Second, an examination is undertaken that looks more closely at the claim that social theory is, in fact, a means for both understanding *and* improving social practice by asking, "How is it that theory achieves its capacity to affect social practice?" Next, a more disturbing question is raised: "Why has action-research downplayed catalytic theorizing in its work with organizations?" It is here that we move to the heart of the chapter. After a critical review of some of the disciplines' most cherished assumptions, it is argued that action-research has been constrained by an overcommitment to a problem-oriented view of the world. Another stance is proposed that calls for a fundamentally different perspective toward our life-world, one that admits to its mysteries, wholeness, and unexplicable miraculous nature. Appreciative inquiry and problem-solving inquiry are seen as two different forks emanating from the same road. Finally, it is posited that the actual fork one takes is based on choice and that, through our assumptions and choice of method, we largely create the world we later discover.

A Socio-Rationalist Foundation for Action-Research

At the heart of socio-rationalism is the assumption of *impermanence*, or fundamental instability of the social order: That is, no matter what the durability to date, virtually any pattern of social action is open to infinite revision. Accepting for a moment the cultural argument that social reality, at any given point, is a product of broad social agreement (shared meanings), and further granting a linkage between the conceptual schemes of a culture and its other patterns of action, then we must seriously reckon with the idea that alterations in conceptual practices, in ways of symbolizing the world, hold tremendous potential for guiding changes in the social order. To understand the importance of this set of assumptions and their meaning for social science, let us quote Gergen (1982) at length:

Is not the range of cognitive heuristics that may be employed in solving problems of adaptation limited only by the human imagination?

One must finally consider the possibility that human biology not only presents to the scientist an organism whose actions may vary in an infinity of ways, but it may ensure as well that novel patterns are continuously emerging...variations in human activity may importantly be traced to the capacities of the organism for symbolic reconstructuring. As it is commonly said, one's actions appear to be vitally linked to the manner in which one understands or construes the world of experience. The stimulus world does not elicit behavior in an automatic, reflex-like fashion. Rather, the symbolic translation of one's experiences virtually transforms their implications and thereby alters the range of one's potential reactions. Interestingly, while formulations of this variety are widely shared within the scientific community, very little attention has been paid to their ramifications for a theory of science. *As is clear, without such regularities, the prediction of behavior is largely obviated...to the extent that the individual is capable of transforming the meaning of stimulus conditions in an indeterminate number of ways, existing regularities must be considered historically contingent—dependent on the prevailing meaning systems or conceptual structure of the times.* In effect, from this perspective, the scientist's capacity to locate predictable patterns of interaction depends importantly on the extent to which the population is both homogeneous and stable in its conceptual constructions (pp. 16-17, emphasis mine).

While this type of reasoning is consistent with the thinking of many social scientists, the ramifications are rarely taken to their logical conclusion:

Virtually unexamined by the field is the potential of science to shape the meaning systems of the society and thus the common activities of the society and thus the common activities of the culture (Gergen, 1978, p. 1379).

Virtually unexamined is the important role that science can—and does— play in what might be called the scientific construction of social reality.

One implication of this line of thought is that, to the extent that social science conceives of its role in the logical positivist sense, with its goals being prediction and control, then not only does it serve the interests of the status quo (i.e., you can't have "good science" without stable replication and verification of hypotheses), but it also seriously underestimates the power and usefulness of its most important product, namely theory. It underestimates the constructive role science can have in the development of the groups and organizations that make up our cultural world. According to Gergen, this realization furnishes the opportunity to refashion a social science of vital significance to society. To do this, we need a bold shift in attention whereby theoretical accounts need no longer be judged in terms of their *predictive capacity*, but instead are judged in terms of their *generative capacity*: the ability to foster dialogue about that which is taken for granted and the capacity for generating fresh alternatives for social action. Instead of asking, "Does this theory correspond with the observable facts?" the question for evaluating good theory becomes, "To what extent does this theory present provocative new possibilities for social action, and to what extent does it stimulate normative dialogue about how we can and should organize ourselves?" The serial logic for such a proposal is summarized in the following ten points:

1. The social order, at any given point, is viewed as the product of broad social agreement (tacit or explicit).

2. Patterns of social-organizational action are not fixed by nature in any direct biological or physical way; the vast share of social conduct is virtually stimulus-free, capable of infinite conceptual variation.

3. From an observational point of view, all social action is open to multiple interpretations, no one of which is superior in any objectified sense. The interpretations (for example, "whites are superior to blacks") favored in one historical setting may be replaced in the next.

4. Historically embedded conventions govern what is taken to be true or valid, and to a large extent govern what we, as scientists and lay persons, are able to see. All observation, therefore, is theory-laden and filtered through conventional belief systems and theoretical lenses.[2]

5. To the extent that action is predicated on ideas, beliefs, meanings, intentions or theory, then people are free to seek transformations in conventional conduct by changing conventional codes (idea systems).

6. The most powerful vehicle communities have for transforming their conventions (i.e., agreements on norms, values, policies, purposes, ideologies, etc.) is through the act of dialogue made possible by language. Alterations in linguistic practices, therefore, hold profound implications for changes in social practice.

7. Social theory can be viewed as a highly refined language with a specialized grammar all its own. As a powerful linguistic tool (created by trained linguistic experts, i.e., scientists), theory may enter the conceptual meaning system of a culture—and in this way alter patterns of social action.

8. Whether intended or not, all theory is normative and has the potential to influence the social order.

9. Because of this, all social theory is morally relevant—it has the potential to affect the way people live their ordinary lives in relation to one another. This point is a critical one because there is no such thing as detached/technical/scientistic mode for judging the ultimate worth of value claims.

10. Valid knowledge or social theory is, therefore, a communal creation. Social knowledge is not "out there" in nature to be discovered through detached, value-free, observational methods

---

2. As physicist Jeremy Hayward (1984) put it, "I'll see it when I believe it," or oppositely "I won't see it because I don't believe it." The point is that all observation is filtered through belief systems that act as our personal theories of the world. Thus, what *counts* as a "fact" depends largely on beliefs associated with a theory and, therefore, on the community of scientists holding this belief system.

(logical empiricism); nor can it be relegated to the subjective minds of isolated individuals (solipsism). Social knowledge, from this perspective, resides in the interactive collectivity; it is created, maintained, and put to use by the human group. Dialogue, free from constraint or distortion, is necessary to determine the "nature of things" (socio-rationalism).

In Table II-1, the metatheory of socio-rationalism is summarized and contrasted to commonly held assumptions of the logical empiricist view of science. Especially important to note is the transformed role of the scientist when social inquiry is viewed from the perspective of socio-rationalism. Instead of attempting to present oneself as an impartial bystander or dispassionate spectator of the inevitable, the social scientist conceives of him or herself as an active agent, an invested participant whose work might well become a powerful source of change in the way people see and enact their worlds.

Table II-1
Comparison of Logical Empiricist and Socio-Rationalist Conceptions of Social Science

Dimension for Comparison	Logical Empiricism	Socio-Rationalism
1. Primary Function of Science	Enhance goals of understanding, prediction, and control by discerning general laws or principles governing the relationship among units of observable phenomena.	Enhance understanding in the sense of assigning meaning to something, thus creating its status through the use of concepts. Science is a means for expanding flexibility and choice in cultural evolution.
2. Theory of Knowledge and Mind	Exogenic—grants priority to the external world in the generation of human knowledge (i.e., the preeminence of objective fact). Mind is a mirror.	Endogenic—holds the processes of mind and symbolic interaction as pre-eminent source of human knowledge. Mind is both a mirror and a lamp.

Dimension for Comparison	Logical Empiricism	Socio-Rationalism
3. Perspective on Time	Assumption of temporal irrelevance; searches for transhistorical principles.	Assumption of historically and contextually relevant meanings; existing regularities in social order are contingent on prevailing meaning systems.
4. Assuming Stability of Social Patterns	Social phenomena are sufficiently stable, enduring, reliable and replicable to allow for lawful principles.	Social order is fundamentally unstable. Social phenomena are guided by cognitive heuristics, limited only by the human imagination; the social order is a subject matter capable of infinite variation through the linkage of ideas and action.
5. Value Stance	Separation of fact and values. Possibility of objective knowledge through behavioral observation.	Social sciences are fundamentally non-objective. Any behavioral event is open to virtually any interpretive explanation. All interpretation is filtered through prevailing values of a culture. "There is no description without prescription."
6. Features of "Good" Theory	Discovery of transhistorically valid principles; a theory's correspondence with fact.	Degree to which theory furnishes alternatives for social innovation and thereby opens vistas for action; expansion of "the realm of the possible."
7. Criteria for Confirmation or Verification (Life of a Theory)	Logical consistency and empirical prediction; subject to falsification.	Persuasive appeal, impact, and overall generative capacity; subject to community agreement; truth is a product of a community of truth makers.

Dimension for Comparison	Logical Empiricism	Socio-Rationalism
8. Role of Scientist	Impartial bystander and dispassionate spectator of the inevitable; content to accept that which seems given.	Active agent and co-participant who is primarily a source of linguistic activity (theoretical language) that serves as input into common meaning systems. Interested in "breaking the hammerlock" of what appears as given in human nature.
9. Chief Product of Research	Cumulation of objective knowledge through the production of empirically disconfirmable hypothesis.	Continued improvement in theory-building capacity; improvement in the capacity to create generative-theoretical language.
10. Emphasis in the Education of Future Social Science Professionals	Rigorous experimental methods and statistical analysis; a premium is placed on method (training in theory construction is a rarity).	Hermeneutic interpretation and catalytic theorizing; a premium is placed on the theoretical imagination. Socio-rationalism invites the student toward intellectual expression in the service of his or her vision of the good.

Driven by a desire to "break the hammerlock" of what appears as given in human nature, the scientist attempts to build theories that expand the realm of what is conventionally understood as possible. In this sense, the core impact of socio-rationalist metatheory is that it invites, encourages, and requires that students of social life rigorously exercise their theoretical imagination in the service of their vision of the good. Instead of denial, it is an invitation to fully accept and exercise those qualities of mind and action that make us uniquely human.

Now we turn to a question raised earlier: How is it that theory achieves its capacity to affect social practice and what are some of the specific characteristics of *generative theory*?

The Power of Theory

The socio-rationalist vision of science is of such far-reaching importance that no student, organizational scientist, manager, educator or *action-researcher* can afford to ignore it. As discussed, good theory is certainly to be regarded as one of the most powerful means we have for helping social systems evolve, adapt, and alter their patterns over time. Building further on this metatheoretical perspective, we can talk about five ways theory achieves its potency:

1. Establishment of a perceptual and contextual frame

2. Providing presumptions of logic

3. Transmitting a system of values

4. Creation of group-building language

5. Extending visions of possibility or constraint

1. *Establishment of a perceptual and contextual frame.* To the extent that theory is the conceptual imposition of order upon an otherwise "booming, bustling, confusion that is the realm of experience" (Dubin, 1978), the first order of business of the theorist is to specify what is there to see, to provide an "ontological education" (Gergen, 1982). The very act of theoretical articulation, therefore, highlights not only the parameters of the topic or subject matter, but *becomes an active agent as a cueing device*, a device that subtly focuses attention on particular phenomenon or meanings while obscuring others. As kind of a telescope or lens, a new theory allows one to see the world in a way perhaps never before imagined.

For example, when American eugenicists used the lens of biological determinism to attribute diseases of poverty to the inferior genetic construction of poor people, they literally could see no systematic remedy other than sterilization of the poor. In contrast, when Joseph Goldberg theorized that pellagra was not genetically determined but culturally caused (as a result of vitamin deficiency and eating habits of the poor), he could discover a way to cure it (Gould, 1981). In a similar way, theories of "survival of the fittest" might very well help executives locate "predators," "hostile environments" and a world where self-interest reigns, where "it is eat or be eaten." Likewise, theories of leadership have been known to quickly facilitate the discovery of Theory X or Theory Y interaction. Whatever the theory, it provides a potential means for members of a culture to navigate in an otherwise neutral, meaningless, or chaotic sea of people, interactions and events. By providing an "ontological education" of what is there, a theory furnishes an important cultural input affecting people's cognitive set. In this sense:

> ...the world is not so constituted until the lens is employed. With each new distinction the groundwork is laid for alterations in existing patterns of conduct (Gergen, 1982, p. 23).[3]

2. *Providing presumptions of logic.* Theories are also powerful to the extent to which they help shape common expectations of causality, sequence, and relational importance of phenomena within a theoretical equation.

Consider, for example, the simple logic underlying most every formal performance appraisal system. Stripped to essentials, the theoretical underpinnings state something like this: "If you want to evaluate performance (P), then you must evaluate the individual employee (E); in other words, $P = E$." Armed with this theory, many managers have entered the performance appraisal meeting shaking with the thought of having to pass god-like judgment on some employee. Similarly, the employee arrives at the meeting with an arsenal of defenses, designed to protect his or her hard-won self-esteem. Very little genuine communication occurs during the meeting and virtually no problem-solving takes place. The paperwork

---

3. As the reader may already surmise, there is an important moral issue beginning to emerge. Part of the reason that theory is, in fact, powerful is that it shapes perceptions, cognitions, and preferences often at a pre-conscious level, much like subliminal communications or even hypnosis. Haley (1976) talks about how Milton Erickson has made this a central feature of his psychotherapeutic work. But Lukes (1974) cautions that such thought control may be "the supreme and most insidious exercise of power," especially when it prevents people from challenging their role in the existing order of things and when it operates counter to their real interests.

is mechanically completed, then filed away in the personnel office until the next year. So powerful is this subtle equation that virtually unnoticed is the alternative Lewinian theory that states that behavior (performance) is a function of the person and the environment (in this case the environment refers to the organizational situation, "OS," in which the employee works). Following this line, the theory underlying performance appraisal would have to be expanded to now read $P = E \times OS$. That is, $P \neq E$. To adequately assess performance, there must be an assessment of the individual *in relation to* the organizational setting in which he or she works and vice versa. What would happen to the performance appraisal process if this more complete theory was used to re-design appraisal systems in organizations throughout the corporate world? Isn't it possible that such a theory could help shift the attribution process *away from person-blame to systems analysis?*[4]

By attributing causality, theories have the potential to create the very phenomenon they propose to explain. Karl Weick, in a recent article examining managerial thought in the context of action, contends that thought and action are part and parcel of one another, where thinking is best viewed as a kind of activity, and activity as the ground of the thought. For him, managerial theories gain their power by helping people overlook disorder and presume orderliness. Theory *energizes* action by providing a *presumption of logic* that enables people to act with certainty, attention, care and control. Even if the theory is originally inadequate as a description of current reality, if it is forceful it may provoke action that brings into the world a new reality that *then confirms* the original theory. Weick (1983) explains:

> Once the action is linked with an explanation, it becomes more
> forceful, and the situation is thereby transformed into something
> that supports the presumed underlying pattern. Presumptions

---

4. A group of colleagues and I are presently engaged in a two-year study of a major industrial plant where introduction of this simple theory has led to changes in job design, work relations, training programs, motivational climate, and hierarchical ideology. For an introduction to this work see Pasmore, Cooperrider, Kaplan and Morris, 1983.

[theories] enable actions to be tied to specific explanations that consolidate those actions into deterministic events...

The underlying explanation need *not* be objectively "correct." In a crude sense, any old explanation will do. This is so because explanation serves mostly to organize and focus the action. The focused action then modifies the situation in ways that confirm the explanation, whatever it is. Thus, the adequacy of any explanation is determined by the intensity and structure it adds to potentially self-validating actions. More forcefulness leads to more validation and more perceived adequacy. Accuracy is subordinate to intensity. Since situations can support a variety of meanings, their actual content and meaning are dependent on the degree to which they are arranged in sensible, coherent configurations. More forcefulness imposes more coherence. Thus, those explanations that induce greater forcefulness become more valid, not because they are more accurate, but because they have a higher potential for self-validation...the underlying explanations they invoke (for example, "This is war") have great potential to intensify whatever action is underway (1983, pp. 230-232).

Thus, theories are generative to the extent that they are forceful (e.g., Marx), logically coherent (e.g., Piaget), and bold in their assertions and consistency (e.g., Freud, Weber). By providing a basis for focused action, a logic for attributing causality, and a sequence specification setting expectations for action and reaction, a theory goes a long way in the forming of common expectations of the future. "And with the alteration of expectation, the stage is set for modification of action" (Gergen, 1982, p. 24).

3. *Transmitting a system of values.* Beyond abstract logic, it is often the affective core of social theory that provides its true force and appeal allowing it to direct perception and guide behavior. From the tradition of logical positivism, good "objective" theory is to be value-free, yet upon closer inspection we find that social theory is infused with values and domain assumptions throughout. As Gouldner (1970) so aptly put it:

Every social theory facilitates the pursuit of some, but not all, courses of action and thus, encourages us to change or accept the world as it is, to say yea or nay to it. In a way, every theory is a discreet obituary or celebration of some social system.

Nowhere is this better exemplified (negatively) than in the role scientific theory played in the arguments for slavery, colonialism, and belief in the genetic superiority of certain races. The theory that is being referred to again is the theory of biological determinism: the belief that social and economic differences between human beings and groups—differences in rank, status, political privilege, educational privilege, etc.—arise from inherited, natural endowments, and that existing social arrangements are justified as an accurate reflection of biological limits. So powerful was this theory during the 1800s that it led a number of America's highest ranking scientific researchers to unconsciously miscalculate "objective" data in what has been brilliantly described by naturalist Steven Jay Gould (1981) as a "patchwork of fudging and finagling in the clear interest of controlling a priori convictions" (p. 54). Before dismissing this harsh judgment as simple rhetoric, we need to look closely at how Gould arrived at it. One example will suffice.

When Samuel Morton, a scientist with two medical degrees, died in 1851, the *New York Tribune* paid tribute saying, "Probably no scientific man in America enjoyed a higher reputation among scholars throughout the world than Dr. Morton" (in Gould, 1981, p. 51). Morton gained this reputation as a scientist who set out to rank racial groups by "objectively" measuring the size of the cranial cavity of the human skull (as a measure of brain size). He had a beautiful collection of skulls from races throughout the world, probably the largest in existence. His hypothesis was a simple one: The mental and moral worth of human races could be arrived at objectively by measuring physical characteristics of the brain. By filling the cavities of the skulls with mustard seed or lead shot, accurate measurement of brain size was possible. Morton published three major works. These were reprinted repeatedly as objective, "hard" data on the mental worth of races. Gould comments:

Needless to say, they matched every good Yankee's prejudices—whites on top, Indians in the middle, and blacks on the bottom; and among whites, Tuetons and Anglo-Saxons on top, Jews in the middle, and Hindus on the bottom...Status and access to power in Morton's America faithfully reflected biological merit (p. 54).

Without much doubt, Morton's work was influential. When he died, the South's leading medical journal proclaimed: "We of the South should consider him as our benefactor for aiding most materially in giving the Negro his true position as an inferior race" (in Gould, 1981, p. 69). Indeed, he did more than give "the Negro his true position" as the following remarks by Morton himself convey:

Negroes were numerous in Egypt, but their social position in ancient times was the same as it is now, that of servants and slaves.

The benevolent mind may regret the inaptitude of the Indian civilization...[but values must not yield to fact]. The structure of his mind appears to be different from that of the white man, nor can the two harmonize in social relations except on the most limited scale. [Indians] are not only averse to restraints of education, but for the most part are incapable of a continued process of reasoning on abstract subjects (in Gould, 1981, p. 53).

The problem with these conclusions—as well as the numerical data that supported them—was that they were not based on "fact;" they were based simply on cultural fiction, on Morton's belief in biological determinism. As Gould meticulously showed, all of Morton's data was wrong. Gould himself reworked it completely. He concludes:

Morton's summaries are a patchwork of fudging and finagling in the clear interest of controlling a priori convictions. Yet—and this is the most intriguing aspect of the case—I find no evidence of conscious fraud; indeed, had Morton been a conscious fudger, he would not have published his data so openly.

Conscious fraud is probably rare in science...The prevalence of *unconscious* finagling, on the other hand, suggests the general conclusion about the social context of science…prior prejudice may be found anywhere, even in the basics of measuring bones and totaling sums (pp. 55-56).

This is a telling example of the power of theory, not only as a shaper of expectation and perception but also as a peddler of values under the misleading typecasting of "dispassionate inquiry" into scientific fact. Hence it is argued here that science is better off abandoning the myth of "value-freedom" and that theoretical work "must be understood as a social phenomenon, a gutsy, human enterprise, not the work of robots programmed to collect pure information" (Gould, 1981, p. 21). Even if Morton's data were correct, his work still could not be counted as value-free: His data and theories not only were shaped by the setting in which he worked, but were also used to support broad social policy. This is akin to making nature the source of cultural values, which of course it never can be (i.e., "what is" does not equal "what should be").

4. *Creation of group-building language.* The socio-rationalist perspective is more than a pessimistic epitaph for a strictly logical positivist philosophy. It is an invitation to inquiry that raises the status of theory from mere appendage of scientific method to an actual shaper of society. Once we acknowledge that a primary product of science is language and that language is a key resource for the creation of groups, then the stage is set for theory-building activity intended for the use and development of human society, for the creation of human options.

Students of human behavior have been aware of the group as the foundation of society since early periods of classical thought. Aristotle, for example, discussed the importance of bands and families. But it wasn't until the middle of this century that scientific interest in the subject exploded into a flurry of general inquiry and systematic interdisciplinary research (for a sample review of this literature, see Hare, 1976). Among the conclusions of this work was the crucial insight that:

...the face-to-face group working on a problem is the meeting ground of individual personality and society. It is in the group that personality is modified and socialized; and it is through the workings of groups that society is changed and adapted to its times (Thelen, 1954, p. vi).

Similarly, in the field of organization development, Srivastva, Obert and Neilsen (1977) have shown that the historical development of the discipline has paralleled advances in group theory. And this is no accident, they contend, because:

...emphasis on the small group is responsive to the realities of social change in large complex organizations. It is through group life that individuals learn, practice, develop, and modify their roles in the larger organization. To enter programmatically at the group level is both to confront and potentially co-opt an important natural source of change and development in these systems (p. 83).

It is no secret that groups are formed around common ideas, expressed in and through some kind of shared language which makes interaction possible. What is less clear, though, is the exact role that science plays in shaping group life through the medium of language. The fact that science frequently does have an impact is rarely questioned, however. An explosive example reported by Andre Gorz (1973) brings clarity to this point.

In the early 60s, a British professor of sociology by the name of Goldthorpe was brought in from a nearby university to make a study of the Vauxhall automobile workers in Luton, Great Britain. At the time, management at the factory was worried because workers in other organizations throughout the U.K. showed great unrest with working conditions, pay and management. An extensive number of strikes were being waged, most of them wildcat strikes, called by the factory stewards, not by the unions themselves. Goldthorpe was called in to study the situation at Vauxhall, to find out for management if there was anything to worry about at their factory. At the time of the study there were no strikes, no disruptions and no challenges by workers. Management wanted to know why. What were the chances that acute conflict would break out in the "well managed" and "advanced" big factory?

After an extensive period of research—an investigation lasting two years—the professor drew together his conclusions. Management, he said, had little to worry about.

According to the study, the workers were completely socialized into the system. They were satisfied with their wages and neither liked nor disliked their work—in fact, they were indifferent to it, viewing it as boring but inevitable. Because it was not intrinsically rewarding, most people performed their labor to get rid of it so they could go home and work on other more worthwhile projects and be with family. Work was marginal and instrumental. It was a means to support other interests outside the factory where "real life" began. Based, then, on his observations, Goldthorpe theorized that management had nothing to worry about: Workers were found to be apathetic and well integrated into the system. They behaved according to middle class patterns and showed no signs of strength as a group (i.e., no class consciousness). Furthermore, most conflict with management belonged to the past.

The sociologist's report was still at the printers when some employees obtained a summary of the findings. They had the conclusions copied and passed out to hundreds of co-workers. Also, around this time, a report on Vauxhall's profits was circulated. Profits were not shared with employees. The next day something happened. It was reported by the *London Times* in detail:

> Wild rioting has broken out at the Vauxhall car factories in Luton.
> Thousands of workers streamed out of the shops and gathered in
> the factory yard. They besieged the management offices, calling
> for managers to come out, singing the "Red Flag," and shouting,
> "String them up!" Groups attempted to storm the offices and battled
> the police which had been called to protect them (quoted in Gorz,
> 1973).

The rioting lasted for two days. All of this happened, then, in an advanced factory where systematic research showed workers to be apathetic, weak as a group, and resigned to accept the system. What does it all mean? Did the researchers simply misread the data?

To the contrary. Goldthorpe knew his data well. He articulated the conclusions accurately, concisely and with force. In fact, what happened was that the report gave workers a *language* to begin talking with each other about their plight. It brought them into interaction and, as they discussed things, they discovered Goldthorpe was right. They all felt alike—apathetic but frustrated—and they *were* apathetic because, as individuals in their isolated jobs, no one could do anything to change things. But the report gave them a way to dialogue about the situation. And, as they talked, things changed, they changed. People were not alone in their feelings and they did not want to feel the way they did anymore. As an emergent group they now had a means to convert apathy to action, non-involvement to involvement, and individual powerlessness into collective strength. Gorz analyzes:

> In other words, the very investigation of Mr. Goldthorpe about the lack of class consciousness helped tear down the barriers of silence and isolation that rendered the workers apathetic...(p. 334).

The case is an important one for a number of reasons. At the general level, it demonstrates that our knowledge in the social sciences differs in quality and kind from our knowledge generated in the physical sciences. For instance, our knowledge of the periodic chart does not change the elements and our knowledge of the moon's orbit does not change its path. But, our knowledge of a social system is different. It can be used by the system to change itself, thus invalidating or disconfirming the findings immediately or at any time. Thus, the human group differs from objects in an important way: Human beings have the capacity for symbolic interaction and, through language, they have the ability to collaborate in the investigation of their own world. Because of the capacity for symbolic interaction, the introduction of new knowledge related to the social world has the strong likelihood of changing the phenomena itself.

Gergen (1982) refers to this as the "enlightenment effect" of scientific work, meaning that once the formulations of scientific work are made public, human beings may act autonomously to either disconfirm or validate the propositions. According to logical positivist philosophy, potential enlightenment effects must be reduced or ideally eliminated through experimental controls. Thus, in social psychology, for example, deception plays a crucial role in doing research. Enlightenment effects are viewed as contaminants to good scientific work. Yet there is an alternative way to look at the reactive nature of social research: It is precisely because of the enlightenment effect that theory can and does play an important role in the positive construction of society. In this sense, the enlightenment effect—which is made possible through language—is an essential ingredient making scientific work worthwhile, meaningful, and applicable. It is an invitation, therefore, to each and every theorist to actively participate in the creation of his or her world by generating compelling theories of the good, the just, or the desirable in social existence.

5. *Extending visions of possibility.* The position taken by the socio-rationalist philosophy of science is that the conduct of inquiry cannot be separated from the everyday negotiation of reality. Social-organizational research is, therefore, a continuing moral concern, a concern of social reconstruction and direction. The choice of what to study, how to study it, and what is reported each imply some degree of responsibility. Science, therefore, instead of being considered an end point, is viewed as one means of helping humanity create itself. Science in this sense exists for one overarching purpose. As Albion Small (1905) proposed almost a century ago, a generative science must aim "at the most thorough, intense, persistent and systematic effort to make human life all that it is capable of becoming" (pp. 36-37).

Theories gain their generative capacity by extending visions which expand to the realm of the possible. As a general proposition, it can be suggested that theories designed to empower organized social systems will tend to have a greater enlightenment effect than theories of human constraint. This proposition is grounded in an important consideration that relates to the unity of theory and practice. The consideration is a simple one: is it not possible that scientific theory gains its capacity to affect cultural practices in very much the same way powerful leaders inspire people to new heights? Recent research on the functioning of the executive mind (Srivastva, 1983; 1985) raises a set of intriguing parallels between possibilities of a generative science and the workings of the executive mind.

The essential parallel is seen in the primary role that ideas (ideals) play in the mobilization of diverse groups in the common construction of a desired future. Three major themes from the executive mind research stand out in this regard:

1. *Vision*: The executive mind works largely from the present and extends itself out to the longer term future. It is powerful to the extent it is able to envision a desired future state which challenges perceptions of what is possible and what can be realized. The executive mind operates beyond the frontier of conventional practice without losing sight of either necessity or possibility.

2. *Passion*: The executive mind is simultaneously rational and intuitive, which allows it to tap into the sentiments, values, and dreams of the social collectivity. Executive vision becomes "common vision" to the extent it ignites the imaginations, hopes and passions of others—and it does so through the articulation of self-transcending ideals which lend meaning and significance to everyday life.

3. *Integrity*: The executive mind is the mental muscle that moves a system from the present state to a new and different future. As such, this muscle gains strength to the extent it is founded upon an integrity able to withstand contrary pressures. There are three

dimensions to executive integrity. The first, *system integrity*, refers to the fact that the executive mind perceives the world (the organization, group or society) as a unified whole, not as a collection of individual parts. The second type of integrity is *moral integrity*. Common vision leadership is largely an act of caring. It follows the "path of the heart" which is the source of moral and ethical standards. Finally, there is *integrity of vision,* which refers to consistency, coherence and focus. Executive vision—to the extent to which it is compelling—is focused and unwavering, even in the midst of obstacles, critics, and conflicting alternatives.

Interestingly, these thematic dimensions of the executive mind have their counterparts in recent observations concerning the utilization of organizational research. According to Beyer and Trice (1982), it is the "affective bonding" that takes place which largely determines the attraction of social science results and generates commitment to utilize their implications. For example, Henshel (1975) suggests that research containing predictions of appealing futures will be utilized and preferred over research pointing to negative or repelling futures: "People will work for predicted states they approve of and against those they detest" (p. 103). Similarly, Weiss and Bucavalas (1980) report that results which challenge the status quo are most attractive to high level executives because they are ones expected to make new things happen, at least at the level of policy. And, as it relates to passion and integrity, Mitroff (1980) urges social scientists to become caring advocates of their ideas, not only to diffuse their theories but also to challenge others to prove them wrong and thus pursue those ideas which have integrity in action.

This section has explored a number of ways in which social theory becomes a powerful resource for change and development in social practice. The argument is simple: Theory is agential in character and has unbounded potential to affect patterns of social action—whether desired or not. As we have seen, theories are not mere explanations of an external world lying "out there" to be objectively recorded. Theories, like powerful ideas, are formative. Through the establishment of perceptual cues and frames, by providing presumptions of logic, by transmitting subtle values, by creating new language, and by extending compelling visions of possibility or constraint—in all these ways social theory becomes a powerful means whereby norms, beliefs and cultural practices may be altered.

Igniting the Theoretical Spirit of Action-Research

The upshot of all this boils down to one point: Instinctively, intuitively, and tacitly we all know that important ideas can, in a flash, profoundly alter the way we see ourselves, view reality and conduct our lives. Experience shows that a simple economic forecast, political poll, or technical discovery (like the atomic bomb) can forever change the course of human history. Thus one cannot help but be disturbed and puzzled by the discipline of action-research as it is widely practiced. Not only does it continue to underrate the role of theory as a means for organizational development (Friedlander and Brown, 1974; Bartunek 1983; Argyris, 1983), but it appears to have become locked within an assumptive base which systematically distorts our view of organizational reality and inadvertently helps reinforce and perfect the status quo (Brimm, 1972).

But why the lack of generative theorizing in action-research? And, more important, what can be done to rekindle the spirit, excitement and passion required of a science that wishes to be of vital significance to organizations? Earlier this chapter addressed a philosophy of science congenial to the task. Socio-rationalism, it was argued, represents an epistemological point of view conducive to catalytic theorizing. Ironically, though, it can be argued that most action-researchers *already do* subscribe to this or a similar view of science (Susman and Evered, 1978). Assuming this to be the case, then it becomes an even greater puzzle why contemporary action-research continues to disregard theory building as an integral and necessary component of the craft. In this section, discussion will be taken a step further by taking a look at some of the metaphysical assumptions embedded in our conventional definitions of action-research, assumptions which can be shown to govern our thought and work in ways inimical to present interests.

Paradigm I: Organizing-is-a-Problem-to-be-Solved

The intellectual and spiritual origins of action-research can be traced to Kurt Lewin, a social psychologist of German origin who coined the term "action-research in 1944". The thrust of Lewin's work centered on the need to bridge the gap between science and the realm of practical affairs. Science, he said, should be used to inform and educate social practice, and subsequent action would then inform science. He writes, "We should consider action, research and training as a triangle that should be kept together" (Lewin, 1948, p. 211). The two-fold promise of an action science, according to Lewin, was to simultaneously contribute to the development of scientific knowledge (i.e., propositions of an if/then variety) and to use such knowledge for bettering the human condition.

The immense influence of the man is a complete puzzle if we look only to his writings. The fact of the matter is that Lewin published only two papers—a brief 22 pages—directly concerning the idea of action-research (Peters and Robinson, 1984). Indeed, it has been argued that the enduring influence of Lewin stemmed not from these writings but from the sheer force and presence of the man himself. According to biographer Alfred Marrow (1968), Lewin was a passionate and creative thinker, continuously knocking at the door of the unknown, studying "topics that had been believed to be psychologically unapproachable." Lewin's character was marked by a spirit of inquiry that burned incessantly and which affected all those in contact with him, especially his students. The intensity of his presence was fueled further by the belief that inquiry itself could be used to construct a more democratic and dignified future. At least this was his hope and dream, for Lewin had *not* forgotten his experience as a refugee from fascism in the late 1930s. From this perspective, then, it is clear why he revolted so strongly against a detached ivory-tower view of science immersed in trivial matters, tranquilized by its standardized methods, and limited in its field of inquiry. Thus, the picture we have of Lewin shows him to have been a committed social scientist, pioneering unchartered territory for the purpose of creating new knowledge about groups and societies which would advance the democratic ideal (see, for example, Lewin, 1952). It was this spirit—relentless curiosity coupled with a conviction in the need for knowledge-guided societal development—which marks Lewin's creative impact on both his students and the field.

Much of this spirit is now gone from action-research. What is left is a set of assumptions about the world which exhibit little, if any, resemblance to the process of inquiry as Lewin lived it. While many of the words are the same, they have been taken too literally and, in their translation over the years, have been bloated into a set of metaphysical principles, assumptions about the essence of social existence, which directly undermine the intellectual and speculative spirit. Put bluntly, under current norms, action-research has largely failed as an instrument advancing social knowledge of consequence and now risks being (mis)understood as little more than a crude empiricism imprisoned in a deficiency mode of thought. A quick sketch of six sets of assumptions embedded in the conventional view will show exactly what we are talking about while also answering our puzzle over the discipline's lack of contribution to generative theory:

1. *Research equals problem solving. To do good research is to solve "real" problems.* So ingrained is this assumption that it scarcely needs documentation. Virtually every definition found in leading tests and articles equate action-research with problem solving—as if "real" problem solving was the virtual essence of the discipline. For example, as French and Bell (1978) define it, "Action-research is both *an approach to problem solving*— a model of paradigm, and a *problem-solving process*—a series of activities

and events" (p. 88).[5] Or, in terms of the Bradford, Gibb, and Benne (1964) definition, "It is an application of scientific methodology in *the clarification* and *solution of practical problems...*" (p. 33). Similarly, Frohman, Sashkin and Kavanaugh (1976) state "Action-research describes a particular process model whereby behavioral science knowledge is applied to help a client (usually a group or social system) *solve real problems and not incidentally learn the process involved in problem solving...*" (p. 203). Echoing this theme, that research equals problem solving, researchers at the University of Michigan's Institute in Social Research state, "Three factors need to be taken into account in an organization development [action-research] effort: the behaviors that are problematic, the conditions that create those behaviors, and the interventions or activities that will correct the conditions creating the problems. *What* is it that people are doing, or not doing, that is a problem? *Why* are they doing or not doing these particular things? *Which* of a large number of possible interventions or activities would be most likely to solve the problems by focusing on why problems exist?" (Hausser, Pecorella, and Wissler, 1977 p. 2). Here it is unmistakably clear that the primary focus of the action-research approach to organizational analysis is the ongoing array of concrete problems an organization faces. Of course, there are a number of differences in the discipline as to the overall definition and meaning of the emerging action-research paradigm. But this basic assumption—that research equals problem solving—is not one of them. In their recent review intended to discover elements of metatheoretical agreement within the discipline, Peters and Robinson (1984) discovered that out of 15 different dimensions of action-research studied, only two had univocal support among leaders in the field. What were the two elements of agreement? Exactly as the definitions above define: Social science should be "action-oriented" and "problem-focused."

2. *Inquiry in action-research terms is a matter of following the standardized rules of problem solving. Knowledge is the result of good method.*

---

5. Emphasis in each of these definitions are mine to underscore the points being made.

"In essence," writes Blake and Mouton (1976) "it is a method of empirical data gathering that is *comprised of a set of rather standardized steps: diagnosis, information gathering, feedback, and action planning*" (pp. 101-102). By following this ritual list, they contend that virtually any organization can be studied in a manner that will lead to usable knowledge. As Chiles (1983) puts it, "The virtue of the model lies in the sequential process… Any other sequence renders the model meaningless" (p. 191). According to Friedlander and Brown (1974) this sequence has served a special purpose: "…to develop data collection methods that are clearly relevant to organizational problem solving…" (p. 318). The basic idea behind the model is that "in management, events proceed as planned unless some force, not provided against by the plan, acts upon events to produce an outcome not contemplated in the plan" (Kepner-Tregoe, Inc., 1985, p. 3). Thus a problem is a deviation from some standard and, without precise diagnosis (step one), any attempt to resolve it will likely fail by not penetrating surface symptoms to discover true causes. Hence, like a liturgical refrain which is seldom questioned or thought about, Cohen, et al. (1984) tell the new student that knowledge is the offspring of processing information through a distinct series of problem-solving stages: "Action-research begins with an identified problem. Data are then gathered in a way that allows a diagnosis which can produce a tentative solution, which is then implemented with the assumption that it is likely to cause new or unforeseen problems that will, in turn, need to be evaluated, diagnosed, and so forth. *This action-research method assumes a constantly evolving interplay between solutions, results, and new solutions…This model is a general one applicable to solving any kind of problem in an ongoing organization*" (pp. 359-360).

3. *Action-research is utilitarian or technical, that is, it should be initiated and designed to meet a need in an area specified by the organization, usually "top management." The search is controlled by the "felt need" or object of inquiry: Everything that is not related to this object should be dismissed as irrelevant.* As we are beginning to see, action-research,

as conventionally understood, does not really refer to research per se but rather to a highly focused and defined type of research called problem solving. Taken almost directly from the medical model, the disease orientation guides the process of inquiry in a highly programmed way. According to Levinson (1972), diagnostic action-research: "...like a therapeutic or teaching relationship should be an alliance of both parties to discover and resolve these problems...[The researcher] *should look for experiences which appear stressful to people. What kinds of occurrences disrupt or disorganize people?*" (p. 37). Hence, in a systematically limiting fashion, the general topic of research is largely prescribed—before inquiry even begins. As we would guess then: "Typical questions in [action-research] data gathering or 'problem sensing' would include: What problems do you see in your group, including problems between people that are interfering with getting the job done the way you would like to see it done? And what problems do you see in the broader organization? Such open-ended questions provide latitude on the part of the respondents and encourage a reporting of problems as the individual sees them" (French, 1969, pp. 183-185).

In problem solving it is assumed that something is broken, fragmented, not whole; it needs to be fixed. Thus the function of problem solving is to integrate, stabilize, and help raise to its full potential the workings of the status quo. By definition, a problem implies that one already has knowledge of what "should be," thus one's (re)search is guided by an instrumental purpose tied to what is already known. In this sense, problem solving tends to be inherently conservative and, as a form of research, tends to produce and reproduce a universe of knowledge that remains sealed. As Staw (1984) points out in his review of the field, most organizational research is biased to serve managerial interests rather than exploring broader human and/ or social purposes. But, even more important, he argues, the field has not even served managerial interests well since research has taken a short-term problem focus rather than having formulated logics of new forms of organization that do not exist. It is as if the discipline's concept of social system development means only clearing up distortions in current functioning (horizontal development) and does not include a conception which refers to stage-based movement to an altogether new or transformed reality (vertical development or second order change).

4. *Action-research should not inquire into phenomena that transcend the competence of human reason. Questions that cannot be answered should not be asked and issues that cannot be acted upon should not be explored (i.e., action-research is not a branch of political philosophy, poetry or theology).* This proposition is a "smuggled in" corollary to the preceding assumptions. It would appear that once one agrees with the ground rules of a pragmatic problem-solving science, then the universe for inquiry is largely pre-determined, defined, and de-limited in scope. Specifically, what one agrees to is a secularized view of the human universe that is controllable and rational, sequentially ordered into a series of causes and effects. As both a credit and a weakness, the problem-solving mode narrows our gaze in much the same manner that a blinder over one eye narrows the field of vision and distorts one's perception of depth. As part of a long-term movement evidenced in social sciences, a contemporary action-research embodies the trend toward metaphysical skepticism and denial (Quinney, 1982). That is, it operates out of a sacred void that cuts off virtually any inquiry into the vital forces of life. Indeed, the whole promise of modern science was that it would finally banish illusion, mystery, and uncertainty from the world. An inquiry process of immediate utility (problem solving), therefore, requires an anti-religious, secular spirit which limits the realm of study to the sphere of the known. And, because of the recognition that the formulation of a problem depends largely on one's views of what constitutes a solution (Rittle and Webber, 1972), then it is not surprising to find that *research on the utilization of research* shows a propensity for social scientists and organizations to collude to study only those variables that can be manipulated (Beyer and Trice, 1982). As one might well imagine, such a view has crippling implications for generative theorizing. For example,

as typically practiced, action-research does little in the way of theorizing about or bringing beauty into organizational life. Does this mean there is no beauty in organizing? Does this mean that the realm of the aesthetic has little or nothing to do with organizational dynamics?

The tidy imagery of the problem-solving view is related to what Sigmund Koch (1981) has called in his presidential address to the APA the syndrome of "ameaningful thinking." One element of this syndrome is the perpetuation of the scientistic myth which uses the rhetoric of prediction and control to reassure people that their lives are not that complex, their situations not all that uncertain—and that their problems are, indeed, manageable through causal analysis. In the process, however, science tends to trivialize, and even evade, a whole class of issues which "transcend the competence of human reason," yet are clearly meaningful in the course of human experience. One way the field of inquiry is restricted is through one's choice of methodology. Hence, writes Koch: "...there are times and circumstances in which able individuals, committed to inquiry, tend almost obsessively to frustrate the objectives of inquiry. It is as if uncertainty, mootness, ambiguity, cognitive infinitude were the most unbearable of the existential anguishes...*Ameaningful* thought or inquiry regards knowledge as the result of 'processing' rather than discovery. It presumes that knowledge is an almost automatic result of gimmickry, an assembly line, a 'methodology.' So strongly does it see knowledge under such aspects that it sometimes seems to suppose the object of inquiry to be an ungainly and annoying irrelevance" (1981, p. 259).

To be sure, this is not to argue that all action-research is "ameaningful" or autistically tied to a standardized problem-solving method. In fact, much of the success that action-research has achieved to date may be attributed to its restricted attention to that which is "solvable." However, it is important to recognize that the problem-solving method of organizational inquiry paints a picture of organizational life in which a whole series of colors are considered untouchable. In this way, the totality of being is obviously obscured, leading to a narrowed conception of human nature and cultural possibility.

5. *Problems are "out there" to be studied and solved. The ideal product of action-research is a mirror-like reflection of the organization's problems and causes. As "objective third party," there is little role for passion and speculation. The action-researcher should not be a passionate advocate nor inspired dreamer (utopian thinker).* One of the laudable and most significant values associated with action-research has been its insistence upon a collaborative form of inquiry. But, unfortunately, from a generative theory perspective, the term collaboration has become virtually synonymous with an idealized image of the *researcher as facilitator and mirror*, not an active and fully engaged social participant. As facilitator of the problem-solving process, the action-researcher has what is generally agreed as three "primary intervention tasks": to help generate valid organizational data; to enable others to make free, informed choices on the basis of the data; and to help the organization generate internal commitment to their choices. Elaborating further, Argyris (1970) states: "One condition that seems so basic as to be defined as axiomatic is the generation of *valid information... valid information is that which describes the factors, plus their interrelationships, that create the problem*" (pp. 16-17). Furthermore, for data to be useful, there must be a claim to neutrality. The data should represent an accurate reflection of the observed facts. As French and Bell (1978) describe it, it is important for the action-researcher to stress the objective fact-finding features: "A key value included in organizational members is a belief in the validity, desirability and usefulness of the data..." (p. 79). Then, through feedback which "refers to activities and processes that 'reflect' or 'mirror' an objective picture of the real world" (p. 111), the action-researcher facilitates the process of prioritizing problems and helps others make choices for action. And, because the overarching objective is to help the organization develop its own internal resources, the action-researcher should not play an active role or take an advocate stance which

solved, real living equals problem solving, and living better is an adaptive learning process whereby we acquire new and more effective means for tackling tough problems. The good life, this image informs, depends on solving problems in ways that problems of utility are identified and solutions of high quality are found and carried out with full commitment. As one leading theorist describes: "For many scholars who study organizations and management, the central characteristic of organizations is that they *are* problem-solving systems whose success is measured by how efficiently they solve problems associated with accomplishing their primary mission and how effectively they respond to emergent problems. Kilmann's approach (1979, pp. 214-215) is representative of this perspective: 'One might even define the essence of management as problem defining and problem solving, whether the problems are well structured, ill structured, technical, human, or environmental...' In this view, the core task of the executive is problem management. Although experience, personality and specific technical expertise are important, the primary skill of the successful executive is the ability to manage the problem-solving process in such a way that important problems are identified and solutions of high quality are found and carried out with the full commitment of organizational members" (Kolb, 1983, pp. 109-110).

From here it is just a short conceptual jump to the idealized aim of paradigm one research, as the following two quotes indicate: "Action-research describes a particular process model whereby behavioral science knowledge is applied to...solve real problems and *not* incidentally learn the process involved in problem solving..." (Frohman, Sashkin and Kavanaugh, 1976, p. 203). "Action-research tends to build into the client system an institutionalized pattern for continuously collecting data and examining the system's processes, as well as for the continuous review of *known* problem areas. *Problem solving becomes very much a way of organizational life*" (Margulies and Raia, 1972, p. 29).

These few pages have attempted to highlight the almost obvious point that the deficiency/problem orientation is pervasive and holds a subtle but powerful grasp on the discipline's imagination and focus. Furthermore it can be argued that the generative weakness of contemporary action-research is securely interlinked to the discipline's guiding metaphor of social-organizational existence. As noted by many scholars, the theoretical output of the discipline is virtually non-existent and what theory there is, is largely problem focused (i.e., theories of turnover, intergroup conflict, processes of dehumanization, etc. See Staw, 1984 for an excellent review). Thus, our theories like windsocks, continue to blow steadily onward in the direction of our conventional gaze. Seeing the world as a problem has become "very much a way of organizational life..."

It is the feeling of this author that the discipline has reached a level of fatigue arising from repetitive use of its standardized model. Fatigue, as Whitehead (1929) so aptly surmised, arises from an act of excluding the impulse toward novelty which is the antithesis of the life of the mind and speculative reason. To be sure, there can be great adventure in the process of inquiry. Yet not many action-researchers return from their explorations refreshed and revitalized, like pioneers, returning home with news of lands unknown but most certainly there. Perhaps there is another root metaphor from which to work.

Foundations for a Second Dimension

The effort here is but one of a small yet growing attempt to generate new perspectives on the conduct of organizational research which will yield the kind of knowledge necessary for both understanding and transforming complex social-organizational systems (Torbert, 1983; Van Manaan, et al., 1982; Mitroff and Kilmann, 1978; Smirchich, 1983; Forester, 1983; Argyris, 1970; Friedlander, 1968). It is no secret that among the different and emerging views there is frequently great tension. Often the differences form the battleground for fierce debate over theories of truth, the meaning of "facts," political agendas, and personal assertions of will. But more fruitfully what can be seen emerging is a heightened sensitivity and inter-disciplinary recognition that, based on "the structure of knowledge" (Kolb, 1984), there may be multiple ways of knowing—each valid in their own realm according to their own set of unique and essential assumptions and purposes. In this sense there are many different ways of studying the same phenomenon and the insights generated by one approach are at best partial and incomplete. According to Habermas (1970) different perspectives can only be evaluated in terms of their specified "human interests" which can broadly be differentiated into the realms of practical rationality or techni-cal rationality. In more straightforward language, Morgan (1983) states:

> This selection of method implies some view of the situation being
> studied, for any decision on *how* to study a phenomenon carries
> with it certain assumptions or explicit answers to the question,
> *"What is being studied?"* Just as we select a tennis racquet rather
> than a golf club to play tennis because we have a prior conception
> as to what the game of tennis involves, so, too, in relation to the
> process of social research; we select or favor particular kinds of
> methodology because we have implicit or explicit conceptions as to
> what we are trying to do with our research (p. 19).

Thus, in adapting one mode over another, the researcher directly influ-ences what he or she will discover and accomplish.

It is the contention of this dissertation that advances in generative theo-rizing will come about for action-research when the discipline decides to expand its universe for exploration, seeks to discover new questions, and rekindles a fresh perception of the extraordinary in everyday organizational life. In this final section a description is offered concerning the assump-tions and philosophy of an applied administrative science which seeks to embody these suggestions in a form of organization study we will call *appreciative inquiry*. In distinction to conventional action-research, the knowledge-interest of appreciative inquiry lies not so much in problem solving as it does in social innovation: Appreciative inquiry refers to a research perspective which is uniquely intended for discovering, under-standing and fostering innovations in social-organizational arrangements and processes.[6] Its purpose is to contribute to the generative-theoretical aims of social science and to use such knowledge to promote egalitarian dialogue leading to social system effectiveness or integrity. Whatever else it may be, social system effectiveness is defined here quite specifically as a congruence between social-organizational values (i.e., the ever chang-ing normative set of values, ideals, or interests that system members hold concerning the question; "How should we organize ourselves?") and every-day social-organizational practices (cf. Torbert, 1983). Thus, appreciative inquiry refers to both a search for knowledge and a theory of intentional collective action which is designed to help evolve the normative vision and will of a group, organization, or society as a whole. It is an inquiry process that affirms our symbolic capacities of imagination and mind as well as our social capacity for conscious choice and cultural evolution. As a holistic form of inquiry, it asks a series of questions not found in either a logical-positivist conception of science or a strictly pragmatic, problem-solving mode of action-research. Yet as shown in Figure II-1, its aims are both sci-entific (in a socio-rationalist sense) and pragmatic (in a social innovative sense) as well as metaphysical and normative (in the sense of attempting to ethically affirm all that social existence really is and should become).

---

6. Following Whyte, (1982), a social innovation will be defined as: (1) a new element in organizational structure or interorganizational relations; (2) innovative sets of procedures, reward systems, or technologies for shaping new forms of human interaction and activity and the relations of human beings to the natural and social environment; (3) a new administrative policy in actual use; (4) new role or sets of roles; and (5) new belief systems or ideologies transforming basic modes of relating.

Figure II-1
Dimensions of Appreciative Inquiry

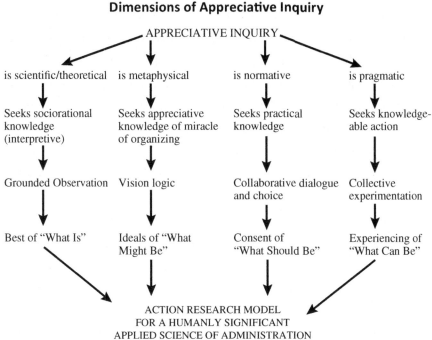

As a way of talking about the framework as it is actually practiced, four guiding principles will first be examined:

Principle #1. Research into the social (innovation) potential of organizational life should begin with appreciation. This basic principle assumes that every social system "works" to some degree (i.e., is not in complete state of entropy) and that a primary task of research is to discover, describe, and explain those social innovations, however small, which serve to give "life" to the system and activate members' competencies and energies as more fully functioning co-participants in the formation and transformation of organizational realities. That is, the appreciative approach takes its inspiration from the current state of "what is" and seeks a comprehensive understanding of the factors and forces of organizing (e.g., ideological, techno-structural, cultural) that serve to heighten the total potential of an organization in ideal-type human and social terms.

Principle #2. Research into the social potential of organizational life should be applicable. To be significant in a human sense, an applied science of administration should lead to the generation of theoretical knowledge that can be used, applied, and thereby validated in action. Thus, an applicable inquiry process is neither utopian in the sense of generating knowledge about "no place" (Sargent, 1982) nor should it be confined to academic circles and presented in a way that have little relevance to the everyday language and symbolism for whom the findings might well apply.

Principle #3. Research into the social potential of organizational life should be proactive. Here it is considered axiomatic that an organization is, in fact, an open-ended indeterminate system capable of: (1) becoming more than it is at any given moment, and (2) capable of learning how to actively take part in guiding its own evolution. Hence, appreciative knowledge of what is (in terms of "peak" social innovations in organizing) is suggestive of what might be and can be used to generate images of realistic developmental opportunities that can be experimented with on a wider scale. In this sense, appreciative inquiry can be both pragmatic and visionary. It becomes provocative to the extent that the abstracted findings of a study take on normative value for members of organizations which can happen only through their own critical deliberation and choice (i.e., "We feel that this particular finding is for [or is not] important for us to envision as an ideal to be striving for in practice on a wider scale"). It is in this way that appreciative inquiry allows us to put intuitive, visionary logic on firm empirical footing and to use systematic research to help organizational members shape their worlds according to their own imaginative and moral purposes.

Principle #4. Research into the social potential of organizational life should be collaborative. This overarching principle points to the assumed existence of an inseparable relationship between the process and content of inquiry. A collaborative relationship between the researcher and members of an organization is, therefore, deemed essential on the basis of both epistemological (Susman and Evered, 1978) and practical/ethical grounds

(Habermas, 1970; Argyris, 1970). Simply put, a unilateral approach to the study of social innovation (jointly bringing something new into the world) is a direct negation of the phenomenon itself.

The spirit behind each of the four principles of appreciative inquiry is to be found in one of the most ancient archetypes or metaphorical symbols of hope and inspiration that humankind has ever known—the miracle and mystery of the being. Throughout history people have recognized the intimate relationship between being seized by the unfathomable and the process of appreciative knowing or thought (Marcel, 1963; Quinney, 1982; Jung, 1958; Maslow, 1968; Gandhi, 1958). According to Schweitzer (1969), for example, it is recognition of the ultimate mystery which elevates our perception beyond the world of ordinary objects, igniting the life of the mind and a "reverence for life." He writes:

> In all respects the universe remains mysterious to man...As soon as man does not take his existence for granted, but beholds it as something unfathomably mysterious, thought begins. This phenomenon has been repeated time and time again in the history of the human race. Ethical affirmation of life is the intellectual act by which man ceases simply to live at random...[Such] thought has a dual task to accomplish: to lead us out of a naïve and into a profounder affirmation of life and the universe; and to help us progress from ethical impulses to a rational system of ethics (p. 33).

For those of us breastfed by an industrial giant which stripped the world of its wonder and awe it feels, quite bluntly, like an irrelevant, absurd, and even distracting interruption to pause, reflect deeply, and then humbly accept the depth of what we can never know—and to consider the ultimates of living for which there are no coordinates or certainties, only questions. Medicine cannot tell me, for example, what it means that my newborn son has life in motion and soul, any more than the modern physicist can tell me what "nothingness" is, which, they say, makes up over 99 percent of the universe. In fact, if there is anything we have learned from the great physicists of our time it is that the promise of certainty is a lie (Hiesenberg, 1958), and by living this lie as scientistic doctrine, we cut short the gift of complementarity—the capacity for dialectically opposed modes of knowing which adds richness, depth, and beauty to our lives (Bohr, 1958). Drugged by the products of our industrial machine we lose sight and connection with the invisible mystery at the heart of creation, an Ultimate Power beyond rational understanding.

In the same way that birth of a living, breathing, loving, thinking human being is an inexplicable mystery so, too, it can be stated in direct and clearly spoken terms that *organizing is a miracle* of cooperative human interaction, of which there can never be final explanation. In fact, to the extent that organizations are indeed born and re-created through dialogue, then they truly are unknowable as long as such creative dialogue remains. At this point in time there simply are no organizational theories which provide adequate account of the life-giving essence of cooperative existence, especially if one delves deeply enough. But somehow we forget all this. We become lulled by simplistic diagnostic boxes, content to transfer our conceptual curiosity over to "experts" who finally must know. Instead of explorers we become mechanics.[7]

This, according to Koch (1981), is the source of "ameaningful" thinking, or as Kierkegaard (1954) suggests, is the essence of a certain dull-minded routine called "philistinism."

> Devoid of imagination, as the Philistine always is, he lives in a
> certain trivial province of experience as to how things go, what
> is possible...Philistinism tranquilizes itself in the trivial...(pp.
> 174-175).

As we know, a miracle is something beyond all possible verification but nonetheless is experienced as real. As a symbol, the word "miracle"

---

7. The dilemma faced by action-research in terms of its creative contribution to knowledge is summed up perfectly in the title of a well-known article by one of the discipline's major advocates of action-research. The title by Marv Wiesbord (1976) has proven prophetic: "Organizational Diagnosis: Six Places to Look for Trouble, With or Without a Theory."

represents unification of the sacred and secular into a realm of totality which is at once terrifying and beautiful, inspiring and threatening. As it relates to the rejuvenation of social theory, Quinney (1982) has suggested that such a unified viewpoint is necessary and can have a powerful impact on the discipline precisely because in a world that is at once sacred and secular there is no place, knowledge, nor phenomenon without mystery. The "miracle" then is pragmatic in its effect when sincerely apprehended by a mind that has not chosen to become "tranquilized in the trivial." In this sense, the metaphor "life is a miracle" is not so much an idea as it is *or* can be a central feature of experience enveloping our: (1) perceptual consciousness; (2) our way of relating to others, the world, and our research; and (3) our way of knowing. Each of these points can be highlighted by a suggestive and diverse literature.

In terms of the first, scholars have suggested that the power of what we call the miracle lies in its capacity to advance one's perceptual capacity to what Maslow (1968) has called a "B-cognition" or growth versus deficiency orientation, or what Kolb (1984) has termed "integrative consciousness." Kolb writes:

> The transcendental quality of integrative consciousness is precisely that, a "climbing out of"…This state of consciousness is not reserved for the monastery, but is a necessary ingredient for creativity in any field. Albert Einstein once said, "The most beautiful and profound emotion one can feel is a sense of the mystical…It is the power of all true science" (p. 158).

Secondly, as Marcel (1963) explained in his William James lectures at Harvard on *The Mystery of Being*, the central conviction of life as a mystery creates for one a distinctly different relationship to the world than the conviction of life as a problem to be solved:

> A problem is something met which bars my passage. It is before me in its entirety. A mystery on the other hand is something I find *myself* caught up in, and whose essence is therefore not before me in

its entirety. It is though in this province the distinction between "in me" and "before me" loses its meaning (p. 80).

Berman's (1981) recent analysis comes to a similar conclusion. The re-enchantment of the world gives rise to a "participatory consciousness" where there is a sense of personal stake, ownership and partnership with the universe:

> The view of nature which predominated the West down to the eve of the Scientific Revolution was that of an enchanted world. Rocks, trees, rivers, and clouds were all seen as wonderous, alive and human beings felt at home in this environment. The cosmos, in short, was a place of *belonging*. A member of this cosmos was not an alienated observer of it but a direct participant in its drama. His personal destiny was bound up with its destiny, and this relationship gave meaning to his life.

Thirdly, as so many artists and poets have exhibited, there is a relationship between what the Greeks called thaumazein—an experience which lies on the borderline between wonderment and admiration—and a type of intuitive apprehension or knowing that we call appreciative. For Keats, the purpose of his work was:

> ...to accept things as I saw them, to enjoy the beauty I perceived for its own sake, without regard to ultimate truth or falsity, and to make a description of it the end and purpose of my appreciations (in Abrams, 1953).

Similarly for Shelley:

> Poetry thus makes immortal all that is best and most beautiful in the world...it exalts the beauty of that which is most beautiful...it strips the veil of familiarity from the world, and lays bare the naked and sleeping beauty, which is in the spirit of its forms (in Abrams, 1953, p. 236).

And in strikingly similar words, learning theorist David Kolb (1984), analyzes the structure of the knowing mind and reports:

Finally, appreciation is a process of affirmation. Unlike criticism, which is based on skepticism and doubt (compare Polanyi, 1958, pp. 269ff), appreciation is based on belief, trust, and conviction. And from this affirmative embrace flows a deeper fullness and richness of experience. This act of affirmation forms the foundation from which vital comprehension can develop...Appreciative apprehension and critical comprehension are thus fundamentally different processes of knowing. Appreciation of immediate experience is an act of attention, valuing and affirmation, whereas critical comprehension of symbols is based on objectivity (which involves a priori controls of attention, as in double blind controlled experiments), dispassionate analysis, and skepticism (pp. 104-105).

There various thinkers have been cited in detail for several reasons; first, to underscore the fact that the powerful images of problem and miracle (in)form qualitatively distinct modes of inquiry which then shape our awareness, relations, and knowledge, and second, to highlight the conviction that the renewal of generative theory requires that we enter into the realm of the metaphysical. The chief characteristic of the modern mind has been the banishment of mystery from the world and along with it, an ethical affirmation of life which has served history as a leading source of values, hope, and normative bonding among people. In historical terms, we have steadily forgotten how to dream.

In contrast to a type of research that is lived without a sense of mystery, the appreciative mode awakens the desire to create and discover new social possibilities which enrich our existence and give it meaning. In this sense, appreciative inquiry seeks an imaginative and fresh perception of organizations as "ordinary magic", as if seen for the first time or perhaps the last (Hayward, 1984). The appreciative mode, in exploration of ordinary magic, is an inquiry process that takes nothing for granted, searching to apprehend the basis or organizational life and working to expand those possibilities proclaiming a better existence.

The phenomenology of appreciation is important because it heightens our living experience of awe and wonder which leads us to the wellspring of new questions, much like a wide-eyed explorer without final destination. Only by raising innovative questions will innovations in theory and practice be found. It must also be noted that in action-research this appears to have been the source of Lewin's original and catalytic genius. So, too, we must re-awaken this spirit. To the extent that our questions determine what we find, then we should place a premium on that which informs our curiosity and thought. The *metaphysical* question of what makes social existence possible will never go away. The *generative-theoretical* question of compelling new possibilities will never go away. The *normative* question of what kind of social-organizational order is best, most dignified, or just, will never go away. Nor will the *pragmatic* question of how to move closer to the ideal, ever go away.

In its pragmatic form, appreciative inquiry represents a data-based-theory-building methodology for evolving and putting into practice the collective will of a group or organization.[8] In this it has one and only one aim: to provide a generative-theoretical springboard for normative dialogue allowing for self-directed experimentations in social innovation. It must be noted, however, that the conceptual world which appreciative inquiry creates remains—despite its empirical content—an illusion. This is important to recognize because it is precisely because of its visionary content, placed in juxtaposition to grounded examples of the extraordinary, that appreciative inquiry opens the status quo to possible transformations in collective action. It appreciates the best of "what is" to ignite intuition of the possible and then firmly unites the two logically, caringly, and passionately into a theoretical hypothesis of an envisioned future. By raising ever new questions of an appreciative, applicable, and provocative nature, the researcher collaborates in the scientific construction of his or her world.

---

8. Details of the methodology are described in the next chapter.

III

The Inquiry Setting and Processes of Observation

If the craftsmen in ideas have a belief in the possibilities of human society and a sense of the dignity of ordinary people, that will be the best safeguard of those ultimate standards of validity we call science and truth.

– Max Lerner

Introduction

THIS CHAPTER PROVIDES A DESCRIPTIVE account of the appreciative inquiry process as it unfolded. It is presented in six parts: (1) the setting of the research; (2) the choice of topic; (3) the articulation of normative theory; (4) the consensual validation of normative theory; (5) experimentations with normative theory; and (6) revisitation of normative theory.

The Setting of the Study

This inquiry was conducted at the medical group practice of the Cleveland Clinic Foundation (CC), a private, non-profit, tertiary care center located in Northeast Ohio.

In contrast to the typical image associated with the word "clinic", the CC is one of the largest medical centers in the world. Beginning in 1921 as a small group practice engaged in patient care, medical research, and post-graduate medical education, the CC has evolved into a multi-faceted institution with a technical complex of over 38 specialties and 67 areas of subspecialization. The physician group practice itself is made up of more than 300 members (the second largest in existence) and is complemented by an employee population of about 7,000 personnel. Presently the CC records some 30,000 annual admissions to its hospital and by 1987 it anticipates yearly service in the form of ambulatory care to more than 450,000 outpatients. With this and an annual operation budget in excess of four hundred million dollars—plus a current expansion program estimated at a billion dollars—the CC represents a large, economically viable, and rapidly developing organization.

The tremendous growth of the organization has been due, in part, to its reputation as a "cutting edge" professional organization capable of providing high quality patient care in the treatment of the most complicated of diseases. Recognized nationally, the United States Congress has formally awarded the CC the title of "National Health Resource" because of its "pioneering advances in basic clinical research, the responsible development and integration of new technology into patient care and the education of future generations of physicians and those physicians already in practice" (*Cleveland Press*, 1980). As just one example why this congressional award was given, the Cleveland Clinic's Department of Cardiology and Cardiovascular Surgery has become the largest of its kind in the world. More than 3,100 heart operations are performed there annually.

Beyond its medical contribution, however, the group practice of the CC is of theoretical interest as a social innovation. Even as a professional bureaucracy, the CC has a number of unique features (see Jensen, 1982 for a detailed analysis). Perhaps most notable is that—from the perspective of the physician group practice—the CC is wholly managed and governed by the productive workers themselves. CC physicians have taken total responsibility for the operation of their organization. While all physicians (including those in leadership positions) continue to practice medicine, a dynamic self-regulating system of cooperative governance has been established whereby the traditional class distinction between management and labor has been eliminated. Those who do the specialized work of the organization also control all aspects of the organization—medical and administrative—through a

has now come to be called "the Revolution of 1968."

Either through death or retirement, the diminishment of the founders' influence in the 1940s left a leadership vacuum. Observers pointed out that it "was clear that the child could walk but the problems of adolescence still had to be met." Devoid of leadership, key members of the Board of Trustees brought in a business consulting firm to help decide how the Clinic should be run. One result was a proposal for a committee system of operation. The other was a formal plan of hierarchical organization clearly placing final responsibility for policy and administration in the hands of the Board of Trustees. This led to what the healthcare literature refers to as a "dual hierarchy" between professional and administrative affairs. Thus, a fundamental of this particular plan called for policy proposals to emerge through committee, whereas *authority* for decision making would be vested in individual offices according to a formalized bureaucratic chain of command. As an organization, the system would follow the bureaucratic blueprint as conventionally practiced by most any corporation in the industrial world.

However, within a decade, staff members began raising concerns of the gradual hardening of the lines of authority. They felt the current bureaucracy inhibited their direct involvement in the affairs of the organization. They felt exploited and voiced their distaste over the fact that there were no democratic processes by which they, as individual members, could register either protests or preferences. The problem was partially solved in 1955 when the Board of Governors (BOG) was formed as a democratically elected forum of physicians. As a representative group of the staff, the BOG would now have final authority over *medical affairs*. However, it was made explicit that the business of the Foundation, the non-professional administration of the Clinic and the hospital, and the administration of the research and education divisions were to continue to be the responsibility of the Trustees. Only those matters pertaining to the practice of medicine would be under the democratic jurisdiction of the group practice via the

Board of Governors. There was a serious weakness, however, with this new plan: The issue of democratization had not adequately been addressed. Soon it would become "evident that the business and professional affairs of the CC could not forever remain entirely separate."

By the end of the sixties, the inadequacies of the plan of organization were directly challenged in what later became called "an ideological confrontation...the revolution of 1968." According to most standards, the use of the word "revolution" is probably too strong: There were no hints of violence, riots, or bloodshed. But, for those taking part in this period, there were definite risks both personally and professionally. There was a cause to fight for and, out of the political and intellectual exchanges, there would be the formation of a fundamentally different social order. From this perspective, the idea of revolution was reality.

While details of the events remain clouded, one meeting stands out for almost everyone. As one of those involved described it to the author:

> I can remember very distinctly 30 of us getting together and going to the Trustees and saying, "We want this place restructured so that we can run it ourselves as a group—or else we'll go..." In short, we said we could run it better.

After months of corridor negotiations, a united coalition of 30 prominent staff members produced a white paper calling for a physician-run organization. Then, following the ideological confrontation, the Trustees conferred their consent to the proposal. Legally responsible to the Board of Trustees (based on state law in Ohio), the CC would henceforward be governed—both administratively *and* professionally—by an elected group of peers, the Board of Governors. The chairman of this body would be considered the chief executive operating officer.

In 1976, the new board chairman went out of his way to make it clear that the affairs of the organization would continue to be conducted on the merits of the staff itself as a group. A special relationship was then formed between the Clinic and Case Western Reserve University's doctoral pro-gram in Organizational Behavior. This relationship was led by the innova-tive work of Suresh Srivastva and his colleagues at CWRU and was based quite simply on a joint agreement with the CC to ongoing learning and experimentation with more effective forms of organizing. While a descrip-tion of the events throughout this period deserves a complete study by itself, this is not our purpose here.

Before ending this sketch of our research setting, it needs to be pointed out that in the last 15 years since the formation of the worker-governed system, the CC has continued to grow at a phenomenal rate, beyond that of comparable industry averages. As alluded to earlier, a major expansion program is now being completed and it has been forecast that by 1986 the CC will:

1. Be responding to more than 450,000 outpatient visits per year.

2. Provide service to more than 42,000 hospital in-patient admissions.

3. Employ an additional 1,000 individuals, bringing its total labor force to more than 8,000.

4. Continue to be recognized as the largest private post-graduate medical facility in the U.S.

5. Continue to break new ground and contribute to medical knowl-edge in its more than 105 specialty and subspecialty areas.

6. Continue in its leadership not only as a national resource but as a local resource as well. As Cleveland's Mayor Voinovich recently commented: "There are few institutions in the city that have shown faith in Cleveland like the Foundation. No busi-ness or industry in Cleveland has grown in employment like the Foundation."

These facts, as well as the brief historical sketch, have been given to highlight the position that the CC is a viable, growing organization that has been experimenting with new processes and structures of organizing that depart significantly from the bureaucratic model. Of interest from the appreciative point of view, the CC is an innovative, post-industrial organization that might well portray a number of the features of the prototype to come. Following Bell (1973), a number of dimensions of post-industrialization do, in fact, apply:

1. *Economic Sector*: As a medical center, the CC represents one of the dominant organizations in the *service* economy.

2. *Professional Occupational Character*: The CC, as a professionalized organization, is marked by the pre-eminence of a highly educated professional and technical operating core.

3. *Axial Principle*: The Clinic's success depends upon the use and creation of ideas, information, and knowledge. It is a prototype system as found in the "information society."

4. *Future Orientation*: Because of the complexity of its environment, the CC requires ongoing strategic adaptation and innovation in the development of intellectual and societal technologies.

5. *Decision making*: Because of the centrality of knowledge—and the communal (public) nature of knowledge—decision making will increasingly encompass both technical *and* political realms through increased levels of member involvement and participation (for example, the CC's revolution of 1968 making the CC's governance structure a collectively controlled mechanism, eliminating the distinction between those who manage and those who do the work).

Topic Choice as an Appreciative Act of Valuing

According to the socio-rationalist foundation of appreciative inquiry, good theory may be one of the most powerful means action-researchers have for contributing to change and development in the groups and organizations in which they do their work. As discussed in the previous chapter, theory is agential or formative in character and cannot be separated from the ongoing negotiation of everyday social reality. Because of this, all social-organizational research is a moral concern, a concern of social construction and direction. The choice of what to study, how, and what is offered to the public in terms of results each imply some degree of responsibility. It also implies opportunity: *The very choice of research topic—positive or negative—may be the single most critical determinant of the kind of world the scientific construction of reality helps bring to focus—and, therefore, fruition.*

In its practical form the appreciative theorist begins with a *positive imaging* and asks: What makes cooperative existence possible…and what would I like to see *more of* in organizational life? Is there something that I care deeply about? What is it that moves me to the point where I would seek every possible avenue to shed new light on the object of inquiry, even if new understandings meant that I might have to change my convictions? Are there some higher values of life seeking expression through my work? Perhaps values of dignity? Equality? Beauty? Excellence? Joy? Justice?

As it was argued in Chapter II, social theory gains its power to affect cultural practice precisely because it provides people with an "ontological education" of what is there to see. It becomes an active agent as a cueing device, a subtle input that serves to focus attention on a particular phenomenon while obscuring others. It also serves as a source of connection among people, and through the language of possibility or constraint serves as a shaper of expectation directing perception and possible behavior. Thus, the images formed by the theorist are important ones, whether they are negative in the sense of the Weberian "iron cage" or Marxist "psychic prison of domination"—or, in a more positive sense, as a meaningful "play" form (Huizinga, 1949) or purposeful interactive system of "cooperative action" (Barnard, 1938).

The appreciative researcher frames the topic of study through positive imaging based on the realization that our images do in fact have a consequence and that choice of topic is "value-relevant" (Weber, 1968). While only suggestive, recent investigations indicate a powerful relationship between belief systems, positive images, and such phenomenon as diverse as the concerted action of a whole people or nation (Burns, 1978; McCluskey, 1976) and the release of our body's own "healing systems" (Cousins, 1981). More specifically, research reported by Matlin and Stang (1979) shows that people: (1) understand positive concepts more quickly and accurately than negative or unpleasant ones; (2) spend more time thinking about positive rather than negative concepts; (3) have better recall of positive concepts; and (4) judge positive concepts to be more intense, more important and more worthwhile in terms of their commitments. Other research links positive imagery to a holistic or synthetic form of intuitive knowing that is generally understood as the gift of the right brain (Rudolph, 1974). And research by Wilkinson (1974) suggests that constructive imagery, in terms of faith in people, is positively related to willingness or desire to accept innovation.

Using experience as a simple example, I've found that the game of golf is clearly affected by the direction of my images, positive or negative. When, for instance, my partners provide "helpful" cues by asserting "Dave, watch out for the woods over there!" I find that in a preponderance of cases I will, in fact, hit the ball into the woods. On the other hand, if they say "Dave, go ahead now and sink this putt right down the middle of the cup!" I often find myself doing just that. It is as if the mind has difficulty negating a negative image and would rather follow a negative image than none at all. In this case, it is as if the mind had extreme difficulty negating the negation of trees into a compelling image of a shot flying straight down the middle of the fairway. A negative image of trees still registers visually then, as trees. While we do not know much about this process, appreciative inquiry seeks to provide compelling, positive images and begins its construction with a very choiceful framing of the research topic.

The excitement for this exploration at the Cleveland Clinic was ignited during an earlier study in 1981 concerned with the question of how professionally trained individuals translate or apply their "professional instincts" to the management of organizational activities (Jensen, 1982; Srivastva, Jensen, and Cooperrider, 1981). During this research at the CC it became readily apparent that the general spirit and guiding logic behind the organization's growth was qualitatively different than predominant bureaucratic rationality of efficiency and effectiveness (Thompson, 1967). Consensus about the primary task of organizing went beyond the economizing functional one (to make profits or fulfill a market demand) and centered around a broader, open-ended psychosocial one. The efficiency logic of instrumental rationality was by no means inoperable or rejected, it was simply circumscribed by the professionals' practical concern for the ongoing development of an active, responsive and cooperative social system in an organization committed to a democratic/ participatory process.

For example, it was no accident that the theme dramatizing the Clinic's history in a major book was entitled, *To Think and Act as a Unit*. Primary concern for the health of the *social system* was at the focal point, early on, in the awareness of each member of the group practice; yet the full implication of this for a coherent theory of administration was admittedly fraught with ambiguity, myth and mystery:

> It is like Ezekiel's vision of the wheels, in which the big wheel moved by faith and the little wheel moved by the grace of God. The keys to success are the participants' desire to do what is best for the Clinic and their confidence in one another's integrity. Businessmen looking at this "unhierarchical" organization feel as mystified as Ezekiel did about what made the wheels work. But they do and the reason why can best be summarized in the expression of "esprit de corps"! (CC, 1971)

This effort began, therefore, as an attempt to understand this "spirit" in terms of *participation potential* and soon progressed into a broader exploration seeking to generate grounded theory (Glaser and Strauss, 1967) of the defining dimensions, categories, and dynamic properties of the emerging egalitarian organization.[10]

As described earlier, the appreciative mode awakens the desire to discover and create new social possibilities that enrich our existence and give it meaning. As a methodology for evolving the collective will of a group or organization, it is a value-relevant form of inquiry that begins with an affirmatively phrased topic of study. As shown in Figure III-1, the topic choice serves as a stabilizing core, around which revolves the various phases of the appreciative approach. Much like the firm yet permeable base of a potter's clay material, the affirmative topic provides a centering point shaping the articulation of theory, consensual validations of theory, and possible experimentations with theory. As Maslow (1968) suggests, good science has a marriage-like quality to it whereby one becomes "wedded" to the phenomenon of interest and concern. In this sense, topic choice is akin to taking on a partner in one's life: It becomes a living power able to reciprocally shape and be shaped by the investigation. So often in social-organizational research we avoid personal attachment. Without commitment, the research process easily becomes crowded with everything in sight. We pay attention to so many noises, acts, utterances, and observations that singular attachment or focused appreciation becomes near impossible. Part of this is caused by the seductive pull of the problem-solving view whereby the grip of practical affairs exerts its own kind of tyrannical pull away from our noblest aspirations. What was discovered in this study, therefore, is that the *discipline* of appreciative inquiry requires commitment, focus

---

10. It is important to note the affirmative phrasing of the topic. As Dachler and Wilpert (1978) point out in their extensive review of the literature in this area, most studies on participation are worded in deficiency terms (e.g., barriers to participation) and, therefore, immediately cut short our understandings of the potential of participatory systems. The deficiency orientation is inherently conservative, they argue, because (1) the pathology is usually defined by those who hire the researchers, and (2) the statement of deficiency implies an a priori set of assumptions about what is "normal".

and care and combines these three elements into an affirmative topic that becomes a living light, infusing the whole process with a subtle but important directionality.

Figure III-1
Phases in the Process of Appreciative Inquiry

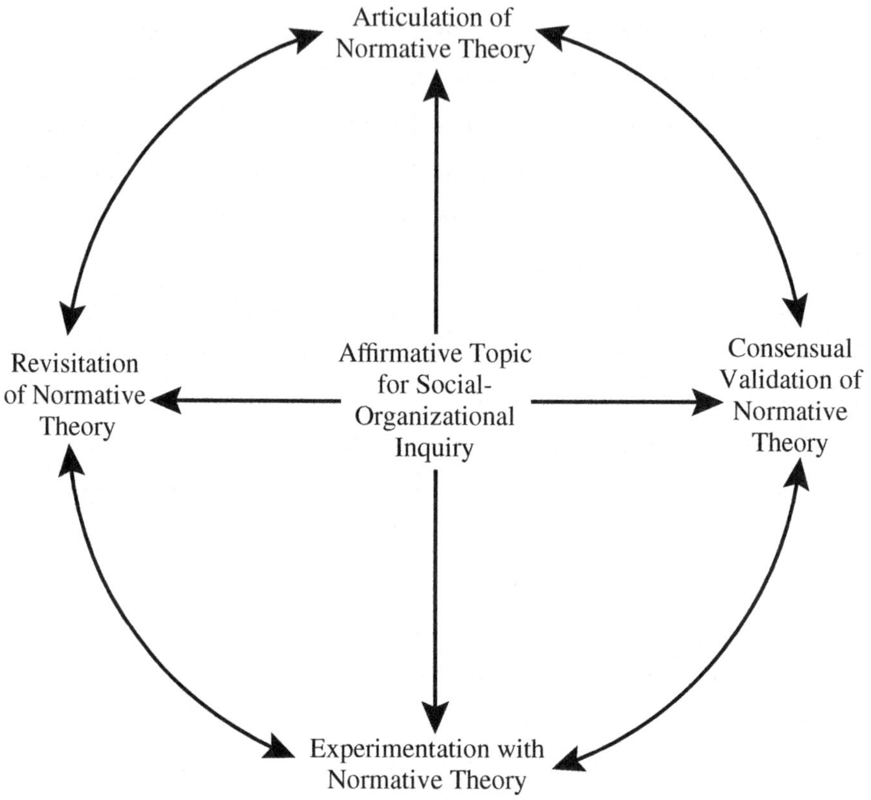

The Articulation of Normative Theory

This particular study of the Cleveland Clinic began in 1979 and to date continues on in the form of a number of large-scale (whole divisions) social experiments designed to help the system move closer to its ideals as first articulated in a normative theory constructed in 1981. In this section, the methods of data collection and analysis used to construct the theory will be presented along with a brief discussion about the qualities of mind required for generative theorizing.

Collection of Data

Data for the initial theory-building activity were collected throughout a two-year period of time (1979-1981) using multiple social science methods including:

1. *Interviews*—Open-ended formal interviews were conducted with 55 members of the CC group practice including all members of the Board of Governors, all division and department chairpersons, the director of Professional Affairs, and all members of the Medical Division Council. Each interview lasted from one to two hours and covered a range of general questions about their involvement in organizational affairs, their work, relationships within and between departments, decision processes, rewards, reasons for the institution's "cooperative spirit," factors associated with success, and perceptions about the future.

2. *Historical Documents*—Newspaper articles, books, unpublished papers and minutes of the governing board were reviewed and content analyzed. The most prominent historical document used in the analysis was a published book, *To Act as a Unit: The Story of the Cleveland Clinic Foundation* (Crile and Bunts, 1971).

3. *Observations*—Numerous board, committee and departmental meetings were attended, providing a direct experiential basis for understanding and complementing the interview data.

4. *Surveys and Group Discussion of Data*—Following each interview a survey was given asking the interviewees to rate their peers on measures of professional and organizational effectiveness. The purpose of this survey was to provide convergent validation around norms of successful membership within the system. The survey was a simple one, asking members to rate

each of their peers (the current leaders of the institution) on a five-point scale on three variables: how they were viewed by their peers as professionals, "professional effectiveness"; how they were viewed by their peers in their "organizational effectiveness"; and how they were viewed by their peers in terms of "overall effectiveness." In a second phase of the research, another survey was developed to again provide convergent validity to the interview data and is described in detail in the section on consensual validation of normative theory.

The use of multiple methods allowed for a cross-referencing of data and a more holistic approach to understanding and appreciation. While conflict is often felt between the use of various methodologies, this study agreed with the assessment of Glaser and Strauss (1967) that there is no fundamental clash between qualitative and quantitative modes of inquiry. What clash there is usually concerns the primary emphasis on verification or generation of theory and, since our focus was on generation, it was felt the inquiry would be strengthened by a multi-method holistic perspective (see Diesing, 1971).

Analysis of Data

The data were handled in two ways. First, all interviews were taped or transcribed verbatim, resulting in more than 350 typed pages of material. An initial reading of the data provided the 30 general themes used in a later survey and became the basis for an organizational report and discussion with the board. From these early activities emerged a preliminary description of a set of characteristics loosely coupled to the concept of "the potential of participatory social systems." Taken together, this set of characteristics pointed to what a number of members referred to as the "common ground" between the person and the organization. Viewed as a substantive and dynamic ideal-type, this common ground was later termed the *ideal membership situation* (see Table III-1). While the concept was not totally clear nor based on operational precision, it could be intuitively grasped as an integral experiential medium governing organizational activity as well as an important consequence of organizational activity. Representing a sphere, Kanter (1968, p. 499) notes "arises at the intersection of organizational requisites and personal experience," the notion of the ideal membership situation provided an important analytic tool for linking phenomenological (subject world) and structural-functioning (object world) considerations as pictured in Figure III-2.

Guided by the theoretical heuristic of the ideal membership situation, the data were then reanalyzed, *appreciatively*, looking specifically at the cultural meanings and factors of organizing associated with the intensity, breadth, and duration of the ideal type of situation. Thus, the coding process was a *highly* selective one, attending more to the centrality and importance of certain features of organizing rather than a summative quantitative assessment. It was a coding process based on "whether, not how much" (see Mitroff, 1978 for support of this technique).

Table III-1
Dimension of the Ideal Membership Situation[11]

1. *Commitment/Conviction:* Refers to an internally regulated willingness to engage with others to address the inevitable problems, conflicts and opportunities arising on the basis of the developmental nature of organizing. It represents a belief that there is something serious, meaningful and purposefully significant about one's existence as an organizational participant: One is convinced about the need to "willingly engage with others."

2. *Critical Control/Ownership:* Critical control refers to the experience of being an integral co-participant in the creation, maintenance and transformation of organizational realities. Based on a self-confident belief that one has the authority to offer up ideas for effectual action, the experience of having critical control is realized when organizational members feel that the organizational world about them reflects the unique expression of their own creative powers. Having selectively (critically) tapped the system's balance of forces in a way that builds on feelings of efficacy, empowerment and responsibility,

---

11. The use of the word "ideal" is used to indicate a state where the structures and processes of organizing maximize each of these dimensions for all members throughout an organization.

the processes of organizing become infused with members' own special contributions and meanings. Hence, members take possession of the organization: They are not "owned" by it, rather it becomes their "own."

3. *Normative Consciousness:* One of the prerequisites and outcomes of existing critical control is the experiencing of increased levels of practical (normative) awareness. This dimension refers to the experience of having the capacity and opportunity to bring one's sharpened thinking, sensing, feeling, and intuiting to bear on normative questions of organizing. It relates to a capacity to participate in strategic dialogue around common organizational issues of what is, what isn't, what could be and how it might become so. Hence, it represents a radical spirit of inquiry whose aim is to bring the best available knowledge to bear on public questions of what is possible and what ought to be.

4. *Colleagueship/Community:* This dimension is related to the desire to increase one's feelings of self-worth, learning and discovery, and productive contribution through an intimate task involvement with a community of "competent" others. Fueled by a deep desire to believe that one can count on the competence, challenge and support of one's colleagues, this factor rests upon the assumption that the collegial group is more than the sum of its individual parts and that the individual becomes more as a result of an active participatory association with the whole. The colleagueship ideal refers to a profound faith in others: a belief that the self and others in the organization can find within their own collegial setting the support, affirmation, challenge and divers talent for setting in motion generative interactions leading to the ongoing discovery and achievement of selected values.

Figure III-2
Analytic Dimensions for Studying
the Potential of Participatory Systems

Normative Theory Building

Appreciation adorns life and amplifies it at its best, providing a kind of synoptic connection between the realms of possibility and practice. As in all theory building, appreciative inquiry represents a process of systematic study that leads to knowledge stated in propositions, seeking to provide an explanatory logic for the dynamic interrelations among dimensions, categories, and properties of a selected phenomenon. But, unlike propositions designed to meet the empirical criteria of a correspondence theory of truth, the normative theory produced by appreciation seeks to meet the generative criteria of a socio-rationalist vision of science: It seeks to construct a world that is derived from, yet is other than, the existing one. As practiced in this study, appreciative theory building is best characterized as a process of systematic *grounded speculation*. In *The Function of Reason*, Whitehead (1929) gives an account of the kind of intuitive speculation we are talking about. For him the essence of such speculation lies in its transforming power—it is used to convert the decay of one order into the birth of its successor. He writes:

> It is the essence of such speculation that it transcends immediate fact. Its business is to make thought creative of the future. It effects this by its vision of systems of ideas, including observation but generalized beyond it (p. 82).

As practiced in this study, normative theory building began with thematic analysis of the data which, according to socio-rationalist assumptions, was aimed at building *empathetic understanding* of the unique meanings and logics that gave coherence, pattern, and context to the actions and activities observed throughout the organization. The process of empathetic understanding proceeded on three fronts simultaneously. First, the author read and re-read the text of the observational and interview data listening with a "third ear," living with the uncertainties presented in the data by engaging in a process of "free-floating attention" whereby no attempt was made to analyze, classify, or judge the data. It was a process of getting a *feel* for the system of meanings, attempting to see the world from the shoes of the other.

Next the author engaged in a mode of inquiry akin to Bion's (1961) "as if" hypothesis testing, i.e., "This system is behaving as if it were important to live up to a norm of..."

Finally, empathetic understanding was achieved by using the author himself as an instrument for knowing. Throughout the past five years, he has worked in almost every part of the system in various capacities: as consultant, project coordinator, writer, friend, task force participant, advocate, after-work-drinker, and learner. Regular activities included well over 200 meetings of one kind or another where the author was always active, responsive and, at times, confrontive in terms of passionately taking on a certain position. As an *observant participant* he was able to build contextual understanding of the organization's most intimate meaning systems. Indeed, as a long term participant, the author was able to secure the trust and confidence of many people, not unlike that found in the privacy of an analyst's couch.

As various themes emerged, data were cross-referenced according to their meaningful relation to what we called the ideal membership situation (see Appendix A for a complete listing of the original "emergent themes"). Some of the themes suggested directions for other sources of data (i.e., historical documents, secondary analysis, new observations, etc.). But mostly the themes and quotes were used to ignite the author's theoretical imagination, leading to a "wandering beyond."

Appreciation is kindled by what we care about, by eros. In this sense, it represents a drive toward union with what belongs together. It seeks, as May (1969) so brilliantly understood, to unite possibility and practice into one esthetic unity. He writes:

> We participate in forming the future by virtue of our capacity to conceive and respond to new possibilities, and to bring them out

of imagination and try them out in actuality. This is the process of active loving. It is the eros in us responding to the eros in others and the world of nature (p. 92).

Similarly, the purpose of the appreciative eye, according to Wordsworth, is to bring "A lasting inspiration, sanctified/By reason, blest by faith: what we have loved/others will love..." (in Abrams, 1953).

Appreciative theorizing risks sometimes being equated with a simple-minded romanticism. Rooted in the Platonic view, we are accustomed to thinking of "ideal" and "real" as dualistic opposites. It seems, however, that this dichotomy has serious limitations and is yet further evidence of the powerful grip that a problem view of life carries. It is as if the ideal were equated with the good and beautiful, while the real is somehow tarnished and exists only on entropic approximation of some distant perfection. Because of this, perhaps it is more productive to talk about possibility and practice rather than the ideal and real. Appreciative inquiry accepts the notion that possibility and practice are, in fact, complementary and seeks, therefore, not the negation of problems but the actualization of possibility, that is, clear realization of possibilities that are embedded in practice and can be illuminated through imagination. Appreciation breaks down into simplistic "positive thinking" or pollyanish avoidance at that point where possibility and practice are dichotomized as contradictory terms, when, in fact, they are complementary. It is, for example, the complementary contrast between light and darkness that allows us to see light. In this sense, appreciation does not deny darkness in seeking more light. It uses them both to shed greater luminosity on possibilities for humanly significant social advancement.

During the beginning phases of theory building, the appreciative theorist experiences a childlike zest: The researcher lives with his or her eyes wide open, heart pounding, flooded by questions. Like the six-year-old, he or she asks: What is life? What made this possible? Why does this work? How did that happen? He or she lives so expectantly that little of value escapes recognition and whatever is judged to hold meaning is carefully recorded and used for the work of theoretical articulation. Later the theorist becomes more of what Keen (1983) has called a "creative rebel": a dreamer, a visionary, a fighter of hope for a new social order. Unlike the sentimentalist who clings to the observed order contending we already live in the best of all possible worlds, the appreciative theorist follows the path of the speculative mind affirming that, indeed, we could *and* should live in the best world we can possibly construct. Appreciative theory is, therefore, profoundly normative: It is a systematically presented proposition of what can and should be. Chapter V presents the theory that emerged from this kind of work.

The appreciative mode invites the theorist to see conjointly with observation, empathy, imagination, and intellect. He or she must be able to live in a realm of experience that at the same time departs from and highlights what is given to the senses, able to challenge the world of purely pragmatic affairs without abandoning one's pragmatic (grounded) base. Through empathetic interpretation of recurrent themes and through the construction of normative theory, the researcher gives words, tone, and image to a forward-looking propositional logic that is ready not for technical validation but consensual validation.

Consensual Validation of Normative Theory

The value of good normative theory is determined less by its empirical truth content and more by its capacity to foster collective dialogue about concerns of normative direction, i.e., "What kind of organizational world do we want to construct together?" "What ideals do we feel the organization ought to live up to and be evolving toward?" As argued throughout, social theory can be viewed as a powerful language and as a linguistic tool, may enter into the conceptual meaning systems of a culture—and in this way alter patterns of social action. Because of this, all social theory is morally relevant; it has the potential to affect the way people live their ordinary lives in relation to one another. Hence, when we approach a group or organization as a cultural system, we are dealing within the realm of the symbolic that is subject to normative rather than technical laws. There simply is no such thing as a detached/technical/scientistic mode for judging the ultimate "validity" or worth of value claims. Valid knowledge or social theory is, therefore, a communal creation. The only law of a generative science that is defensible is the law of agreement: Dialogue free from constraint or distortion is necessary to determine the "nature of things"; truth about "what ought to be" requires the consensual validation of the human group.

In this study, consensual validation of normative theory took two primary forms. First, a 30-page report was compiled that listed some 26 "emergent themes" that related to dimensions identified earlier as the ideal membership situation. Each theme was clearly articulated and then elucidated through numerous direct quotes that were taken from our appreciative analysis of 350 pages of interview data. Next this report was circulated in 1981 to all members of the Board of Governors. Members were asked to come to the next meeting prepared to discuss, debate, and determine if these themes, indeed, were a reflection of what they felt the institution ought to be living up to.

At the next meeting, a clear consensus emerged that not only was each and every theme important, but that the themes should somehow be communicated to others, and that the institution should make a systematic effort to: (1) see if others also agreed that the ideals were indeed important, and (2) find ways to help those that wanted to, to move closer to their agreed upon ideals. Participation in such an effort would be voluntary.

The second phase of consensual validation consisted of constructing a 30-item survey instrument that translated the emerging theory into terms that could easily be communicated. Thirty affirmative statements were constructed. For each one, respondents were asked to consider two ratings:

I. To what extent do you feel the statement *is important as an ideal* to be pursued by the organization?

P. To what extent is the statement actually *reflected in practice*?

The normative statements were described on the survey as "a set of appreciative and provocative set of ideas, beliefs and assumptions that signify important ideals members feel their organization ought to live up to and be evolving toward." Each item was to be rated on a 7-point Likert scale ranging from 1 (to a *very little* extent) to 7 (to a *very great* extent).

The purpose of the survey was two-fold. The primary function, it was decided, would be to use the survey itself as a means for educating people and encouraging dialogue about the thematic dimensions of the emerging theory. Because of this, the survey was constructed a bit differently than most surveys intended solely for statistical analysis and measurement. The major difference was that the survey items often contained numerous concepts linked together, as opposed to the simple, concise one-concept items used in "scientifically" designed survey items. For example, the following statement has at least three different concepts in it, linked together, showing the relations and causality among concepts, *as if it were a theory*:

> #23. In this group practice there are minimal bureaucratic constraints because members are able to initiate changes when formal rules, procedures, or structures are no longer useful or relevant. There is nothing sacred or fixed about any organizational arrangement that shouldn't be questioned or changed once it has lost its usefulness.

Hence, as a vehicle for *communicating* the normative theory, each item was phrased in ways that mirrored the theory and preserved the integrity of the theoretical language form (i.e., causality, relations, among units, etc.).

The second function of the survey was to collect quantitative data concerning members' agreement or disagreement with the ideals as they related to their experience. This quantitative data would then serve not so much as proof or disproof but would serve as yet *another form of theoretical language that again would enter the common culture of meaning through processes of feedback.* In this sense, then, numbers play an important role in generative theorizing because they are a concise, rhetorical device that (in our culture) carries a great deal of authority and hence, has the power to stimulate dialogue, debate, and consideration of alternatives (the survey is reproduced in Appendix B).

To test whether or not the survey represented an accurate reflection of the egalitarian theory, scales were created and tested for their reliability using Cronbach's alpha. Each "ideal" scale was constructed to reflect a specific dimension of the egalitarian theory, including:

I. Egalitarian Ideology (made up of subscales "inclusion," "consent," and "excellence"; alpha = .79)

  A. Inclusion (items #4, #15, #16; alpha = .74)

  B. Consent (items #2, #3, #5; alpha = .62)

  C. Excellence (items #8, #18, #19; alpha = .56)

II. Egalitarian Structures of Interaction (made up of subscales "shared governance" and "catalytic task structure"; alpha = .73)

  A. Shared Governance (items #7, #21, #24; alpha = .54)

  B. Catalytic Task Structure (items #1, #10, #16, #26; alpha = .56)

III. Social Paradigms (made up of subscales "epistemic structure" and "relational structure"; alpha = .74)

  A. Epistemic Structure (items #11, #14, #25, #29; alpha = .64)

  B. Relational Structure (items #4, #17, #24, #28; alpha = .63

Taken together, the grand mean of all the scales had an alpha reliability of .66 that seemed to indicate that, in the translation from theory to survey, the scales did indeed "hang together" as conceptually figured in the emerging theory.

The initial sample from which the ideals were tested for this "consensual validity" and reliability had an N of 177 people. Four major divisions requested to take part in this initial consensual validation. Included were three professional-medical divisions (physicians only) and one administrative division (including directors, managers, exempt professional staff and non-exempt support staff). Out of a possible 270 people, 177 returned the mailed-out survey for a total return rate of 65.5 percent. While data from this survey are reported in chapter V, it can be pointed out now that the median score for the 30 ideal-type themes was 6.15 ("very great importance") on a 7-point Likert scale, providing a high level of cross-validation for our thematic analysis.

Experimentation with Normative Theory

In contrast to conventional action-research, the aim of appreciative inquiry lies not so much in problem solving as it does in social innovation. Its purpose is to contribute to the generative-theoretical aims of social science and to use its theoretical articulations to foster innovations in social-organizational structures and processes. Thus, a primary contention of this dissertation is that for action-research to reach its potential as a vehicle for human development and organizational transformation, it needs to elevate the status of theory building and to learn more about how theory and the process of theorizing becomes an active agent in the construction of social reality.

At this point, we need to make something clear: At no point during the last six years of this "project" did this author make a contract with the organization that a long-term project would be taking place in order to help the system develop or improve functioning. The only thing that was agreed upon was that some dissertation research, a kind of basic research, would be conducted to learn more about how professionals approach managerial activities (see Jensen, 1982 for more detail). The only condition of our initial "contract" was that the results of the investigation would be shared with the Board of Governors.

This is mentioned because early on it *was not* intended to use our inquiry as an organization-wide intervention. But as events unfolded, it was discovered that the theory began taking on a life of its own. After the Board of Governors reviewed it, four different divisions came forward and wanted to discuss the theory throughout their sections. Later, two of those divisions decided to experiment directly with the theory, to try to use it to move closer to their ideals. In one of those divisions alone, more than 80 meetings have been held since June of 1981, each devoted to discussion and planning on how to practically implement the ideals. Another division recently contacted the author for the same purpose. Also, numerous copies of the more complexly written theory (see Chapter V) have been requested either by phone or mail and future meetings are being planned to make the "emergent themes" a formal part of: (1) socialization programs for new incoming members, and (2) the physician-in-management annual two-week training program. The basic proposition, therefore, that theory may be one of the most important tools that action-researchers have to offer the groups and organizations in which they work, seems to be a powerful hypothesis that deserves a great deal more attention than it has received to date.

"Experimentation with normative theory" refers here to any activity explicitly aimed at helping a group narrow the gap between its consensually validated ideals and its actual practice (i.e., how it organizes itself). As mentioned, two divisions, one a medical division and the other an administrative division, have undertaken major steps to move closer to their agreed upon values and ideals. A third is just getting underway.

In each of the divisions, the author has been involved as consultant, participant-observer, and survey researcher. In Chapter IV, these cases are described and analyzed based on observations and analysis of survey data across two periods. Recognizing that a part of the overall research goal was to learn more about how theory itself becomes an active agent in organizational change, both field projects were allowed to emerge by themselves and there was no attempt to force or set up a formal experimental design to test the effects of various interventions. Because of this, there are no control groups. The time one and time two t-test statistics and correlational analysis are reported, therefore, descriptively and in an exploratory *indicative* mode, not a predictive mode.

Revisitation of Normative Theory

In February of 1985, one of the physicians whom the author had worked with during the initial survey project set up an appointment to see the author at the university. He had just read the paper that is presented in Chapter V on "The Emergence of the Egalitarian Organization." The physician showed a great deal of excitement about the paper but was concerned that perhaps things had changed so much in terms of the medical environment that the egalitarian principles were becoming even more distant as a driving force. He said, "I don't know if you can say we're really living up to these things anymore; and there are many of us growing increasingly concerned."

At the time of the meeting, this physician was involved in a graduate program in business administration and was working on an independent study course. After this talk, the author and the physician came up with the idea of a kind of re-enactment of the initial study in 1981 leading to the "emergent themes." Only this time he would do the study.

In terms of the data collection method, the physician used the original process of semi-structured interviews with individuals serving in leadership positions on the Board of Governors, the management group, and division and department chairmen. A representative sample of 24 people was identified and interviewed. Data from the interviews were transcribed into more than 100 pages of typed material. The average interview covered "an intense one-half hour period and frequently extended beyond this time frame." Each interview began in an open-minded way after the individuals had a chance to revisit and reflect on a listing of the initial 26 themes from 1981. Key findings from this study are reported in the epilogue of the concluding chapter.

IV

Consensual Validation and Social Experimentation with Normative Theory[12]

The final actuality is accomplished in face-to-face relationships by means of direct give and take. Logic in its fulfillment recurs to the primitive sense of the word: dialogue. Ideas which are not communicated, shared, and reborn in expression are but soliloquy and a soliloquy is but broken and imperfect thought.

– John Dewey

WHETHER OR NOT SOCIAL SCIENCE theory represents "the way things should be" is a fundamental concern to a socio-rationalist approach to action-research. As the quote by Dewey indicates, social knowledge is but broken and imperfect thought until submitted to the test of dialogue and actual experience of the human group. In this sense, it is through the *process* of interaction that normative theory validates itself as a form of knowledge more "truthful" than ivory tower speculation and/or simple-minded romanticism. It recognizes that it is through dialogue that ideas become creative of the future and thus find mature completion in the social act.

First, this chapter describes how the (emerging) egalitarian theory was used as a springboard for normative dialogue. Data are presented showing the degree to which members of the CC valued the theory and felt that it represented a provocative image of what the institution should be evolving toward. Second, the chapter tells the story of two divisions that

---

12. Throughout this chapter, when referring to "normative theory," *the author is really talking about the theory as it was emerging*. The final articulation of theory did not occur until after the processes of the consensual validation and experimentation. In this sense, this chapter represents yet another important element in the process of developing generative theory. "The theory" is not, therefore, presented until the very last chapter.

have consciously attempted to enact a set of organizational policies and practices that seek congruence with the consensually validated elements of the theory. The first case is important because it broadens the potential scope of the egalitarian theory beyond the physical group to the rest of the organization. The "Administrative Division" experiment shows that the theory is applicable and appealing not only to highly educated physicians or professionals but also to more bureaucratically trained administrators, technical specialists, and clerical support staff.[13] It also highlights some of the promises and pitfalls of making the transformation from bureaucratic to egalitarian principles. Finally, the second case describes an experiment undertaken by the physician group in one of the CC's medical divisions. This case is particularly significant in that it demonstrates just how *rapidly* human beings can, in fact, alter their practical activities to reflect elements of a commonly constructed will.

How Much Value Do Cleveland Clinic Members Place on the Egalitarian Theory?

During the process of articulation, the theory was translated into the "Survey of Group Practice Ideology" as discussed in the methods chapter. Themes from the theory were then presented to the Board of Governors who, as a group, consensually agreed that every theme was important. But just how important? And how much value did members throughout the system place on such ideals?

Table IV-1 summarizes the survey data based on the question: "To what extent do you feel the statement *is important as an ideal* to be pursued by the organization?" Included in this "time-one" sample of 177 people were three medical divisions and one administrative division.

---

13. The names of the division/departments are fictitious and are simply referred to as the Administrative Division and Medical Division.

Table IV-1[14]
Importance of Normative Theory:
Summary Scales for "Ideal" Means,
Stand Deviations, and Rank Ordering*

Scales and Subscales	X	SD	Rank Ordering
			Importance of Ideals
I. Egalitarian Ideology/Ethos	6.15	.53	I
A. Inclusion	6.09	.72	4
B. Consent	5.95	.77	6
C. Excellence	6.43	.52	1
II. Structures of Interaction	6.13	.60	II
A. Shared Governance	6.03	.68	5
B. Catalytic Primary Task	6.17	.61	3
III. Social Paradigms	6.02	.56	III
A. Epistemic Structure	5.85	.71	7
B. Relational Structure	6.21	.57	2

N = 177
*Rank ordering among composite scales is indicated by Roman numerals.

Analysis of the scaled items shows that all dimensions of the egalitarian theory were viewed as important ones, i.e., ones that the organization feels it ought to be living up to or evolving toward. On a 7-point scale where 7 equaled "to a very great extent," the dispersion of means was quite narrow, ranging from a low of 5.85 to a high of 6.43. The highest ideals were: (1) devotion to excellence; (2) the need for an egalitarian relational structure; and (3) the need for a catalytic primary task. The least important scale, which still approached 6 on the 7-point rating, had to do with the epistemic structure. In particular, as we show next, two items had a major impact here pulling this normative dimension below a mean of 6. The first had to do with how much members valued a "tolerance for uncertainty" (item #11) and the second had to do with how much they valued looking at important

---

14. Rank ordering among composite scales is indicated by Roman numerals.

decisions "as experiments to be learned from" (item #14). While observations showed that these two items were important to the well-being of an egalitarian system, the survey data indicates that they are not, in relative terms, valued as much as the other dimensions of the theory.

Table IV-2 presents the means, standard deviations, and rank ordering of all ideals from highest to lowest. Examination of the five highest items presents the following ideal-type portrait: Members of the CC value the pursuit of excellence and feel that their organization should be designed in a way that inspires people's energies. It should be a system that supports ongoing learning and discovery as well as collegial relationships where individuals can become more than they ever could have if they had worked alone as solo practitioners. In such a system, information about what is happening should be shared openly, leading to a widespread level of awareness of all members. And, finally, it should be a system which exists for some important societal purpose, thereby engendering a sense of commitment and conviction that the work of the organization is significant in a larger scheme of things.

In contrast to this portrait, the five lowest ideals suggest that members do not as strongly value a system where there is: (1) a high tolerance for uncertainty; (2) a communal political philosophy; (3) experimentations in decision making; (4) collective authority; and (5) unity of purpose. It should also be noted that the standard deviations of the five lowest items are about twice that of the top five ideals. This, among other things, indicates that there is not as much "common vision" at the CC as it concerns those ideals ranked lowest. However, as it relates to answering our basic question, it appears that *even among the lowest items there is a great deal of agreement that the normative theory is viewed as important to CC members.*

Table IV-2
Importance of Normative Theory:
Time One (all four divisions) Means,
Standard Deviations and Rank Ordering of Ideals

			Importance of Ideals
Item #	X	SD	Rank Ordering
1. Unity of Purpose	5.93	1.19	26
2. Shared Ownership	6.15	.97	17
3. Collective Authority	5.75	1.13	27
4. Face-to-Face Interaction	5.95	.94	24
5. Consensus Decision Making	5.94	.87	24
6. Communal Political Philosophy	5.66	1.15	29
7. Free and Informed Choice	5.98	.98	21
8. Ongoing Learning and Discovery	6.53	.66	2
9. Candid Debate	6.32	.71	10
10. Collaborative Work Relations	6.33	.87	8
11. Tolerance for Uncertainty	5.37	1.22	30
12. Reward Diversity	6.26	.87	13
13. Ideas on Merit	6.22	.86	14
14. Spirit of Inquiry	5.66	1.09	28
15. Opportunity for Involvement	6.19	.85	15
16. Collective Reward System	6.14	.87	18
17. Trust and Confidence	6.38	.78	7
18. Innovative Organization	6.17	.84	16
19. Devotion to Excellence	6.58	.57	1
20. Inspirational System	6.50	.69	3
21. Colleague Control	5.97	.96	22
22. Developmental Leadership	6.28	.79	11
23. Minimal Bureaucracy	6.27	.83	12
24. Democratic Partnership	6.12	.94	20

Item #	X	SD	Rank Ordering
25. Permanent Dialogue	5.94	1.15	25
26. Significant Work	6.38	.69	6
27. Self-authority	6.12	.89	19
28. Developmental Colleagueship	6.39	.67	5
29. Shared Information	6.41	.67	4
30. Democratic Leadership	6.32	.73	9

N = 177

Table IV-3 takes the analysis one step further by comparing the means and the rankings of ideals by group. This data set is remarkable in terms of its consistency. For example, as it concerns item 19 (devotion to excellence) the three medical divisions all ranked this item number one, while the administrative division ranked it within its top six. Similarly, as it concerned item 11 (tolerance for uncertainty), three groups ranked it 30th in terms of its relative importance, and the other ranked it 27th. In not one case was there disagreement of up to one point or more. Finally, the differences in scores between the medical division and administrative division are not statistically significant but a number of items deserve attention. First, it appears in item #1 that the administrators may value "unity of purpose" more than the physician group. This finding corresponds to observations made throughout our study that showed administrators to be divided as a group and in this sense perhaps more desiring of unity than the physician group. Second, data in Table IV-3 indicates that the medical divisions placed a higher value on "candid debate" (item #9) than the administrative division. Similarly, they also placed a higher value on the importance of rewarding diverse activities (item #12) and on the importance of having an innovative organization (item #18). However, it is important not to take these differences too far because: (1) they were not statistically significant, and (2) the means among all items are considered to be quite high, indicating that, in general, the CC values the normative theory as articulated.

Agreement in abstract principle is probably to be found throughout the organization. As one member put it: "How could anyone not agree with the tone and thrust of the themes—they represent a world everyone would like to see."

Table IV-3

Means and Rank Ordering of Ideals by Division

Divisions/Departments

Item #	MD_1 N = 55	MD_2 N = 17	MD_3 N = 56	AD_1 N = 49
1. Unity of Purpose	5.48* (29)**	5.87 (18)	5.83 (27)	6.18 (13)
2. Shared Ownership	5.96 (22)	6.06 (16)	6.33 (12)	6.14 (17)
3. Collective Authority	5.50 (28)	5.50 (24)	5.96 (25)	5.85 (29)
4. Face-to-Face Interaction	5.67 (25)	5.56 (22)	6.16 (23)	6.00 (26)
5. Consensus Decision Making	5.87 (23)	5.50 (25)	6.14 (19)	5.93 (27)
6. Communal Political Philosophy	5.51 (27)	4.68 (30)	5.74 (28)	5.87 (28)
7. Free and Informed Choice	5.82 (24)	6.00 (20)	6.00 (24)	6.12 (18)
8. Ongoing Learning and Discovery	6.46 (3)	6.31 (5)	6.67 (2)	6.50 (4)
9. Candid Debate	6.27 (9)	6.25 (8)	6.42 (5)	6.26 (16)
10. Collaborative Work Relations	6.33 (5)	6.25 (9)	6.42 (8)	6.26 (12)
11. Tolerance for Uncertainty	5.06 (30)	5.43 (27)	5.24 (30)	5.79 (30)
12. Reward Diversity	6.20 (12)	6.56 (2)	6.37 (9)	6.06 (20)
13. Ideas on Merit	6.06 (20)	6.13 (13)	6.26 (15)	6.37 (8)

Item #	MD$_1$ N = 55	MD$_2$ N = 17	MD$_3$ N = 56	AD$_1$ N = 49
14. Spirit of Inquiry	5.56 (26)	5.5 (14)	5.29 (29)	6.06 (19)
15. Opportunity for Involvement	6.12 (16)	6.31 (6)	6.25 (16)	6.16 (15)
16. Collective Reward System	6.16 (14)	6.19 (11)	6.19 (22)	6.04 (22)
17. Trust and Confidence	6.33 (6)	6.19 (12)	6.51 (4)	6.31 (10)
18. Innovative Organization	6.32 (8)	6.06 (17)	6.17 (18)	6.02 (24)
19. Devotion to Excellence	6.60 (1)	6.63 (1)	6.69 (1)	6.40 (6)
20. Inspirational System	6.38 (4)	6.25 (10)	6.64 (3)	6.53 (1)
21. Colleague Control	6.11 (17)	5.18 (29)	6.01 (21)	6.04 (21)
22. Developmental Leadership	6.09 (18)	6.06 (18)	6.32 (13)	6.48 (5)
23. Minimal Bureaucracy	6.13 (15)	6.13 (15)	6.33 (11)	6.39 (7)
24. Democratic Partnership	6.09 (19)	6.13 (14)	6.25 (17)	6.00 (25)
25. Permanent Dialogue	5.98 (21)	5.31 (28)	5.89 (26)	6.02 (23)
26. Significant Work	6.24 (10)	6.31 (7)	6.43 (7)	6.51 (3)
27. Self-authority	6.19 (13)	5.56 (23)	6.12 (20)	6.18 (14)
28. Developmental Colleagueship	6.47 (2)	6.06 (19)	6.50 (6)	6.27 (11)
29. Shared Information	6.33 (7)	6.50 (3)	6.36 (10)	6.51 (2)
30. Democratic Leadership	6.24 (11)	6.44 (4)	6.32 (14)	6.34 (9)

*The first figure reported is the mean score for each variable
**The second figure is the rank ordering from most important (1) to least important (30).

Is the Egalitarian Theory Provocative?

As suggested in Chapter II, theory may gain its power to affect social practice in ways not unlike the workings of the executive mind. That is, theory will tend to be generative to the extent to which it expands the conventional realm of the possible by its:

1. *Vision*: Generative theory is presumed to work largely from the present and extends itself out to the longer term future. It is provocative to the extent it is able to envision a desired future state that simultaneously challenges perceptions of what is possible and what can be realized. It situates itself beyond the frontier of conventional practice without ever losing sight of such practice.

2. *Passion*: The generative mind is simultaneously rational and intuitive, which allows it to tap into the sentiments, values, and aspirations of the organized collectivity. Normative theory transforms itself into common will to the extent to which it ignites the imagination, hopes and passions of others.

3. *Integrity*: To be truly generative, a social theory must be morally daring (i.e., challenge the social order to become better than it presently is) and must do so through logical consistency, coherence and focus. Viewing the system as a whole, the generative theorist seeks to tap into a set of higher values that provide the energy needed to move a whole group or organization and not just isolated parts.

It would appear from our consensual validation that the egalitarian theory does indeed begin to tap into the hopes and values of participants at the Cleveland Clinic. But is it provocative? Does it represent a challenging step beyond current cultural practice?

Table IV-4 takes a look at our total data set of three medical divisions and one administrative division and compares the organization's values or ideals to its actual practices. As is readily apparent from the mean discrepancy scores, it would appear that the theory does represent a challenge to the CC in virtually every dimension. The five highest discrepancies (see Figure IV-1, <page >) are in areas that are key, at least theoretically, to the long-term health and well-being of an egalitarian system. Each of the five is listed below exactly as stated on the survey form:

#7. *Free and Informed Choice*: Future plans and directions of the organization are based on free and informed choice of the members (X discrepancy of 2.31).

#29. *Shared Information*: Information about what is happening is openly shared, leading to a widespread level of awareness among all members (X discrepancy of 2.24).

#15. *Opportunity for Involvement*: All members have an equal opportunity to become involved in the affairs of the organization and to help it become what it can potentially become (X discrepancy of 2.36).

#22. *Developmental Leadership*: The leadership is more concerned with the development of others than the control of others. Thus, the leadership process is essentially an educative process (X discrepancy of 2.31).

#24. *Democratic Partnership*: The organization is a "partnership" of members who govern themselves through highly democratic processes (X discrepancy of 2.22).

Table IV-4
Cleveland Clinic Ideals, Practices and Discrepancies:
Means, Standard Deviations and Rankings

Item #		X	Ideal (s.d.)	Rank Order	X	Actual Practice (s.d.)	Rank Order	X	Discrepancy Rank Order
1.	Unity of Purpose	5.88	(1.16)	26	3.91	(1.41)	25	1.95	13
2.	Shared Ownership	6.17	(.94)	16	4.07	(1.49)	22	2.1	9
3.	Collective Authority	5.76	(1.15)	27	3.59	(1.53)	29	2.16	8
4.	Face-to-Face Interaction	5.99	(.93)	22	4.36	(1.55)	13	1.62	19
5.	Consensus Decision Making	5.97	(.91)	23	.425	(1.36)	16	1.74	15
6.	Communal Political Philosophy	5.67	(1.14)	28	3.72	(1.35)	38	1.54	20
7.	Free and Informed Choice	6.00	(.94)	21	3.47	(1.41)	30	2.50	1
8.	Ongoing Learning and Discovery	6.48	(.67)	3	5.06	(1.31)	2	1.40	24
9.	Candid Debate	6.35	(.71)	10	4.36	(1.61)	14	1.97	11
10.	Collaborative Work Relations	6.37	(.83)	7	4.57	(1.42)	8	1.79	14
11.	Tolerance for Uncertainty	5.53	(1.26)	30	4.07	(1.36)	21	1.46	23
12.	Reward Diversity	6.29	(.84)	12	4.62	(1.66)	7	1.63	17
13.	Ideas on Merit	6.21	(.89)	15	4.15	(1.44)	19	2.00	10
14.	Spirit of Inquiry	5.64	(1.10)	29	4.28	(1.66)	7	1.63	18
15.	Opportunity for Involvement	6.24	(.87)	18	4.18	(1.44)	18	1.63	18

Item #	X	Ideal (s.d.)	Rank Order	X	Actual Practice (s.d.)	Rank Order	Discrepancy X	Rank Order
16. Collective Reward System	6.14	(.87)	18	4.18	(1.44)	18	1.63	18
17. Trust and Confidence	6.36	(.76)	8	4.68	(1.49)	6	1.69	16
18. Innovative Organization	6.16	(.83)	17	4.77	(1.39)	5	1.37	25
19. Devotion to Excellence	6.58	(.58)	1	5.22	(1.22)	1	1.34	28
20. Inspirational System	6.50	(.67)	2	4.53	(1.40)	9	1.96	12
21. Colleague Control	5.94	(.96)	24	4.40	(1.32)	12	1.25	29
22. Developmental Leadership	6.31	(.76)	11	4.01	(1.45)	24	2.31	4
23. Minimal Bureaucracy	6.28	(.78)	12	4.10	(1.61)	20	2.17	7
24. Democratic Partnership	6.13	(.90)	19	3.89	(1.56)	26	2.22	5
25. Permanent Dialogue	5.95	(1.17)	25	4.42	(1.39)	11	1.47	22
26. Significant Work	6.41	(.71)	5	4.89	(1.36)	4	1.49	21
27. Self-authority	6.12	(.87)	20	4.45	(1.55)	10	1.34	21
28. Developmental Colleagueship	6.37	(.70)	6	5.02	(1.42)	3	1.34	27
29. Shared Information	6.43	(.67)	4	4.01	(1.55)	23	2.42	2
30. Democratic Leadership	6.35	(.70)	9	4.17	(1.51)	17	2.18	6

N = 232

Includes three medical divisions (physicians only) and one administrative division (managers, technical specialists, and support staff).

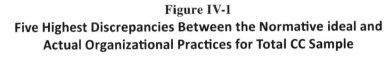

Figure IV-1
Five Highest Discrepancies Between the Normative ideal and
Actual Organizational Practices for Total CC Sample

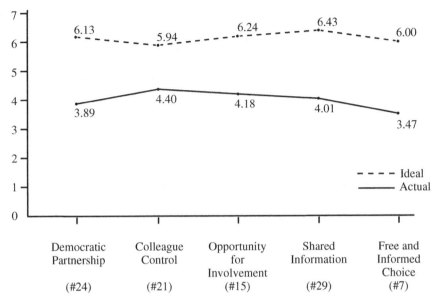

The data appears to support the intended aim of producing theory that could be used to help move the CC to perhaps a higher level of development. While we have no way of quantifying the "passion" exuded by its propositions, we do know that the theory was viewed by members as having a great deal of focus, consistency, and logical coherence. Figure IV-2 and Table IV-5 show the positive interrelationships among the major dimensions and subscales of the normative theory. Interrelations among the grand scales were very high, all significant at or beyond the .001 level. Similarly, correlations among subscales were all significant and ranged from moderate to very high positive association. The lowest correlations were between consent and inclusion (r = .35) and the highest were between inclusion and an egalitarian relational structure (r = .80).

Figure IV-2
Correlation Coefficients Among Egalitarian Theory

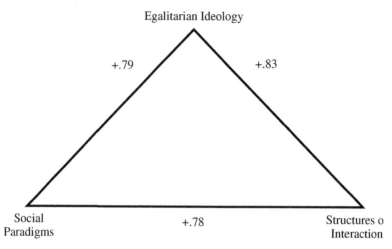

Correlations are significant at or beyond the .001 (two-tailed) test.

Table IV-5
Interrelationships Among Egalitarian Theory Subscales (Ideals)

	1	2	3	4	5	6	7
1. Inclusion	—	.49	.50	.58	.70	.46	.80
2. Consent		—	.35	.56	.61	.46	.53
3. Excellence			—	.47	.55	.47	.61
4. Shared Governance				—	.59	.57	.69
5. Catalytic Primary Task					—	.55	.69
6. Epistemic Structure						—	.50
7. Relational Structure							—

Note: N = 77. All correlations are significant at or beyond the
.001 level (two-tailed test).

Clearly, for this sample, the egalitarian represented a normative ideal that could be embraced as important by a wide range of organizational participants. Also, data indicate that perhaps it is a provocative, internally consistent theory capable of inspiring dialogue and experimentation with new social arrangements. Let us now turn to a descriptive analysis of our experimentations with normative theory.

Social Innovation in an Administrative Division

The first case took place in a 55-person division that provided administrative and technical services to the CC as a whole. The division was structured nominally as a four-tiered bureaucratic pyramid with a fairly well routinized division of labor and clear chain of command (see Figure IV-3). The total group was made up of one division head, seven department directors, 25 technical specialists, and 23 support staff including receptionists, secretaries, data-assistants and clerks. The atmosphere was production-service oriented and was segmented in terms of "territorial" boundaries between departments. Other than its extremely rapid growth rate (the division went from 10 to 55 people from 1970-1980), there is little of note about the division in terms of its organization or management. It was very much like most any administrative organization found in other corporations with which we've studied or worked.

Figure IV-3
Administrative Division Organizational Structure

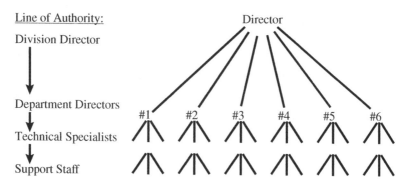

No "Felt Need," No Contract

Unlike most action-research, the author's work with the Administrative Division did not begin with a definition of the problem, contract for help, or diagnosis. In fact, early on it was not even considered a project. It had no plan nor clear objective and yet—as a project—it continues to evolve after almost five years.

In 1981, the author was asked by a colleague at Case Western Reserve University to join him as a facilitator at a one-day planning meeting with all the directors of the division. At one point during the meeting, conversation turned to questions about the "confusing and different physician culture." It was about this time also that the author had submitted an initial report of the appreciative analysis of the egalitarian organization to the Board of Governors. Knowing all this, the author was asked to present an overview of the study.

Although unprepared for a formal presentation, the author did have the egalitarian theory (ET) survey instrument available and began outlining some basic assumptions of the study:

1. All organizations are guided by the beliefs and ideals that members make about themselves and the organizations in which they live and work.

2. Organizations are possible in the last analysis because participants who govern and sustain them carry in their minds a shared image of what the organization is, how it should function, and what it might become.

The basic ideas involved in the egalitarian theory of organizing were described by going over each ideal-type statement in the ET survey. It was explained that the instrument was being used by physicians in the medical divisions to help them collaboratively discuss and discover:

1. How important are these ideals to members of the CC?

2. Which are most important?

3. For those felt to be most important, which ones need to be set out as priorities for change or development?

The directors were intrigued. First, someone said, "We should take this right now ourselves to see how we compare to the physician culture." Another said, "No, this is important enough that not only should we study ourselves but we should include all exempt staff [technical specialists] as well…Could you give us the survey and have it analyzed for us within a month?"

So, within a ten-minute period after presentation of the normative theory, a decision was made to send out the survey to be voluntarily completed by all directors and technical specialists. This was the extent of the contract. The survey was sent out the next day.

The serendipitous first meeting was an exciting one personally and represented the beginning of the author's own first-hand education into the essential unity between theory and practice and the potential power of ideas as a means for social-organizational reconstruction.

Table IV-6 lists the major activities that later emerged from this experience. Out of the activities, three broad phases can be discerned that serve to differentiate significant elements of the project:

(1) confirmation; (2) contradiction; and (3) conscious cultural evolution.

Table IV-6
Appreciative Action-Research in an Administrative Division

Date	Major Activities
June, 1981	Appreciative inquiry into CC group practice
September, 1982	Articulation of normative theory (emergent themes)
October, 1982	Introduce directors to normative theory

collective authority structure encompassing decision making at the operation, tactical and strategic levels. As one member described it:

> This is a unique organization because all the doctors feel that they are a vice-president. That is, everyone has responsibility and say in the place. Everyone is considered on an equal basis...

The system was not always organized in an egalitarian fashion, however.[9] The story of the CC begins just after World War I when four locally and nationally renowned Cleveland physicians—Drs. Crile, Bunts, Lower, and Phillips—jointly committed themselves to the idea of creating a "group practice." The birth of this concept is directly traceable to experiences these men had while serving as medical officers in World War I. Stationed in Rouen, France, near the battlefields, Drs. Crile, Bunts and Lower established and directed the first U.S. military hospital and through this experience became convinced of the need to practice medicine through collective effort where people are able "to act and think as a unit" (Crile and Bunts, 1971, p. 3). Using teams of specialists in the diagnosis and treatment of critically wounded medical cases, these physicians became convinced of the practical benefit of group medicine. And while it may have seemed an obvious response to the demands created by wartime conditions, the idea of group practice was, at that time, considered "revolutionary" at home. It threatened the very conception of the patient-client relationship which rested on a strong tradition of solo practice. It also represented an economic threat to the whole system of solo practice.

In spite of its threat, the CC was established as a tertiary care center in 1921 and from its original four person partnership has now grown to become one of the largest and most esteemed medical institutions in existence. However, its success was never easy; and its history is not without controversy or failure (Hartwell, 1985). Most noteworthy is a period that

---

9. The historical development of the CC into one of the largest privately funded medical organizations in the world is a fascinating and significant story of importance in and of itself. While this history is only touched upon here, more information is available from Crile and Bunts (1971) and more recently, Hartwell (1985).

Date	Major Activities
October, 1982	Egalitarian theory (ET) survey administered to directors and technical specialists
November, 1982	Formation of data-feedback workshop steering group
December, 1982	Three data-feedback workshops
January–February, 1983	Subgroups prepare for total group meeting
March, 1983	Total group meeting: "Declaration Values"
March, 1983	Departments meet as subgroups to prepare for second total group meeting
March, 1983	Second total group meeting: "Intergroup Value Negotiations"
April–May, 1983	Survey administered to all support staff
June, 1983	Three data-feedback workshops run by joint task force
June–July, 1983	Task force appointed to plan first ever division-wide meeting
August, 1983	Division-wide meeting (n = 55): "Building a Common Vision of Excellence"
September–December, 1983	Task force appointed to build charter proposal for a division-wide elected council of representatives
November, 1983	Proposal for council sent to all member
December, 1983	Second division-wide meeting: "Action Planning and Approval of Proposed Council"
January, 1984	Ten-member elected council begins
June, 1984	Council readministers ET survey to assess changes
September, 1984	Total division feedback meeting
September, 1984	Diagnostic workshop with council: "Should we disband?"
November, 1984	Division-wide reaffirmation of ideals (feedback of time one and time two changes)
November, 1984	Division-wide meeting: "Where do we go from here?"
December, 1984	Reconfiguration of council of representatives to become task-focused
January–July, 1985	Council launches three major change projects

Confirmation and the Process of Social Bonding

The first phase refers roughly to a period from the end of 1982 to August of 1983. During this period, there were about 60 different meetings, each in one way or another related to the processes of social bonding and the formation of an integrated group will. It was a complex and dynamic period that began with the introduction of the survey and ended with a proposed restructuring of the entire division whereby the chain-of-command bureaucracy would be transformed into a consensus system of group authority. It was a period marked by a great deal of emotion, particularly feelings of anxiety, hope, euphoria, anticipation, and excitement. It was also a period of great surprise. For the first time, members from throughout the division were able to connect with each other around cherished values that had never reached a level of public declaration. In particular, what was contagious was a sudden shock that there was more agreement in the group than disagreement; that there was more overall connection than disconnection; and that the possibility of working *together as a division* to create a jointly envisioned world was more real than unreal. It was a period of confirmation and affirmation that allowed everyone an enthusiastic voice in the articulation of their highest hopes, ideals, and values.

Following the survey, a steering group was put together to plan the feedback process. The feedback, they decided, should be used to prepare members for a division-wide meeting where there could be a broad-based and public "declaration of values."[15]

The feedback took the form of three one-half day workshop sessions with a third of the division randomly assigned to each. While the author helped design the sessions, the actual leadership of the events was taken on by steering committee members. The agenda for the meetings included:

1. Feedback/review of the data

---

15. This first "division-wide" meeting did not include support staff, which is indicative of how people viewed "the division" early on.

2. Comparison of data to personal experiences

3. Subgroup assignments:

    a. In your own words, what are the three most important ideals?

    b. Why are they important for *this* division?

    c. What are the three most critical discrepancies that we, as a division, should work on?

Subgroups of about six people then met on their own as needed during the month of January. Their task was to be prepared to give a full report on each question. Most groups met about three times, a couple met as many as five times. Everyone took the task seriously, for it was virtually the first time anyone else had been given a lead role at a division meeting other than the director. There were also many unknowns: Why are we doing this? Are the directors really committed to hearing our views? Isn't this kind of idealistic? Is this going to amount to anything in practical terms? Aren't our differences so great that we really should stick to our own work and not even attempt to do anything together as a whole? In fact, what does it mean to act and think "as a division" anyway?

It is no exaggeration to say that a clear 90% of the participants had never considered themselves as agents—as active participants—in the construction of the organizational world they lived and worked in. To think in systemic/group terms was not only foreign, it was antithetical to their entire bureaucratic experience. Thus, emotions soared. Nobody knew quite what to expect.

The first divisional meeting outstripped the expectations of almost everyone and ended in a sincere and passionate round of applause symbolizing the emergence of a new bond, connecting everyone to the division in a somehow different kind of way. Each subgroup stood up and declared its perspectives on the values they and the system ought to be evolving toward. There was no discussion, debate or criticism—only declaration. Out of some 30 members present, 24 of them stood up and voiced their opinion and laid forth their own arguments on why the values were important and what made them critical to the division's future functioning. People talked about sharing information, mutual respect, developmental leadership, collaboration, trust, caring, and unity. They talked about the need for fairness, learning, and joy at work. And they spoke about the need for democracy, freedom, and the courage to treat one another as adults, as partners and as members of a community. After each presentation there were nods of approval. And, after everything was posted on flipcharts, one member summed it all up saying:

> I can't believe how articulate everyone has been. I've never even heard many of you speak before…I was really pessimistic before this meeting but now I'm not. I can't believe how much agreement there is in this room. It feels really good to talk like this as a whole group. But where do we go from here? I'm afraid we have a long way to go!

Time ran out and a new task force was appointed to design another division meeting. The next meeting was similar in terms of hope and optimism but it had a "more practical" thrust. Like the first, there was subgroup pre-work but this time the subgroups were actual functional departments. Their task was to prepare themselves to publicly enter into "intergroup negotiations around values" whereby each department could re-formulate their working relationship with each other group by building agreements around:

1. What we should like to see more of (in terms of our espoused values) from you.

2. What we would like to see less of.

3. What we would like to see the same.

At the end of this meeting, agreements were drawn up and a number of action possibilities were discussed. One of the action items had to do with "eliminating the caste system and really becoming a whole division." It was felt that, "It would be a critical mistake to go one step further without bringing the non-exempt support staff on board."

Another task force, this time representing *all* levels in the division, was formed. From April to June, members of this group managed all aspects of the survey and feedback process with the support staff except for the statistical analysis and summary, which the author prepared. They repeated the designs of the earlier meetings in preparation for the very first *total* division-wide meeting where each peer level group (i.e., directors, technical specialists, and support staff) would present their group's declaration of highest values and most critically experienced discrepancies. The only new event planned for this meeting would be an intergroup mirroring exercise between peer level groups that was intended to:

1. Lead to empathetic understanding of how we see ourselves and each other group in terms of living up to the espoused ideals, and

2. Provide a springboard for dialogue around (a) things we can do more of, (b) things we would like your group to do more of, and (c) things we should continue doing.

It is impossible to portray the richness of the dialogue and the sheer emotion associated with the actual speeches delivered by the subgroups. However, it was a stepping-stone event for everyone present and seemed to the author to be not at all unlike what the term "politics" must have meant to the early Greeks. It was a situation where all the "citizenry" were expected to participate actively and seriously in the life of the *polis*, contributing their thoughts unselfishly in the name of the betterment of the whole life and spirit of the community. Thus, people talked about the need and benefits of building a more inclusive system, a more consensual system, and a system that provided developmental opportunities for all. Symbolizing the flavor of the whole meeting, one group posted a huge and colorful rendition of the Jolly Green Giant stooping over a can of peas, holding down the lid of the can with both hands, shutting it tightly. People questioned who the green giant actually was. Some said it was the directors. Others said it was their own internalized image of what and who they could and should be in a bureaucratic system.

The meeting ended with a commitment to find some "realistic and effective means for transforming the division." It was clear that people shared a common vision in the abstract. Now, as one person shouted in frustration, "Enough talk; words must be put into action." The author then put forward a proposal that received immediate attention:

> Based on the survey data, it appears important for the division to create a shared governing forum whereby all staff have an opportunity to share their ideas for bettering the workings of the division. It should be a forum, where people will be heard and responded to. As an ongoing forum it should be designed to embody the stated ideology of inclusion, consent, and excellence—and it should serve to foster the development of as many members as possible. Whatever it looks like, this forum should take a division-wide focus that seeks continuously to find new and better ways to create a system that engenders in all members a sense of commitment, critical control/ownership, normative consciousness, and a sense of colleagueship and community.

By this point, everyone in the room knew exactly what was being proposed. The words and grammar of the emerging egalitarian logic had now firmly entered the culture; it was no longer a completely foreign language. In its abstract form, the commonly emerging image provided a kind of compelling backdrop, inviting each and every person to project his or her fantasies and hopes. It was this *process* of collective fantasizing that was unique to the group; and it was catalyzed by an egalitarian *language of possibility*. Another task force was then appointed. It was given the near impossible mandate of recommending to the division exactly how their fantasies could be enacted.

Cultural Contradiction

For the next three months the task force met weekly in what was later described as:

> ...a grueling and often painful experience of convincing ourselves that the division's fate really did rest largely on our own choices or non-choices and that we actually could as a group move closer to the ideal.

Another said:

> ...there were so many negative forces to overcome that I found myself becoming more and more disgusted...ET was making things unbearable for me and I almost left to find another job.

The idealized image that was growing throughout the division had become so powerful that every act, utterance, and interaction in the system was now scrutinized in a new way and, in most cases, was found deficient. Contradictions in the form of traditional management practices were found everywhere. Earlier feelings of hope were now challenged by skepticism, doubt, guilt and, in some cases, there was overt hostility and in yet others there was apathy and withdrawal. Over the next few months, a number of clear themes emerged as indicated by the following typical quotes:

1. *Low self-conception (support staff)*: What do we have to offer? The directors are the only ones who know what's going on. Things are too complex and there is too much that I don't know. I think some kind of council will be a waste of everybody's time.

2. *Displacement of responsibility (technical staff)*: The directors will never give up their power. If the division is going to change, it is up to them and I don't think *they* want change.

3. *Guilt of omission (director)*: There is no way we can possibly live up to these expectations. I even see the discrepancies between what I believe and what I'm sometimes forced to do. It hurts to set these kinds of standards.

4. *Guilt of self-authority (support staff and technical specialist)*: Who am I to say how this should be done or that? What makes me so special that I can challenge the directors? They have the authority and final say and they are the ones getting paid to handle things. I feel badly just in the message we're sending them right now by considering a representative council.

5. *Displacement of hostility to peers (technical specialist)*: We're all in a competition with each other for the next level job, which is scarce. You wouldn't believe how we treat each other. Since this ET program, we've tried to work things out in about six closed door meetings, but we've had to stop meeting because of the tension, fighting, and hostility.

6. *Tension between apathy (fate) versus activism (choice) (technical specialist)*: The idea of an elected representative council is okay, but it will never work or do any good. Things are the way they are for a reason and they will continue to be done in the same way no matter what. The directors will continue to run the show and I'll continue to just do my job; and that's fine with me.

In spite of all this, an elected representative council was formed to provide policy level input into the affairs of the division. By the time the proposal was finally drawn up, fully 80% of the division's members had attended and contributed to at least one of the task force meetings. Without the affirmative bonding that had taken place earlier, it is not likely that the project would have progressed as it did. Also, the later development of the council itself was never easy or assured. In fact, at one point it was almost abolished because little of importance was being dealt with. The interactional dynamics between hierarchical levels within the council began mirroring older bureaucratic norms. People were afraid to speak their minds and the directors soon dominated discussions. It took almost another full year to achieve any semblance of egalitarian interaction.

Conscious Cultural Evolution

Through processes of confirmation and contradiction, the Administrative Division was able to innovate in a wide range of ways. Unlike the problem-solving approach, the inquiry here did not begin with an analysis of deficiencies to help the system "unfreeze" itself. Instead it began with confirmation, with a vigorous affirmation of a consensually validated system of ideals. In this sense, appreciative inquiry creates a whole different research context or "holding environment" (Winnicott, 1965) whereby a system is actually held and cared for in a deliberately supportive manner. The appreciative context is unique in its capacity, therefore, to surface the urge toward fantasy, caring, empathy, and hopeful imaging; and it invites a bonding among people that allows for individuals to speak and be listened to in the public life of the system. While most action-research begins in a post-mortem atmosphere, appreciative inquiry begins in a pre-natal, maternal one. This, it is contended, is the central difference between problem solving and social innovation.

While it is impossible to claim the project as a total success, there is some evidence that the system is consciously evolving in the direction of its ideals. Table IV-7, for example, provides a listing of the positive changes attributed to ET by members themselves. The most commonly mentioned change was the establishment of a system of shared governance through the creation of the Representative Council. The other was the breakdown of barriers between departments and levels, allowing for the emergence of many new and different temporary project teams. Behaviorally and attitudinally, the system exhibits increased empathy, reciprocity, and mutual respect. And, structurally, it has made a shift from a system of bureaucratic authority to a system of group authority. As shown in Figure IV-4, the system of group is still hierarchical in the sense of having different levels, but it is a different kind of hierarchy. Instead of a chain of command, the system at all levels revolves around a dynamic consent formed and re-formed through the constant interplay between various and multiple groupings that members find themselves in. In this sense, authority flows upward and downward, guided always by an evolving group will.

Table IV-7
Positive Changes Attributed to Appreciative Intervention ("E.T.") by members of the Administrative Division

A. Structural/Procedural Changes

1. Formation of Shared Governance (Representative Council)
2. Increased use and effectiveness of cross-departmental temporary project teams
3. Formation of career ladders (i.e., interim positions
4. Regular division-wide discussion versus informal meetings
5. Division-wide "brown-bag" luncheons
6. Interdepartmental meetings
7. Division representative at directors' meetings
8. Formalized team-building program for each department
9. Implementation of flex-time
10. Development workshops for non-exempts
11. More/new responsibilities given non-exempts
12. Introduction of new performance review system
13. Division-wide job audit
14. More frequent updates on strategic plans
15. Clarified tasks and interrelationships between individuals and departments
16. Monthly "press meeting" luncheons
17. Participative agenda-setting procedures
18. Career development program, cross training, increased educational support
19. Establishment of move coordinators and participative planning process
20. Participation in the planning for new technology (i.e., computerization for the division)
21. New orientation program for division

B. Relational-Behavioral Changes

1. More members taking responsibility for self and their concerns
2. Improved divisional communication and less misunderstanding
3. Improved individual and departmental cooperation

4. Improved divisional work effectiveness through elimination of "cracks" between departments
5. Increased dialogue in all departments and between departments
6. Increased opportunity for exempts and non-exempts to present and represent their ideas to the division
7. More recognition given to non-exempt employees (e.g., speeches at division-wide meetings)
8. Has allowed for more participation and contribution by people not otherwise involved
9. More sharing of information *before* decisions are made
10. Directors are listening more
11. More mentoring between specialists
12. Everyone behaves more as if they have power
13. Less unhealthy competition
14. Stronger, more open leadership
15. Learning group leadership skills among all levels

C. Relational-Attitudinal Changes

1. Heightened awareness of group and individual feelings throughout the division
2. Heightened awareness of the extent to which our practice is short of our ideals
3. Non-exempts are viewed more accurately and positively versus stereotypically
4. Increased readiness to deal with important issues and concerns
5. Non-exempts feel more included, more important
6. Less of a gap between the three levels, more equality
7. Feel like a whole division
8. Increased desire and drive for consistency around values
9. Increased mutual respect
10. More commitment and follow-through on projects
11. More integration of values into day-to-day work with the organization and trying to help others understand and embody the values
12. Increased *shared* awareness of divisions/issues
13. Reduction of the caste system
14. Greater sense of professionalism
15. Feelings of optimism concerning the future

Figure IV-4
The Administrative Division's Conception of Its Authority Structure Before and After the Council

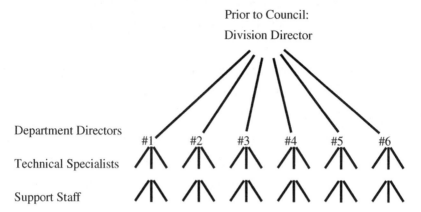

Prior to Council:

Division Director

Department Directors

Technical Specialists

Support Staff

Figure IV-4 (con't.)

After Council:

Evolving Group Will

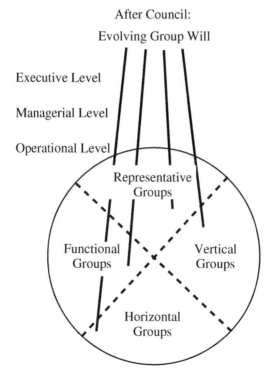

Executive Level

Managerial Level

Operational Level

Representative Groups

Functional Groups

Vertical Groups

Horizontal Groups

In terms of its ideals, Table IV-8 lists the survey means, standard deviations, coefficients of variation and T-values for the Administrative Division from June of 1983 to October of 1984. What this table shows is that, in spite of the let-downs and disappointments following an earlier more romantic phase, the system as a whole did not lower its standards. In fact, it has become even more idealistic as a group. Almost all items went up and seven of them moved significantly. What is most remarkable about this change is that it happened in terms of values that were already rated extremely high to begin with. For example, "devotion to excellence," went from a mean importance of 6.4 to almost 6.7. There just isn't much further to go on a seven-point scale. Figure IV-5 shows these changes in graphic forms.

Table IV-8
Means, Standard Deviations, Coefficients of Variation
and T-Values for Administrative Division "Ideals" Across Time

Item #	X	Time One N = 49 s.d.	c.v.%	X	Time Two N = 40 s.d.	c.v.%	T-Value
1. Unity of Purpose	6.18	.90	14.5	6.05	1.17	19.3	.59
2. Shared Ownership	6.14	.84	13.6	6.17	.81	13.1	-0.18
3. Collective Authority	5.85	1.20	20.5	5.95	1.08	19.1	-0.38
4. Face-to-Face Interaction	6.00	1.08	18.0	6.17	.93	15.0	-.82
5. Consensus Decision Making	5.93	.65	10.9	6.17	1.08	17.5	-1.21
6. Communal Political Philosophy	5.87	1.11	18.9	—	—	—	—
7. Free and Informed Choice	6.12	.74	12.0	6.07	.94	15.4	.29
8. Ongoing Learning and Discovery	6.50	.54	8.3	6.31	.70	11.0	1.33
9. Candid Debate	6.16	.75	12.1	6.50	.76	10.3	-2.18**

Item #	X	Time One N = 49 s.d.	c.v.%	X	Time Two N = 40 s.d.	c.v.%	T-Value
10. Collaborative Work Relations	6.26	1.01	16.1	6.52	.64	9.8	-1.47*
11. Tolerance for Uncertainty	5.79	1.03	17.7	6.37	.83	13.0	-2.80**
12. Reward Diversity	6.06	1.05	17.3	6.37	.80	12.5	-1.52*
13. Ideas on Merit	6.37	.81	12.6	6.22	1.02	16.3	.75
14. Spirit of Inquiry	6.06	.97	16.0	—	—	—	—
15. Opportunity for Involvement	6.16	1.02	16.5	6.45	.98	15.1	-1.34
16. Collective Reward System	6.04	.81	13.4	—	—	—	—
17. Trust and Confidence	6.31	.92	14.5	6.32	.65	10.0	-.07
18. Innovative Organization	6.02	.88	14.6	6.32	.73	11.5	-1.76*
19. Devotion to Excellence	6.40	.67	10.0	6.67	.52	7.7	-2.10**
20. Inspirational System	6.53	.64	9.8	6.57	.54	8.2	-.35
21. Colleague Control	6.04	.89	14.7	—	—	—	—
22. Developmental Leadership	6.48	.64	9.8	6.50	.64	9.8	-.07
23. Minimal Bureaucracy	6.39	.67	10.4	6.50	.50	7.6	-.83
24. Democratic Partnership	6.00	.84	14.0	6.30	.56	8.8	-1.88*
25. Permanent Dialogue	6.02	1.08	17.9	6.15	1.13	18.3	-.55
26. Significant Work	6.51	.64	9.8	6.62	.66	9.9	-.82
27. Self-authority	6.18	.86	13.9	—	—	—	—
28. Developmental Colleagueship	6.27	.76	12.1	6.25	.84	13.4	.12
29. Shared Information	6.51	.76	11.6	6.52	.67	10.2	-.10

Item #	X	Time One N = 49 s.d.	c.v.%	X	Time Two N = 40 s.d.	c.v.%	T-Value
30. Democratic Leadership	6.34	.66	10.4	6.50	.55	8.4	-1.19

*p = .05 one-tailed test of significance

**p = .01 one-tailed test of significance

— These items were taken off the second survey by the Division's newly formed representative council.

Figure IV-5
Significant Changes in Administrative Division's Ideals

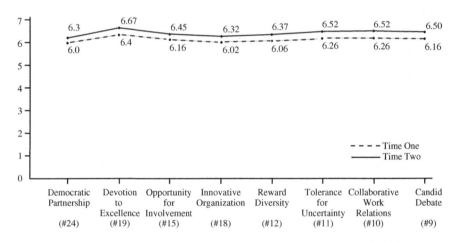

Also of note in Table IV-8 are the changes displayed by the coefficients of variation. As a crude measure of the development of a common will, the coefficient of variation gives us a relative measure to compare the dispersion of an entire set of data with the dispersion of another set. In this case, it shows us how uniform people were in the way they valued the ideals from time one and time two. It appears that agreement or consensus around the ideals did go up. In 68% of the items, the coefficient of variation went down the second time around. Overall, the average coefficient in time one was 14% as compared to a coefficient of 12% in time two. While the change may not be highly significant, the overall pattern is consistent.

Finally, Table IV-9 compares changes in the Administrative Division in terms of actual practice. Here we find that the majority of items showed improvement, while five of the items showed significant change at the .05 level or better. In Figure IV-6, these items are shown graphically. Here we also see that one of the items moved significantly in a negative direction. People felt that at time two there were more constraints on their energies than at time one. It is important to note also that nine other items, while not significant, showed movement in an unexpected negative direction (i.e., away from the stated ideals). To understand this phenomenon, the data were broken out by group-director, technical specialist, and support staff. While we need not go into great detail here, it appears that the technical specialist group (the middle group) actually perceived the division becoming worse in terms of its actual practice.[16] In comparison to the support staff group, for example, the technical specialists saw no significant change in the division's actual practices while the support group saw significant change in ten different areas. In fact, the technical specialists reported significant negative movement in five areas of practice, while the support staff saw none. In terms of the directors, data showed that they became more idealistic than the other groups and saw change occurring in a number of areas of practice, most significantly in terms of consensual decision making processes.

Table IV-9
Means, Standard Deviations, and T-Values for
Administrative Division "Practices" Across Time

Item #	Time One N = 49		Time Two N = 40		
	X	s.d.	X	s.d.	T-Value
1. Unity of Purpose	3.65	1.42	4.05	1.17	-1.44*
2. Shared Ownership	3.83	1.53	3.97	1.29	-0.47

16. These data have been presented elsewhere in more detail in a paper delivered at the 1984 Academy of Management Meetings entitled, "Promoting Workplace Democracy Through the Articulation of Values;" it is available from the author.

Item #	Time One N = 49		Time Two N = 40		
	X	s.d.	X	s.d.	T-Value
3. Collective Authority	3.40	1.59	3.32	1.40	.26
4. Face-to-Face Interaction	4.10	1.63	4.97	1.42	-2.69**
5. Consensus Decision Making	4.04	1.28	4.55	1.76	-1.93*
6. Communal Political Philosophy	3.51	1.31	—	—	—
7. Free and Informed Choice	3.38	1.51	3.45	1.41	-0.21
8. Ongoing Learning and Discovery	4.91	1.59	4.47	1.05	1.54
9. Candid Debate	4.00	1.53	4.00	1.67	.00
10. Collaborative Work Relations	3.93	1.43	4.10	1.46	-.52
11. Tolerance for Uncertainty	4.12	1.31	4.02	1.47	.33
12. Reward Diversity	4.20	1.64	4.65	1.83	-1.18
13. Ideas on Merit	4.20	1.67	3.82	1.39	1.17
14. Spirit of Inquiry	4.58	1.44	—	—	—
15. Opportunity for Involvement	3.12	1.64	3.72	1.89	-1.58*
16. Collective Reward System	3.27	1.40	—	—	—
17. Trust and Confidence	3.76	1.50	3.67	1.43	.29
18. Innovative Organization	4.75	1.45	4.45	1.56	.92
19. Devotion to Excellence	4.65	1.45	4.72	1.20	-.25
20. Inspirational System	4.28	1.51	3.77	1.87	1.78*
21. Colleague Control	4.15	1.38	—	—	—
22. Developmental Leadership	3.77	1.60	3.90	1.37	-0.41
23. Minimal Bureaucracy	4.31	1.81	4.25	1.69	.17
24. Democratic Partnership	3.59	1.51	3.87	1.57	-.84

Item #	Time One N = 49		Time Two N = 40		
	X	s.d.	X	s.d.	T-Value
25. Permanent Dialogue	4.28	1.29	4.58	1.61	-.95
26. Significant Work	4.63	1.66	4.35	1.51	.84
27. Self-authority	3.97	1.73	—	—	—
28. Developmental Colleagueship	4.27	1.63	4.55	1.37	-.87
29. Shared Information	3.87	1.55	3.97	1.52	-.30
30. Democratic Leadership	4.20	1.58	3.95	1.39	.80

*p = .05 one-tailed test of significance

**p = .01 one-tailed test of significance

— These items were taken off the second survey by the division's newly founded representative council.

Figure IV-6
Significant Changes in Administrative Division's Actual Practices

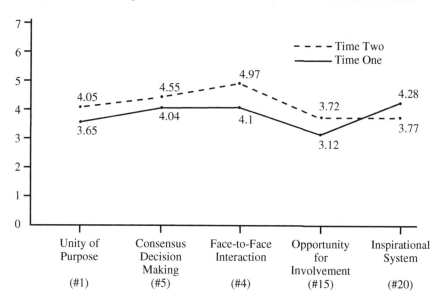

When presented with this data, the technical specialist group was splintered in their reactions. About half of the group denied the accuracy of the data, pointing to numerous changes that had evolved; while the other half held firm to the portrait it depicted. For them, many of the changes were superficial ones and the real work of understanding and enacting a set of egalitarian values had just begun. However, in all groups, there was one area of total agreement: All the ideals were viewed just as important or more important than they were in 1982. After analyzing the total set of data, one of the technical specialists issued a report to the division that concluded:

This information illustrates that:

1. We can be proud about having high ideals and values for how we operate as a division.

2. Collectively we share a common vision in terms of the kind of division we would like to have.

3. We have and *can* make some significant changes in moving closer to our envisioned ideal.

4. There are still some things we need to work on together.

Experimentation in a Medical Division

The Medical Division case is different from, yet shares a number of similar features to, the experimentations in the Administrative Division. The primary difference is found in the role played by the emerging egalitarian theory. Unlike the first case, where the normative theory entered the Administrative Division's culture through serendipity (i.e., the author just happened to be at a meeting where, as chance would have it, members were dealing with issues of trying to understand the physical culture), in the Medical Division case the theory was actively sought. The people involved felt that this *knowledge* (i.e., the theory) could make a difference in the future development of the system. The theory itself, so to speak, was beginning to stimulate thinking and take on a life of its own.

The other important difference between cases is that the Medical Division experiment suggests that conscious evolution of culture can take place rapidly and effectively. That is, it suggests that the transformation of the group will into actual practice can take place about as quickly as it takes human beings to forge agreements around how they want to exist with one another. Such change does not have to be a traumatic struggle nor does it have to begin in deficiency.

The similarities in the two cases boil down to three simple elements: (1) the early development of an appreciative context for inquiry and dialogue; (2) the conscious use of normative theory (in the form of the survey) to provide cues, language, and hope in the constructive potential of normative discourse; and (3) the use of multiple mixed groups for purposes of consensual validation and the evolution of group will. Because of these similarities, the author will not go into nearly as much detail in describing this case but will focus more on a number of considerations that guided the approach. First, data are presented that are suggestive of where and how much change occurred over time, then it is followed with a description of how it came about.

Results from the Medical Division Experimentations

When the author refers to the "Medical Division" (not its real name), referral is to just part of the division, including only the staff of physicians as a group. There were 20 physicians in this area and out of the 20 there was an 80% response rate to the first survey (n = 16) and a 75% response rate to the second (n = 15). The time one survey was administered in August of 1983 at the beginning of the author's work with the division. The time two survey was administered in March of 1985, 17 months from the first.

Table IV-10 presents the means, standard deviations, coefficients of variation and T-values of all the "ideal" survey variables across time. The data indicate, first, that statements in the ET survey do accurately reflect important ideals members feel their division ought to be living up to or evolving toward. Because of the very high degree of shared agreement (i.e., median score of 6.13), we might say that there existed from the beginning a strong basis for evolving a common will in relation to the group's philosophy of organizing.

Table IV-10
Means, Standard Deviations, Coefficients of Variation and T-Values for the Medical Department's "Ideals" Across Time

Item #	X	Time One N = 16 s.d.	c.v.%	X	Time Two N = 15 s.d.	c.v.%	T-Value
1. Unity of Purpose	5.87	.88	14.9	6.06	.70	11.5	-.67
2. Shared Ownership	6.06	.92	15.1	6.46	.74	11.4	-1.34*
3. Collective Authority	5.50	.96	17.4	5.46	.99	18.1	.09
4. Face-to-Face Interaction	5.93	.88	14.8	6.13	.91	14.7	-.61
5. Consensus Decision Making	5.50	1.03	18.7	5.80	.86	14.8	-.88
6. Communal Political Philosophy	5.35	1.27	23.7	5.89	.91	15.5	-1.23
7. Free and Informed Choice	6.00	1.21	20.1	6.13	.74	12.0	-.37
8. Ongoing Learning and Discovery	6.31	.60	9.5	6.33	.72	11.3	-.09
9. Candid Debate	6.25	.68	10.8	6.26	.79	12.6	-.06
10. Collaborative Work Relations	6.25	.68	10.8	6.40	.73	11.4	-.59
11. Tolerance for Uncertainty	5.43	1.03	18.9	5.33	1.64	30.7	.61
12. Reward Diversity	4.00	1.78	44.5	4.13	1.72	41.6	.39
13. Ideas on Merit	6.12	.88	14.3	6.00	.82	15.3	.38
14. Spirit of Inquiry	5.50	.81	14.7	5.53	1.24	22.4	-.09
15. Opportunity for Involvement	6.31	.87	13.7	6.33	.72	11.3	-.07
16. Collective Reward System	6.18	.83	13.4	6.20	.86	13.8	-.04

Item #	X	Time One N = 16 s.d.	c.v.%	X	Time Two N = 15 s.d.	c.v.%	T-Value
17. Trust and Confidence	6.18	.75	12.1	6.40	.82	12.8	-.75
18. Innovative Organization	6.06	.68	11.2	5.66	.72	12.7	1.57*
19. Devotion to Excellence	6.25	.61	9.7	.40	.73	11.4	.92
20. Inspirational System	6.25	.85	13.6	.40	.73	11.1	-.52
21. Colleague Control	5.18	1.37	26.4	.60	.82	14.6	-1.02
22. Developmental Leadership	6.06	.92	15.1	6.26	.70	11.1	-.69
23. Minimal Bureaucracy	6.12	.88	14.3	5.86	.74	12.6	.88
24. Democratic Partnership	6.12	.88	14.3	5.80	1.08	18.6	.91
25. Permanent Dialogue	5.66	1.58	27.9	5.53	1.45	26.2	.24
26. Significant Work	6.31	.79	12.5	6.20	.94	15.1	.36
27. Self-authority	5.56	1.31	23.5	6.26	.70	11.1	-1.87*
28. Developmental Colleagueship	6.06	.77	12.7	6.53	.64	9.8	-1.85*
29. Shared Information	6.50	.63	9.6	6.53	.64	9.8	-.15
30. Democratic Leadership	6.43	.62	9.6	6.40	.73	11.4	.15

*p ≤ .05 (one-tailed test)

Second, the table suggests that the group has, over time, become more idealistic in at least 19 of the 30 variables and shows significant increase in idealism in three areas, including belief in the importance of shared ownership, the importance of self-authority and the importance of having developmental colleague relations (see Figure IV-7). Ten items showed non-significant decreases in the importance of certain values, while one item (the importance of an innovative organization) showed a significant drop. Some reasons for this will be discussed shortly.

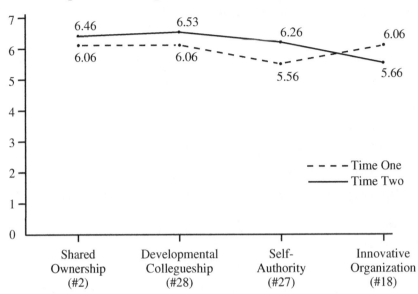

Figure IV-7
Significant Changes in Medical Department's Ideals

Third, examination of the coefficient of variation indicates that, in a majority of the cases, there was less relative dispersion or more agreement within the group over time concerning the ideals. The average coefficient among all items at time one was 16.9 percent and at time two, 14.9 percent. While the total change is not great, it is consistent, indicating the direction of the evolving group will.

Table IV-11 presents the changes in actual organizational practices within the one-and-a-half-year time period. First it needs to be pointed out that, at both time periods, the discrepancies between the ideal and the actual were considered to be high. At time one, for example, the discrepancies between ideal and practice for shared information (#29), opportunity for involvement (#15), democratic leadership (#30), free and informed choice (#7), shared ownership (#2), developmental leadership (#22), and collective authority (#3) were all above a mean discrepancy of 3.00 and together averaged a discrepancy score of 3.49. These were all statistically significant beyond the .001 level. Also, they match members' verbal descriptions of the division at time one, when people consistently referred to the system as a "centralized, benevolent dictatorship."

Table IV-11
Means, Standard Deviations and T-Values for the Medical Department's "Practices" Across Time

Item #	Time One N = 16		Time Two N = 15		
	X	s.d.	X	s.d.	T-Value
1. Unity of Purpose	3.50	1.46	4.60	1.24	-2.26**
2. Shared Ownership	2.81	1.32	4.26	1.32	-3.04**
3. Collective Authority	2.18	1.22	3.33	1.44	-2.37**
4. Face-to-Face Interaction	2.93	1.53	4.40	1.50	-2.65**
5. Consensus Decision Making	2.62	1.20	4.40	1.40	-3.77***
6. Communal Political Philosophy	2.64	1.39	4.33	1.34	-3.32***
7. Free and Informed Choice	2.50	1.41	3.93	1.33	-2.90**
8. Ongoing Learning and Discovery	5.00	.89	5.33	1.59	-.28
9. Candid Debate	3.37	1.58	4.33	1.49	-1.73*
10. Collaborative Work Relations	4.12	1.40	5.00	1.30	-1.79*
11. Tolerance for Uncertainty	3.50	1.46	4.13	1.18	-1.33*
12. Reward Diversity	4.00	1.73	4.13	1.72	-.21
13. Ideas on Merit	3.75	1.52	4.26	1.43	-.97
14. Spirit of Inquiry	3.75	1.48	4.13	1.30	-.77
15. Opportunity for Involvement	2.62	1.40	4.33	1.75	-2.87**
16. Collective Reward System	3.62	1.20	4.00	1.60	-.73
17. Trust and Confidence	4.50	1.46	5.26	.79	-1.83*
18. Innovative Organization	5.00	1.15	4.93	1.28	.15
19. Devotion to Excellence	5.50	1.15	5.46	.99	.09

Item #	Time One N = 16		Time Two N = 15		
	X	s.d.	X	s.d.	T-Value
20. Inspirational System	4.12	1.40	4.65	1.29	-1.12*
21. Colleague Control	3.31	1.49	4.73	.79	-3.33**
22. Developmental Leadership	2.81	1.37	4.00	1.64	-2.17**
23. Minimal Bureaucracy	3.19	1.51	3.66	1.67	-.83
24. Democratic Partnership	2.50	1.50	3.40	1.50	-1.67*
25. Permanent Dialogue	4.00	1.55	3.86	1.55	.23
26. Significant Work	4.43	1.41	5.00	1.04	-1.25
27. Self-authority	3.53	1.50	4.33	1.39	-1.51*
28. Developmental Colleagueship	4.56	1.36	5.26	1.20	-1.48*
29. Shared Information	2.68	1.44	4.26	2.05	-2.46**
30. Democratic Leadership	2.75	1.57	4.26	1.48	-2.76**

*p = .05 (one-tailed test)

**p = .01

***p = .001

Next, Table IV-11 shows that significant change in terms of improvements in actual practice took place in 20 out of 30 items. Eight of these were significant at or beyond the .05 level, ten were significant below the .01 level, and two items were changed significantly below the .001 level. In contrast to the Administrative Division, which is just now beginning to exhibit major change after more than four years, the medical group appears to be experiencing rapid progress in less than half the time. Looking in particular only at the items that are significantly changed at or below the .01 level, we find a clear pattern:

(#1) Unity of Purpose

(#2) Shared Ownership

(#3) Collective Authority

(#4) Face-to-Face Interaction

(#21) Colleague Control

(#29) Shared Information

(#5) Consensus Decision Making

(#6) Communal Political Philosophy

(#7) Free and Informed Choice

(#15) Opportunity for Involvement

(#30) Democratic Leadership

Intercorrelations among these items are quite high, as we would expect, indicating that some kind of major, focused change has taken place, which is exactly what has happened. Structurally, the entire division has been re-designed on the basis of semi-autonomous work group concepts and cultur-ally, as the data indicate, has moved from bureaucratic to more egalitarian relations and governing processes.

Figure IV-8 graphically portrays all the significant changes, while Table IV-12 seeks to summarize the movement in terms of the egalitarian theory scales. As it relates to the egalitarian ideology, the only scale that did not show significant increase was the commitment to excellence which, of course, was already quite high. In terms of the structures of interaction, it was the political structure that shows the most dramatic change while, in the area of social paradigms, it was the relational structure that developed most. Overall, the data indicate that the system has become much more consensual in nature where people relate more as partners and together take ownership for the governance of their shared social-organizational world.

Figure IV-8
Significant Changes in Medical Department's Actual Practices

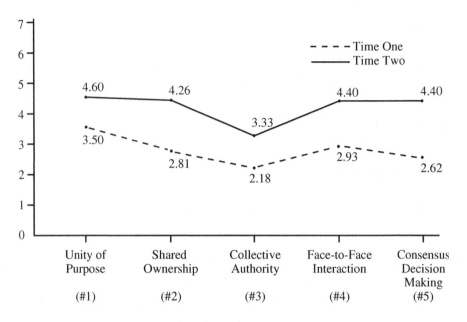

Figure IV-8 (con't.)

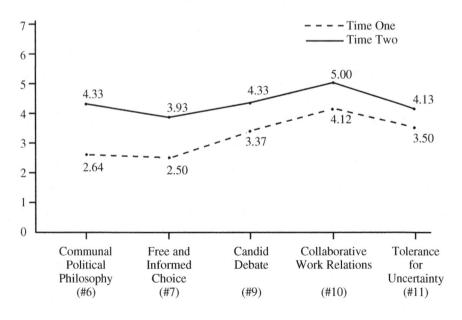

Figure IV-8 (con't.)

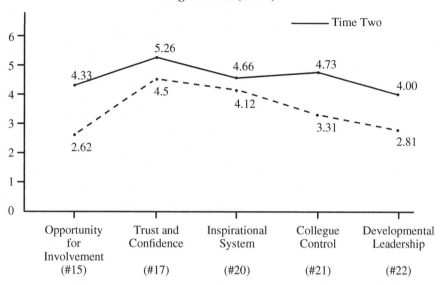

Figure IV-8 (con't.)

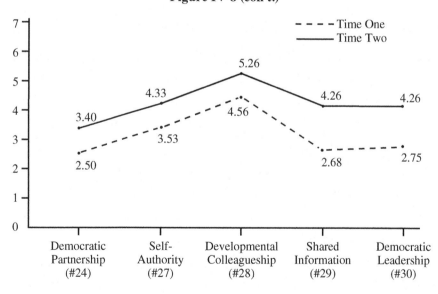

Table IV-12
Medical Department's Actual Changes in Practice: Means,
Standard Deviations and T-Values on Egalitarian Theory Scales

Scales and Subscales	Time One N = 16		Time Two N = 15		
	X	s.d.	X	s.d.	T-Value
A. Egalitarian Ideology	3.74	.72	4.61	.91	-2.90**
1. Inclusion	3.04	1.11	4.24	1.34	-2.66**
2. Consent	2.54	1.05	4.00	1.22	-3.54**
3. Excellence	5.16	.82	5.17	1.14	-.03
B. Structures of Interaction	3.42	.96	4.36	.97	-2.65**
1. Shared Governance	2.77	1.2	4.02	1.04	-3.07**
2. Catalytic Primary Task	3.92	.97	4.58	1.02	-1.82*
C. Social Paradigms	3.57	.87	4.34	1.12	-2.09*
1. Epistemic Structure	3.45	.98	4.10	1.35	-1.50*
2. Relational Structure	3.70	.99	4.58	.95	-2.49**

*p = .05
**p = .01
***p = .001 (all one-tailed tests)

The Subtle Role of Theory in Organizational Change

Of course, in a single-case field study without controls, it is impossible to isolate the agential role that the normative theory played in producing such change. There were, in fact, many different forces operating on the organization during the one-and-a-half-year period we worked with it and there were a multitude of consequential factors that preceded this period. To say that the egalitarian theory or the process of inquiry caused the transformations would be ludicrous. To say that it played a subtle yet important role, however, is a possibility we feel is well worth exploration. The project will now be described in more detail.

The author was called in initially to consult to an internal consultant of the CC, Jim Hardy. Mr. Hardy had been requested by the Medical Division chairman, Dr. Lombardi (fictitious names), to put together a training program on "goal setting." As Jim looked more closely into the situation, he saw that there was a great deal more going on and that the opportunities for helping the division were extensive. Jim called on the author to work with him because, as he put it, "You've worked closely with the physician group over the years and have as much if not more knowledge of the culture here than most anybody." He had recently read a rough draft paper on "The Emergence of the Egalitarian Organization" and felt that it was important to the situation "...because the Medical Division seems to be operating under norms antithetical to the spirit of the rest of the CC group and is in danger of losing some of its best staff because of it."

Actually, it had already lost some of its best staff and perennially it had one of the highest turnover rates among physicians in the whole organization. As we talked, a number of other bits of information came out:

1. The division was considered to be the largest and one of the best of its kind in the world. It was a pioneer in many new areas of clinical technique and high technology and had a good reputation for its contributions to clinical research.

2. The division had grown rapidly and had attained its national and international reputation largely on the basis of the strong, charismatic and scientifically renowned leadership of Dr. Lombardi.

3. Lombardi's management style was said to be "old guard"; it was largely autocratic and distant. He was increasingly on trips away from the institution giving speeches to various groups and presiding over the national college of physicians in his specialty.

4. Morale in the department was low. There seemed always to be a shortage of staff due to turnover and there was an atmosphere of professional competition, secrecy, envy, and mistrust.

5. Staff were demoralized and convinced that nothing would or could change without major changes in leadership. For example, the division had tried unsuccessfully for more than eight years to decentralize into semi-autonomous sub-specialty areas. As one person put it: "Every time we broached the subject, emotions would flare

and discussion would degenerate into disagreement, backbiting and accusations. People were afraid to move into specialty areas and the leadership wouldn't let loose of the reins. The cycle has repeated itself like clockwork to the point where discussions of change are no longer even considered."

As Jim went on, he told the author that he had convinced Lombardi of the need for a diagnosis of the division through interviews with all staff members. Data would be collected and fed back, and problems could be identified and worked out as a group.

The author agreed to become involved, but under a couple of conditions. First, the author suggested that interviews take a more appreciative, opportunity-focused approach as opposed to diagnosis. His reasoning here was that it wasn't likely that a diagnosis, no matter how good or sophisticated, would do much good early on. Based on what he had just heard, it was clear that the group did not need focused education on the subject of how unfortunate its dynamics were. As he suggested to Jim quite crudely:

> Bopping them over the head with a heavy load of intellectual
> problem analysis is not likely to unfreeze them…It is apt to only
> help refine the language they now use and will likely provide cues
> directing their attention into the same frame they've been cyclically
> stuck in.

The frame needed to be broken.

Second, the author suggested that he and Jim use the egalitarian theory as kind of a screen or backdrop to the whole work. He proposed that they *not* bring much formal attention to it, but simply administer the survey at the beginning of the interviews: "…as part of a larger study the author is doing on the physician culture of the CC." They said it was completely voluntary and, as it turned out, almost everyone returned the survey. The author's hypothesis was that the survey would serve as a subtle cueing device providing not only a new frame for the interviews but also for the ensuing project as well. It would raise the level of discussion away from petty concerns of everyday self-interest to more broad and abstract concerns of the group as an *entirety*. Also, it might well provide a new *language of possibility* as opposed to constraint and could provide a special sanctioning to talk about important values and hope of more idealistic concerns. It was at this level that fresh bonding would take place. Also, the author was convinced that the theory would tap into some deep underlying sentiment of the whole group at an almost pre-conscious level and provide a subtle but powerful input guiding the whole process. The theory therefore, would *not* be the agenda, as it had been in the Administrative Division. Instead, it would be planted like a seed to grow. It would move at its own pace in its own direction, and take its own form. The approach would be seminal, not technological. There would be a seeding and nurturing, not a fix-up.

Jim Hardy agreed to experiment with the approach. It was his opinion, too, that the group needed some kind of success before deeper issues could be addressed. Table IV-13 lists the major activities of the project as it unfolded.

Table IV-13
Major Activities in the Medical Division Project

Time	Activities
May, 1983	Chairman requests assistance on goal-setting
August, 1983	Interviews and first administration of the ET survey (all staff)
September, 1983	Division-wide meeting: "Decision to hold a two-day planning retreat"
November, 1983	Training on Vroom "decision charting"
November–January, 1984	Steering committee meets weekly to design retreat
January, 1984	Retreat "Structural and Cultural Re-Designing of the Division"
February, 1984	Creation of semi-autonomous work sections (decentralization)
January, 1985	Interviews with all staff to evaluate progress
February, 1985	Second retreat: "Reaffirmation of Basic Philosophy and Values"

Time	Activities
March, 1985	Second administration of the ET survey
April, 1985	First in an ongoing series of monthly dinner "retreats" for all staff.

After interviews with the staff and introduction of the theory, a division-wide meeting was held. To help build an appreciative context, the meeting was begun with general impressions of what the forces were that had made the group great over the years (see Figure IV-9 for a look at the flipchart presentation). The author and Jim Hardy then identified five areas of opportunity and presented back the picture of the division in the form of general questions. They were careful to use the language of possibility and outlined a number of developmental opportunities. One member of the group suggested the author and Jim were right on the target in terms of what the group would ideally like to imagine itself to be, but had overlooked some of the problems. Someone then proposed:

> Well, this is just a start. Maybe we need to get away together for two or three days to really work through these questions. I think the essence of what we are and what needs to be done has really been captured.

The rest of the meeting resulted in open and candid debate over the pros and cons of a retreat and whether things could actually change or not. Dr. Lombardi did not say much during the debate but came out in favor of the idea once the rest of the group decided to give it a try. Dates were set and a task force was assembled to meet over the next couple of months to plan the agenda.

Figure IV-9
Initial Feedback to Medical Division

A. General Impressions

1. Group devoted to *excellence*, "cutting edge"
2. Group that can be characterized as *"partnership"* of professionals
3. As a professional organization, there is a drive toward professionalism in management, i.e., where colleagueship and cooperative methods are required for managing complex interdependence.

B. Emerging Managerial Issues/Tasks Concerning Partnership, Excellence, Colleagueship, Cooperation

1. *Superordinate Goals:* "What is it we should be working toward ideally?"
2. *Structure:* "Are the sections going to meet our needs? How should the sections be organized?"
3. *Style and Culture:* How can we develop a more cooperative system both managerially and professionally?"
4. *Careers and Rewards:* "How can we jointly optimize professional needs and organizational needs?"
5. *Helpful Mechanisms:* "How can we make our meetings and other communication vehicles more effective, consequential and timely?"

C. Developmental Opportunities

There are but two other things of special note about the case. The first has to do with the actual process of the evolution of the will of the group or organization. Similar to the Administrative Division case, the actual work of reformulating the group's "ideal" state happened through the overlay of multiple memberships within a variety of different subgroups, i.e., representation groups, functional work groups, vertical groups, and horizontal "peer" groups. The representative steering committee, for example, was made up of the eight people who were each members of at least three separate groups in the division. In other words there was the potential for 24 different groupings to become affected by the work the steering group was doing. As it turned out, this group met every Tuesday morning at 7:00, before rounds, for two months. They were not simply building an agenda for the retreat. In fact, much of the real work happened before the retreat ever took place. Much of the *interpretation of wills* took place informally in an interlocked webbing of subgroups. The formal retreat arena, therefore, became a forum whereby informally arrived at agreements were formally declared, celebrated, confirmed and embellished. Jim and the author did not talk for more than 15 minutes during the whole two-day retreat, yet at the end they received an ovation and congratulations for helping to make the whole thing a "splendid success." It was a success. The group made a series of decisions it had not been able to broach for years. The most significant was the establishment of semi-autonomous work units that would be responsible for managing their own budgets, fees, hiring of new staff, performance review, and strategy planning. This decentralized structure was put into effect immediately and observation confirms, as well as the survey data support, the fact that there is more shared ownership, leadership, and a cooperative-egalitarian spirit within the division.

The final thing of note is an example of the subtle role that supposedly descriptive theoretical language plays in governing conscious awareness and action. When the author looks back over his whole field experience at the CC, this one event stands out as most memorable.

After the decision to have the retreat was made, Jim proposed that the staff meet once more as a whole to get some training on group decision making. This he felt would help lay the groundwork for more effective work at the retreat and would reinforce the notion of an appreciative context because it would likely give members a success experience together, without getting heavily into diagnostic problem-solving. He argued, and the author agreed, that the group would probably experience the training as stimulating and perhaps even fun.

The training took place shortly thereafter. It centered around the very well-known model of decision making by Victor Vroom. In brief, the model provides a decision chart structure for helping a superior determine when it is appropriate to include subordinates in group decision making ("GII") and when it is more effective for the superior to make the decision him or herself ("AII"). Articles on the model were handed out prior to the meeting so the lecture was brief, just enough to get people started analyzing a few cases. Things went quite well. The author began thinking that the training was a perfectly good idea. Certainly it would be useful in reinforcing the ideas in the egalitarian theory because, as he recalled, most of the cases showed the reason and need for GII decision making. The author was taken aback, then when during a break, one of the young physicians came up to him and said, "You know this is all bullshit, don't you!" He then said:

I bet if you counted in both the article and your lecture the number of times the word "subordinate" was used, it would be close to fifty times.

The author responded, "I hadn't realized that, but I guess it certainly is interesting." The young physician then continued:

The problem is that these ideas may be all right for the business world but they won't do here. As you said yourself the other day in your survey, we are a *partnership* of physicians. I'm not a subordinate. I'm not just an employee here. I resent what your training is trying to do to us.

The experience was powerful. It made the author think back to his use of this particular training program for years and how he had used the term "subordinate" unthinkingly thousands of times in his work with managers. But, when he got home that night, he mapped out what must have been going on for this young physician (see Figure IV-10).

Figure IV-10
The Ripple Effect Power of Theoretical Language

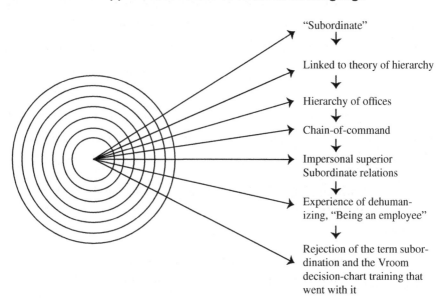

"Subordinate"
↓
Linked to theory of hierarchy
↓
Hierarchy of offices
↓
Chain-of-command
↓
Impersonal superior
Subordinate relations
↓
Experience of dehuman-
izing, "Being an employee"
↓
Rejection of the term subor-
dination and the Vroom
decision-chart training that
went with it

As is obvious now, the word *subordinate* was not just some neutral descriptive term. There is no such thing as a subordinate "out there" some-where in reality that can be pointed to and objectively described. The word "subordinate" is virtually nothing, meaningless as a descriptive term, until it is seen as a key link in a broader theory of bureaucracy, a theory that says that organizations work and work best when there is a hierarchy of offices and a clear chain of command. In such a system, orders are to be issued by those above, and those below have the duty to carry them out. In fact, what makes the whole thing work is that the orders are impersonal, they are issued from offices or roles at a necessary higher level of command. The beauty of the whole thing is that, ideally, everyone just does his or her own job according to the prescribed scheme. As Weber (1968) himself put it, "Bureaucracy advances the more it is dehumanized." There is no such thing—or need—for an emotion-filled sense of partnership, responsibility, and ownership for the whole. What is so memorable, then, was the author's virtual lack of awareness that he himself had, time and time again, helped to support and reproduce, in interaction with others, a powerful bureaucratic theory and ideology.

The language of bureaucracy, like all theoretical language, helps cue our attention on what is there to see; it helps to set expectations about what the world is or should be; and it subtly constrains our attention and our ability to recognize other possibilities. It was not until the young physician rejected the training that the author really began to recognize and ponder the role of theory in the scientific construction of reality. As it was, the egalitarian theory seems also to have had some impact: "I'm not a subordinate," he said, "I'm a partner."

V

Conclusion and Epilogue

Articulation of Normative Theory: The Emergence of the Egalitarian Organization as a Consequence of Appreciative Inquiry

and I remember well
That in life's everyday appearances
I seemed about this time to gain
  clear sight
Of a new world—a world, too, that
  was fit
To be transmitted, and to other eyes
Made visible...

—Wordsworth

THIS CHAPTER FIRST PRESENTS THE theoretical articulation resulting from the five-year appreciative inquiry as described in Chapter III. Figure V-1 shows the major analytic themes of the theory. While each point can be highlighted by numerous instances of data, examples are used only where they are relevant for building a sense of clarity and understanding of the theoretical propositions. As Rothschild-Whitt (1979) has pointed out, no number of examples ever constitute proof. Therefore, it is hoped that this work is judged from a socio-rationalist perspective in terms of its appreciative and provocative qualities, as well as its capacity to be used as a basis for collaborative experimentation and future research.

Figure V-1
Themes Related to the Ideal Membership Situation and
the Emergence of the Egalitarian Organization

	EGALITARIAN ETHOS/IDEOLOGY		
I. Organizational Ethos	Inclusion	Consent	Excellence
	SOCIO-POLITICAL STRUCTURE		SOCIO-TECHNICAL STRUCTURE
II. Developing Catalytic Structures of Interaction	Shared Governance		Catalytic Primary Task
	EPISTEMIC STRUCTURE		RELATIONAL STRUCTURE
III. Predominant Social Paradigms	Co-Inquiry-in-Action		Community of Competence

Following Figure V-1 as a thematic outline, the theoretical articulation is organized into three sections:

I. The Organizational Ethos

II. The Developing Catalytic Structures of Interaction

III. The Predominant Social Paradigms

Each section carefully builds upon the other through a presentation of complexly interwoven themes. Data are presented to bring life and specificity to the themes. Then, at the end of each section, the themes are taken to a higher level of generality through a propositional logic building on key theoretical points.

The chapter ends with an epilogue and summary of the dissertation's key argument. The epilogue comments on yet another phase in which members of the Cleveland Clinic are now taking the theory. The summary highlights key features of the appreciative mode and considers implications for the discipline of action-research.

I. The Organizational Ethos

Any meaningful analysis of the participatory transformations occurring in modern organizational life must attempt to identify the deep underlying aspiration, sentiments and ideological forces shaping the newer, more cooperative forms of organizing. We refer to this complex of forces as the organizational ethos: the general human spirit serving to characterize the disposition of an organization as a dynamically formulated living social system. Used here as an analytic guide, ethos is not equivalent to culture, but is more accurately depicted as a catalytic primordial ingredient of culture. Largely tacit, it can be viewed as an ideologically infused background element of a highly charged nature providing the most general of orientations for the emergence of culture. Drawing on symbolism and metaphor used by one of the clinic members, ethos can be likened to a powerful oceanic tide:

> On the ocean it is easy to see the crest of wave or to feel the surge of the ground swell, but the full flood of the tide may be almost imperceptible even to those who are borne upward on it...[the organizational ethos] may be like a tide...

Central to the concept of the "egalitarian ethos" is a threefold ideal that is viewed as a self-reinforcing system of ideas: inclusion, consent, and excellence. These themes, taken together, form an indispensable visionary scheme for building an understanding of the *processual logic* of the egalitarian organization. Most important, this reinforcing system of ideas helps explain the basic attention given to the "ideal membership situation" and provides, in primitive form, the ideological basis for a theory of organizing that is relatively free of arbitrary forms of hierarchical domination.[17]

The Spirit of Inclusion

This theme can be summarized as follows: Based on inclusion as an organizational member, every person should share in the right and responsibility for *actively* taking part in the creation, maintenance, and transformation of the organization's operating realities. Similarly, and perhaps more congruent with the spirit of the term, inclusion refers to an organizing impulse that seeks a quality of membership that is summed up by the word *partnership*: a cooperative relational stance whereby each participant accepted into an organization has, by sheer definition of membership, an inalienable obligation to take part in the security, well-being and determination of the various patterns of individual and organizational development. It represents, as one respondent in our study put it, "a very high concept of group":

> There is another thing that is important for you to understand. It is not only the concept of the group practice that is important in understanding the CC, but it is a very high concept of group. We deal with each other as professionals here and have to consider one another equal potentials. Dealing with each other goes back to life's first lesson: We have to learn to trust our colleagues and trust them implicitly. It means that anyone who comes into this group and is absorbed into it has to sense the serious level of commitment required.

How serious is the commitment? Another member talked about the inclusive spirit and described it as having a distinctive marriage-like quality:

> At the CC we bring together, under one rooftop, specialists in every area of medical care. We are a partnership of physicians. And like any marriage it continues to require continual interchange, work, tolerant attitudes and trust. But the relationship is non-negotiable. It is not about to be put off, put asunder, or be divorced. We see

---

17 The concept of the ideal membership situation was described in Chapter III. In review, it refers to a situation that *maximizes* organizational members' commitment/conviction, critical control/ownership, critical consciousness, and sense of colleagueship/community.

the same patients, work in the same system, use the same tools, we share space—and we take care of patients together. No matter what our difficulties, they will never amount to a breach...Do we see eye-to-eye on every issue? No. But we work things through.

In functional terms, it can by hypothesized that the inclusionary ideal is one whose integrative aim is to draw upon the totality of member energies and to bring those energies to bear on organizational activities of all kinds. That is, inclusion represents a desire to open the process of organizing up to the latent and existing powers inherent in a collective body of active participants. It represents an explicit desire to cooperate with human energy rather than to control it and, as Baxter (1982) has cogently discussed, it is the ontological basis of an authentic social construction. More concretely, a member of the CC characterized the theme of inclusion as the defining feature of a "real" organization:

What you have to infuse in an institute is that it is a unified, developmental, growth situation...That's the real secret of an institution. And, if you can corral the forces, then you will have a charging animal on your back. Now the CC is still not a real institution in this sense, but it is getting to be one...as you can see there is a tremendous amount of energy flowing through this place.

Ideologically, the theme of inclusion has an important paradoxical quality. On the one hand it is viewed as a journey—a process of bringing in, not closing out. In this sense, it points to the continuing pursuit of a largely mythical state of wholeness, integrity, shared meaning, coordination and balance (e.g., in the CC founder's words, "to think and act as a unit"). On the other hand, inclusion does not imply some distant aim at all. It gains its ideological potency through a simple acknowledgement of "what is"; one which recognizes *a priori* of *relationships* between participants who *share* the same social space, time, and resources. Inclusion, in this sense, is viewed less as a distant aim and more as an original and powerful force that refuses to give itself over to arbitrary barriers of differentiation and stratification making members impervious to one another and their common interests (Cooper, 1983). So, more than a mere economic or legal arrangement, the notion of inclusion bespeaks a subtle yet profound systemic "recognition that we are partners" in an interdependent social life world. In a kind of *declaration of interdependence*, Dr. Will Mayo spoke to this issue at the CC's opening day ceremonies more than 60 years ago:

> The critical feature of medicine of the immediate future will be the development of medical cooperation...properly considered, group medicine is not a financial arrangement, except for minor details, but is scientific cooperation for the welfare of the sick.

Later, in another ceremonial speech elaborating on this ideal, one of the CC founders talked about what he called the "spirit of collective work":

> With the rapid advance of medicine to its present day status in which it invokes the aid of all the natural sciences, an individual is no more able to understand the intricate problems alone. Our institution is designed to meet what we believe to be a public need in a more flexible organization...The result of such an organization will be that the entire staff—the bacteriologist, the pathologist, the biochemist, the physicist, the physiologist, the radiologist, no less the internist and general surgeon—each, we hope and believe we will maintain the spirit of collective work, and each of us will accept as our reward for work done, our respective part in the contribution of the group, however small, to the comfort, and usefulness, and the prolongation of human life.

The spirit of inclusion, of partnership, continues to pervade the culture of the Cleveland Clinic's group practice. Some argue that its ideological overtones are clearly communal or collectivistic. But it is more than that. The inclusive spirit is a powerful ideological commitment that affirms both the individual *and* the group—by affirming the inevitable interdependence between the two. This affirmation has been translated into the construction of organizational arrangements that dramatically depart from the divisive and exclusionary dynamic of more traditional bureaucratic arrangements. Thus, the sentiment and spirit of the inclusionary theme will resonate throughout the rest of this paper, just as it has been felt throughout the more that 60-year history of the CC.

The Spirit of Consent

Amplifying the theme of inclusion, the consensus ideal premises that: (1) organizational decisions, plans, or rules become morally binding to the extent that they emerge from a process where all relevant stakeholders have access to full, active and mutual involvement in their determination; (2) the ultimate basis of authority does not rest with any one individual (or set of individuals) based on ownership, formal position *or* expertise; rather it is based on the dynamic consent of the group; and (3) there is no authority that can unilaterally command obedience, nor any tradition that can demand conformity without seeking to elicit voluntary agreement on the basis of dialogue, persuasion or negotiation, i.e., use of logic, facts, or appeal to values. As an ideology, Gouldner (1976) observes that the consensus ethics has a deep-rooted structure. It is one that:

> ...encompasses and refers to the inner rather than the external, to the chosen rather than the imposed, to the indigenous rather than the alien, to the natural rather than the artificial. It refers to that which is capable of self-movement and self-direction rather than to that which is externally driven (p. 33).

Commenting directly on both the self-governing and group-centered essence of this ideal, a number of members of the CC explained:

> Let me tell you something about this group. When dealing with any major issues, we have to resolve it through consensus because we know that the Board of Governors, although it is made up of elected representatives, will not be able to make its dictates stick by trying to force something on the rest of the group. The issue will keep bubbling to the top...In this kind of (inclusive) environment *where we agree up front to function as a group, it is the only way you can function!*

Echoing this philosophy, another member described the institutional decision-making process in consensual terms:

> In other organizations when an order is given, it goes right down the pecking order and gets carried out. But here, if the Chairman of the Board gives a directive and I don't agree, I may go through channels and dispute it. And I have every right to do that. The Chairman operates here on a year-by-year basis at the pleasure of the Board which is elected by all the staff members. If the members were mobilized around a basic issue, they would have the final say.

Needless to say, the consensus mode as described here is not outcome or even a logical extension of an economizing system of technical rational thought. Nor, however, can it simply be viewed as a rejection of organized activity or the use of power. Instead, it can only be fully appreciated as it reflects an alternative, perhaps higher order logic. Later in the chapter we describe this logic as a relational one, as "interhuman logic." But, for now, it is only important to highlight the point that the egalitarian ideology carries within it the seeds of an alternative administrative logic. For example, consider the logic-in-use embedded in the following quotes:

> Through ongoing discussions we all become aware of the problems. Being part of the process we are not being dictated to. And as a result we learn more about the process and this leads to a higher level of intelligent action among all who work here.

***

> One disadvantage of our system is that decision making isn't that easy...But when finally a decision is made, a consensus is reached, it is probably a far better decision and one which can be embraced by a great number of people...It means that you will have good morale and good relations.

***

> The great opportunity here is one of being involved in the information flow, the dialogue, and the negotiation of decisions...Here each

and every one of the full-time staff is responsible for and allowed to have an impact on the work environment. This is an extremely important asset, opportunity and perhaps, for some, a liability. But as for me, I love the opportunity.

In each of these quotes, one is hard pressed to find traces of traditional bureaucratic rationality. And, unlike bureaucracy which Weber (1968, p. 975) has argued, "advances the more it dehumanizes," the consensus ideal stipulates that a system of collective action is likely to advance the more it calls for the voluntary energies and contributions its members have to offer. *Perhaps more than anything else, it is the consensual spirit that most clearly differentiates the egalitarian ethos from other normative systems, especially that of bureaucracy* (Antonio, 1979). This point cannot be overemphasized.

To cite just one example, we can look at a recent two-day planning meeting with *60* leaders of the CC. Six major action items were on the agenda. The aim of the meeting was to build agreement so that organizational action could be taken around each item. At one point in the meeting, subgroups were formed and asked to write a letter to the Chairman of the Board "telling the Chairman what your group gives its full consent to." At the end of the two-day meeting, after agreements were forged around each strategic issue, the Chairman closed the meeting saying something like the following:

> This, I believe, will be considered a historic meeting for the CC. We have dealt thoroughly with some very complex issues as a group, but we have not balked. We have agreed to action, and we will act swiftly. I want to thank *each of you for empowering me, for giving me the authority* to now move ahead with certainty to make our agreements happen.

The consensus ideal means that ultimate authority rests with the group. It is one that demands an ecology of participants who have the freedom to propose or oppose. It places a high premium on the *face-to-face* meeting between thought and action. And it presupposes that member-generated normative controls are socially and developmentally more effective than coercive, formal-hierarchical or strictly remunerative controls. Thus, throughout our study, there was little surprise when finding open resentment toward the more traditional bureaucratic ethic emphasizing "compliance," "obedience," "discipline," "rule," and "authoritarian power of command" (Antonio, 1980). For example, when asked to comment on the possibility of having a more traditional form of management, one member of the CC forcefully claimed:

> A person trained in management is just an administrator. That type of person hasn't a feel for this kind of organization or our field. They don't know how I think or what motivates someone like me. They only know what motivates them. They want to get to the top of the pyramid and jockey people around. Therefore, they will keep memos on everything and everybody. They just want efficiency. If we ran our department like that, it would be sterile and static.

The Spirit of Excellence

To remain static is antithetical to the egalitarian ideal. In his landmark study of equality, De Tocqueville (1969: pp. 452-456) observed that an egalitarian system:

> ...puts many ideas into the human mind which would not have come there without it and it changes almost all the ideas that were before. [Members of such a system] discover that nothing can confine them, hold them, or force them to be content with their present lot. They are all, therefore, conscious of the idea of bettering themselves.

Furthermore, observed De Tocqueville, as increased levels of inter-action between people are set in motion through the widening of inclu-sionary boundaries, then new facts and truths would be discovered, and changes continuously witnessed. "Then," writes De Tocqueville, under these conditions, "...the human mind images the possibility of an ideal but always fugitive perfection."

Similarly, one of the more striking features of the CC's egalitarian system is an almost insatiable appetite for the new, an optimism toward an uncertain future, and feelings of relatively unlimited opportunities for ongoing development. The egalitarian ethos at the CC is marked by an espoused belief in the infinite perfectibility of self and organization. When asked about this optimistic perspective, a member of the CC reflected on perhaps the most widely shared sentiments discovered throughout our study:

> I see *tremendous potential here*. There are almost no limits if you have ideas...There are very few obstacles here. In fact, my greatest obstacle is myself. I always have to have everything accomplished yesterday.

And, echoing this belief, other members explained (using almost identical words):

> Everyone here has the same opportunity to broaden their perspective and realize their full potential. The main thing is to recognize what the potential is and then go after it. The common goal among all of us is to *have an outstanding medical group* here...We are an idealistic group devoted to becoming the best we can become.

The word "excellence" is itself an indefinite. It has no stable empirical referent and, therefore, refuses precise definition as an administrative science construct (Peters and Waterman, 1982). But as an ideal—and ideology—the symbolism of excellence holds a romantic and imaginative quality that is expressed in a style of organizational life built around commitment to what members in our study continually referred to as "the frontier," and to staying at the "cutting edge" of their own capacities. It was referred to as "a goal without a design," marked by an intensity of becoming more, achieving more, learning more, and directly experiencing more. In sociological terms, the theme of excellence can be translated as the corporate version of society's *modern spirit*: "The self-willed effort of a style and sensibility to remain in the forefront of advancing consciousness" (Bell, 1973, p. 46). Excellence, as a word-symbol, is perhaps the corporate representation of the modernist "self-infinitizing spirit."

For example, on his 80th birthday, one of the retired founders of the CC spoke out and asserted: "We must forever remain flexible and open to the newer and better things that come along." And, more recently, the organization's Board of Governors discussed and agreed with an agenda item that stated: "The Cleveland Clinic is structured for adaptability and rapid change and is predictably unstable—it is in the process of becoming." In fact, members argued that it was precisely because of the devotion to growth and excellence that attracted many of them to the institution:

I think those of us here seek out this kind of organizational setting. And we deserve the opportunities that exist here—the possibilities of developing our skills and being on the cutting edge. Long ago we had a business running this place who told people what to do and how. But not any more. Our greatest growth as an organization has come in the last decade, ever since we were allowed more participation and have become directly involved in the governance of this institution.

This quote is especially important in that it touches directly on an ideological implication of the spirit of excellence. The words from the quote can be translated into a simple equation of associated ideas: excellence = the desire for the cutting edge = the need for active involvement and participation. There is a simple political logic in this equation of ideas that is often overlooked.

The quest for excellence is accompanied by a public recognition of the dynamically emergent nature of organizing. Thus, in a changing organizational setting, how can *a priori* exclusion from the opportunity for active participation in organizational affairs be legitimized? In a transforming system reaching toward higher levels of innovation and development, it

world as deliberately transformable *and* susceptible to rational action.

Proposition #4: The egalitarian ideal gives rise to the emerging *interhuman logic* that supersedes and circumscribes the technical mode as a legitimate basis for organizing, unlike bureaucracy, which deflects our focus away from the sphere of interaction and represents the application of an economizing, atomizing, technical rationality to social activity.

Proposition #5: The primary aim of an interhuman administrative logic is to activate the potential of a work system as a cooperative human social system and it accomplishes this aim *dialogically* through: (a) reducing or eliminating arbitrary barriers to active participation that tend to inevitably arise in organizations, and (b) creating arenas of interaction that are catalytic; interactive forums that cultivate, reinforce, and rely upon the "ideal" membership situation.

In sum, it is proposed that an interhuman logic is one that is activated by egalitarian ideals of inclusion, consent and excellence. As a system of *social-logical* thought, it represents rational administrative orientation that places active participatory contribution at the leading edge of any consideration having to do with the design or development of the organization itself. It means putting conscious effort into keeping an organization "as free as possible of arbitrary barriers to cooperation" so that members can regulate their organizational lives in accordance with publicly agreed upon values, aspirations, and needs.

In an especially clear articulation of this point of view, an account of the CC's research division highlights the centrality of an interhuman logic as it relates to its own theory of administration:

If problems of human beings are to be solved, the solutions must originate with people. In the Division of Research, a *determined effort has been made to ensure the cooperative effort* of scientists in a variety of disciplines…Every effort has been made to keep the

division as free as possible of arbitrary barriers to cooperation…
This has allowed everyone to participate actively…Odd as it may
seem, much effort was required to maintain such a *seemingly structureless* organization because of the inherent tendency of people to
organize and give titles or assume roles (Crile and Bunts, 1971).

It is interesting to note that from an outsider's perspective, the interhuman logic operative at the CC has often appeared mysterious, counter-
intuitive, non-logical or even irrational. For example, we might revisit a
quote used earlier in this chapter:

Businessmen looking at this "unhierarchical" organization feel as
mystified as Ezekiel did about what made the wheels work. But they
do and the reason why can best be summarized in the expression of
"esprit de corps"! (Crile and Bunts, 1971).

We have shown in this section that what "makes the wheels work"
is not so much a result of mysterious forces or non-logical managerial
perspectives; it is a result of a different kind of administrative logic that
goes beyond traditional technical-rational thinking. As we will continue to
elaborate, the interhuman logic is, above all else, a relational logic. It is an
administrative perspective founded upon a belief that the basic problem of
organizing is a problem of human/social organization. "Develop a group
where there is a high degree of commitment to excellence, professional
opportunity, belief in service to the public, and a strong sense of ownership," argued one of the CC's leaders, "and the economic success factors
will take care of themselves." In the next section, we will take a closer look
at how such an ideology is being put into practice.

II. The Developing Catalytic Structures of Interaction

Much of the history of the group practice at Cleveland Clinic can be read
as the emerging application of an interhuman theory of administration. The
perennial challenge has been one that asks: Given this time and place, what
organizational arrangements can we experiment with to optimize the ideal

membership situation and thereby ensure that the cooperative capacity of our system will be reached? How can we continue to heighten, throughout our organization, the experiencing of high levels of commitment, critical control and ownership, normative consciousness, and collegial respect and trust? How can we maintain the "unique esprit de corps" that continues to breathe life into the institution and make it what it is?

In this section, these questions are addressed by viewing the organization as an ensemble of structurally patterned *arenas* of social interaction (Bowles and Gintis, 1981; Giddens, 1979). Specifically, we examine the analytically distinct arenas of work and politics. While we can take the viewpoint that structural arrangements such as definitions, cues, rules, patterned relationships and resources people use in interaction are both a medium and product of interaction, we are primarily concerned here with how they mediate interaction. We are concerned thematically with the exploration of those structural characteristics that support, reinforce and rely on an active cooperative-relational stance among participants. Organizational arrangements that heighten the potential for such interaction are termed "catalytic."

The Political Arena: Shared Governance

In 1954, voices of rebellion echoed throughout the hallways of the CC concerning "the gradual hardening of the lines of authority." About ten years earlier, a plan of organization had been implemented placing final authority for policy and administration in the hands of the Board of Trustees. A fundamental condition of the plan called for policy proposals to emerge through committees, while authority for decision making would be vested in individual administrative offices according to a clearly defined hierarchical chain of command.

For the next few years the institution grew and prospered economically under this conventional form of management. However, in the spring of 1954, staff members voiced their distaste over being "treated as employees" and reacted actively against the fact that there were no open forums whereby they could register either their protests or preferences. Revolted by the "exploitive" character inherent in the monocratic feature of bureaucracy, and fractured by numerous barriers of red tape and secrecy inhibiting their direct participatory involvement in the shaping of policy and goals, members began demanding changes. To justify their critical sentiment, they called upon principles of medical ethics laid down by the American Medical Association, one of which stated:

> A physician should not dispose of their professional attainments or services to a hospital body, or organization, group or individual by whatever name called or however organized under terms or conditions which permit exploitation of the physician...(quoted in Crile and Bunts, 1971).

Debate over the emotion-filled issues continued for months. To channel the energy, an assessment was conducted involving direct consultation with every member of the staff. A report was then issued that set the stage for a search for a more effective governing process, a quest that continues today. The underlying theory behind the report reflected the theme of an interhuman logic: that an organization's governing process can be considered to be a healthy one to the extent that it is: (1) open and responsive to its membership, and (2) is designed in such a way that it enhances, throughout the group, the experiences of commitment, responsibility and ownership. The leading conclusion of the study captures the matter succinctly:

> The government of the Cleveland Clinic must become more democratic so that every member of the staff will feel greater responsibility for the welfare of the institution and have a more definite stake in the future (Crile and Bunts, 1971).

It is now conventional wisdom that organizations are not the "ideal" administrative entities as described in classical Weberian theory. The notion, perpetuated by bureaucratic thought, that organizations are pure and technical-administrative systems devoid of passion and politics has been widely challenged and exposed as myth (Brown, 1978; Weinstein, 1979; Antonio, 1979; Pfeffer, 1978). In fact, as Brown (1978) has demonstrated, the very conception of an instrumentally rational form of administration is itself an achievement of a political form of interaction: It is a symbolic product of non-calculable human interaction resulting in the formation of a shared set of governing beliefs or understandings. Thus, if we take the word "political" to refer to that sphere of interaction dealing with uncertainty, equivocality, or non-agreement concerning means and ends in organizational affairs, then it is the political that might well represent the cutting edge of organizing. No doubt this point is one that would be hotly contested by a great number of organizational theorists. In fact, many continue to argue that organizations are "economic entities" and should not be treated as if they contain a political sphere. However, while the scholarly debate over this issue will, of course, continue, the essential question raised by members of our study was not whether an organization has a political dimension, rather the question was "what kind"? What forms of governance should the organization choose to enact?

Reacting against the monological system of hierarchical authority, members of the Clinic set out to establish a system of *shared governance*. While the espoused logic legitimizing the chain-of-command bureaucratic form is conventionally understood as an economizing one of least cost and instrumental rationality (Bell, 1973), the principal passion associated with shared governance is hypothesized as a drive to heighten the "ideal membership situation" throughout an organization, especially the total level experiencing of *critical control and ownership*. In this sense, *shared governance represents a search for an effective political process that substitutes the processual criteria of participatory efficacy for hierarchical efficiency* and, in so doing, challenges the basic assumption that organizations can only achieve their purposes through hierarchical interactions between those structurally classified as "superiors" and those defined as "subordinates."[18]

---

18 In a provocative analysis, Thayer (1981) reviews the history of the productive value of hierarchy

What then is the role of the leader in such a system? Using the criteria of participatory efficacy, one member of our study defined the leadership task in highly catalytic terms:

I have one firm belief as a chairperson. The chairperson serves only one basic and good purpose. It is to utilize their knowledge and skill and political acumen to incite and charge other younger members with political and professional growth and development. I use every ounce of my energy to see to it that they develop…If a department chairperson doesn't have this goal in mind, then they shouldn't be the chairperson.

Without going into details, it was not until the late 60s that Clinic members realized their aim of becoming the governors (the working managers) of their own group practice. Accounts of the events culminating in the elimination of the system as hierarchical authority remain clouded, but the period is clearly remembered by many as one of "new birth" and major transformation. It was described as a period of "ideological confrontation… the revolution of 1968":

Up until 1968 there was no real group practice democracy except in the limited sense of our being responsible for the hiring of medical staff and the overseeing of the quality of professional practice. There was nothing in the way of the total institution as a democratic system. There was mounting unrest over this fact that then resulted in an ideological confrontation with the Trustees. I can remember very distinctly 30 of us (leading members of the staff) going to the Trustees and saying "We want this place restructured or else we'll go." We said that we could run it better ourselves as a group…so they agreed to let us do it. Since then, there has been the gradual evolution of our own Board of Governors (elected members of the staff) assuming responsibility for the total operation of the institution. The concept of physician-as-manager and CEO was born soon after the ideological confrontation.

(con't)
and suggests that as an assumption it carries little truth value. He concludes, in agreement with our observations, that anything of major significance that is achieved in organizational life is achieved because of a cooperative rather than hierarchical relational stance. He then raises an important question, "Is it possible that the effective conduct of social business occurs *in spite of hierarchy*, not because of it?"

216

Since that time, with the "group in command," an ongoing process of experimentation has been enacted in order to discover and rediscover more effective means of bringing people's talents and energies to bear on the persistent challenge of shared governance within the corporate setting. For members of the CC, the inclusionary ideal of "thinking and acting as a unit" had, in fact, become a realistic concern. There were many who predicted that the "unprecedented" experiment in physician management would fail. But it has not failed. And, based on our observations, there are five thematic characteristics that are essential to an understanding of the *catalytic* features of this egalitarian system of organizational governance:

1. *Power equals the formation of group will.* Power in the shared governing system is viewed as a function of the participatory process leading to the formation of collective public opinion. It is the "growing together" of a unified group will. Power is not, therefore, a person-centered nor position-centered phenomenon; it is a situational and interactive phenomenon that can be measured by a group's capacity for evolving a synthesizing collective vision in response to specific challenges and aspirations. The greater the capacity for mobilizing an integrated collective will, the greater the organizational power.

2. *Classlessness in social authority arrangements.* In a system of shared governance, there is no such thing as a formal hierarchy of authority in which "subordinates" are expected to surrender their own judgment and opportunity to make decisions to the commands of a "superior." The class distinction between the governing and governed is eliminated, not only because it is just or moral, but because it is the only practical means of securing the widest possible cooperative ownership and involvement. While hierarchy remains, it is not hierarchy in the sense of chain of command. Instead it is best depicted as a "chain of consent." The focus is not on ruling, commanding or even power-sharing; the primary focus is on power expansion (advancement of the group will). It is a system where the concept of potential is more important than what is, and where the

mobilizing *power of ideas* is more important than the power itself. Thus, it is an internally responsible system where politics is more a matter of the advancement of the whole rather than a mere balance of interests or control over different groups.

3. *Driven by dialogical substance and temporal group forms.* The substance of shared governance is the *ongoing process of dialogue* in which guiding values are created through the active interplay of relevant individuals, groups or intergroups. This dialogical core is translated into a consensus system of high political intensity that can be roughly measured as the ratio of organizational activities that are guided by publicly derived ideals and policies versus those that are unilaterally or privately determined and imposed. All major governance decisions having to do with new policy, allocation of resources, performance review, membership selection, budgeting and strategic planning emerge through collegial group forums made up of those who do the work of the organization. The political forums include a wide array of intra and interdepartmental groups, committees and councils that are designed to have rotating leadership and membership, and are open to any member who has something to add to the development of consensus.

4. *Requires the learning of group and political skills.* An egalitarian system of shared governance does not mean a leveling of differences but implies a face-to-face meeting of differences. In terms of the participatory process, members are treated equally simply because they are "members" and are assumed to possess unique and valid resources that can potentially empower or disempower the whole. Everyone is considered an "executive" in that each is expected to help the organization become what it can possibly become. The price of membership is, therefore, demanding and requires the ongoing learning of those capacities needed for effective participation in a relatively structureless group setting. The ultimate test of a shared governing system is not past or current performance, but the preparedness of its members for cooperatively managing their common affairs of the future.

5. *Nobody is exempt from the law of common consent.* A shared governing system is not a system without rules, but is a system where the rules are governed by common consent—and are binding on all. There is no such thing as a pyramid of privilege where those at the top are exempt from the consensus of the group. "Management prerogative" as a working concept does not exist. It is a governance process where all are equal in the eyes of the normative "law." It is a system where "if the group were mobilized around a basic issue, it would have the final say."

Each of these five themes is essential in understanding the catalytic nature of shared governance. But the overarching characteristic of such a governing process is its *emergent quality*. It is viewed as a permeable form whose open involvement, fluid structure and intensive interaction are most responsive to the natural rhythms of organizational construction and reconstruction. An account of the Clinic's history puts the matter pragmatically, recognizing the inevitability of change:

> At the present time the form of the Clinic's organization seems close to ideal, but past experience indicates that with time comes change…The plasticity of the Clinic's organization, based as it is on the democratic method, will continue to enable it to meet the challenges of the future (Crile and Bunts, 1971).

Commitment and the Catalytic Task Arena

The egalitarian organization is a complex and dynamic product of human interaction. And, while the ideal of open participation emerges as a consequence of many diverse and often incidental forces, there are concrete factors that are amenable to analysis and purposive action. Here we consider one of the most potent of these: the interactive arena of work. The proposition to be advanced is that *under norms of an interhuman administrative logic, an organization will define and structure its primary task in such a way that it serves as a highly democratizing and group-building force.*

That is, the work of an organization will be socially constructed in ways that catalyze committed interaction, thereby heightening the participation potential of the total system.

What are the catalytic factors? Five thematic characteristics stand out as most important: (1) the *work frontier* is actively pursued in all jobs and is used as a group-building force; (2) intensive *task interdependencies* are developed and contractually prescribed where possible; (3) *systemic rewards* and peer appraisal mechanisms are used to link members promotively to one another; (4) the design of work advances not just technically but progresses in *moral significance* as well; and finally, (5) responsibility for task design is a group-centered, *inclusive design process* where the discretionary elements of work (e.g., goals, roles, procedures) are given meaning and form through the creative interplay of all relevant participants.

The observation that the first theme, the frontier, effectively functions as a unifying and democratizing force is not a new one (De Tocqueville, 1969; Bennis and Slater, 1968; Festinger, 1957). In a recent field study, for example, Blau and Alba (1982) report that the introduction of sheer complexity and uncertainty into an organization can undermine inequalities among bureaucratic units and that a more egalitarian system emerges as complex role relations promote extensive inter-unit communications. Such findings are generally quite consistent in the literature and raise an interesting question for organizational theory: Is it not possible that when people in organizations choose to move along the path of the frontier, in all its uncertainty and possible complexity, that they do so not so much as a reactive response to "objective" environmental stimuli, but do so more as a self-creative means of constructing interactive structures worthy of their committed involvement?

Our observations lend support to this often neglected point of view. Consistent with the egalitarian ideology of inclusion, consent and excellence, the group practice of the CC has "enacted" (Weick, 1977) a complex task environment which, in turn, has made it imperative upon members to perform effectively as a group. The organization itself has largely built its own stimulating external world through defining its technical identity in terms of the frontier. In fact, the CC did what virtually any organization could choose to do: Together, members continue to agree that an essential feature of their work system should be to "forever remain open to the newer and better things that come along." In other words, the work sphere of the Clinic was defined in terms of impermanence, signifying an openness to continuous learning, discovery and diversity. To remain at the "cutting edge" of their own capacities meant the system of work would have to be viewed in highly temporary terms, in a relatively endless state of formation and transformation. Furthermore, it must be pointed out that the decision to enter or not enter into the foreground of change was largely an ideological decision. To enter the frontier was essentially a commitment to operate as a group; it required opening the system to the strengthening contributions each participant would have to offer. As one member at the Clinic clearly explained, the ability to "pounce on new modalities..." was directly associated with their ability to bring a cohesive force together:

> Our strength comes from belonging to a group. Part of the excuse of the CC's existence is its ability to respond to new developments in a timely manner and to get things on board before anyone else. The Clinic has the capacity for rapid change. It has the ability for alteration of configuration, the ability to pounce on new modalities, and the ability to bring a cohesive force together.

The second catalytic element, the intensification of task-based interdependencies, is also viewed as a powerful group development agent. Here the task arena is marked by a belief that all members control critical resources for organizational success (Neilsen, 1984) and that the system's total capacity for achievement and innovation will be higher to the extent that "key" performance interdependencies are clearly agreed upon (Pasmore, *et al.*, 1983). Task interdependence can be said to exist when members perceive one another as essential for the accomplishment of their operative goals and it becomes more intensive when the tasks grow in difficulty, variability, novelty and knowledge content, and when the resources to perform the tasks are distributed among members. The egalitarian organization we hypothesize moves in the direction of a growing intensity of interdependence and, at least, the Clinic has shown that the more fully developed and integrated the network of task-based interaction, the more the system is able to become. It is in this sense then that we can understand the elegant simplicity in the management logic concisely proposed by one of the Clinic's successful leaders:

> I would envision myself as a catalyst who gets people (diverse specialties) working well together toward making this the best department of its kind in the world.

Much like Durkheim's theory of solidarity, realization of technical interdependence gives people cause to act in ways that benefit the whole (Collins and Makowsky, 1978). In the form of a practical theory, another Clinic member put it this way, "Along with ultraspecialization comes the need for ultracooperation." Committed action becomes essential. When summarizing this view and why it works, others said:

> There is little trouble relating because they want something and you want something. We relate technically, share experiences, consult with each other, operate together and educate each other through meetings and the sharing of interests. I think it all boils down to the nature of the CC.

***

> The type of work we're doing here requires us to work together. My whole career has been to work collaboratively—and it has been successful. To make this work, there must be enthusiasm for the excellence of results without striving for personal recognition. It takes a certain kind of person to work here. It takes people who can say, "We did this, the CC group did this."

The third catalytic factor, the systemic approach to rewarding and appraising performance, reinforces the partnership contract. It involves the consideration that all members should benefit through the elevation of the organization as a whole and that the best source of appraisal is a combination of self-appraisal and peer review. It also means creating collective reward structures so that one member's advance is not contingent upon another's failure. Speaking to this theme, one member describes:

> ...it (the compensation program) is a positive thing because then, in a group practice such as this, it means I no longer have to build an empire. And that automatically means there is much more interaction between departments...What we do is for the good of the whole Clinic and we all benefit from the good of the Clinic. For example, everyone knows that our Cardiac Surgery Department generates a tremendous amount of revenue for the institution and that those in that department are not paid what they generate. What they generate is shared by the whole Clinic. Similarly, we have a Department of Pediatrics that doesn't generate much, yet is considered valuable. When you look at the median pay scale between the two, they are very close together. But that is one of the benefits here: We are all in this together.

The fourth catalytic task factor, the moral progression of the work of the organization, is perhaps the most critical thematic element able to explain the maintenance of commitment required to sustain the egalitarian form. What the clinic has called "ultracooperation" was shown to be dependent on the progressive realization of a morally relevant primary task; a mission which, in essence, *calls forth the conviction that there is something serious, meaningful, and humanly significant about one's existence as an organizational participant.* One member, for example, touched on this feeling when he traced his commitment to a sense of larger destiny concerning the institution:

> There is a sense in an institution like this of tithing to the organization. We feel that the CC will go on forever, even after we're gone.

So, psychologically, you say that you are part of it all and you buy in. Many organizations don't have that sense of significant mission, but it is very strong here.

The theme of moral progression points to the idea that whatever separate interests members might hold, they can potentially be synthesized in the pursuit of higher order end-values of their own making (Burns, 1978). Thus, when referring to moral progression, we are not speaking of a specific moral code or even specific level of morality (Kohlberg, 1964): instead, we are talking about the process of surfacing normative differences concerning the work of the organization and seeking to exploit those differences by seeking a synthesis of value at a higher, more inclusive level, a level where a growing consensus emerges that, "Yes, we agree *in principle* that this is a direction or task we should pursue."

Two factors have been found to be especially instrumental in promoting this process of moral progression. The first, as described earlier, is simply that the potential for exploiting multiple perspectives is encouraged through a *primary task definition* emphasizing the ubiquity of incompletion, i.e., "We must forever remain open..." The second factor builds on this open transitory orientation by providing a backdrop of stability through which dynamic and conflicting membership interests can progressively be dealt with. This stabilizing or "centering" factor has been well defined in another detailed study of the Clinic as the "syntonic" leadership type (Srivasta, Jensen and Cooperrider, 1981). Briefly, this type has exhibited itself as a quality of leadership that promotes among institution participants:

1. A sense of timeless *destiny* about the institution;[19] its role in its own field as well as its larger role in its service to society.

2. A *holistic* view of the organization through appreciation and acceptance of all positions.

---

19 Even the word "institution," which was used repeatedly by members in reference to the organization, conjures up a certain sense of destiny, stability and purpose of a higher order. Sociologically, the term institution has been used to describe well established patterns of behavior, such as the institution of marriage. And theologically, "to institute" has meant to assign or invest with spiritual power.

3. A climate where people can picture and debate the *polar opposite* of what has been declared in order to keep alive the possibilities of mobility and progression.

4. A process of decision making where value-relevant matters are not permanently decided but rather are *permanently in dialogue* in order to work through the extremes of dualisms.

Against this backdrop of stability (i.e., sense of destiny, wholeness, acceptance of polar realities, and the role of perpetual dialogue), the institution has enabled itself to enter into the foreground of change, thereby allowing for, or more accurately yielding to, the progression of the system's highest values as translated into its day-to-day work. In this sense, it can be said that one of the more important managerial tasks in an egalitarian system is to find ways to rejuvenate, on an ongoing basis, a shared sense of conviction that the difficult process of direct participation in organizational affairs is, indeed, worth members' voluntary effort.

The last factor, an inclusive task design process, is based on the idea that the designers and implementers of a given work system should be co-designers, or one in the same (Weick, 1981). It is an idea that is directly linked and coterminous with the political arena of shared governance. In fact, being an acknowledged partner in the determination of new goals, roles, procedures or work relation *is* shared governance, distinguishable at the level of the local work process.

So integral is the inclusive task design process as a group-building force that it can be said, perhaps too bluntly, that the task arena will never be catalytic—no matter how much in the frontier, intensively interdependent, collectively rewarding or morally significant—if members are successfully barred from making their creative energies felt in the construction of their own work. Unless people take part in constituting the technical arrangements that shape their lives, they will never view each other as partners. Partnership in this sense is not a thing given or imposed; it is an achievement of the creative collective act. It is a realization that one is a part of an authentic negotiated order, or, as one member of the CC aptly put it:

> We are a partnership of physicians and function as a group which means that if you have a good idea and take the time to educate and sell it to others, then it will go. There is no suppression from the top. I think this evolves from the fact that we govern ourselves.

Summing up this theme, a division chairperson described the primary executive task as the task of building a self-designing system:

> My aim and goal is to contribute to the creation of an atmosphere where each department is strong, has strong leadership, strong performance and to enable it to go as far as it wants to go...We are setting up an organization that can pretty much run itself.

Section II Conclusions: Organizing is Based on an Interhuman Logic

We can now state more clearly, in summary propositional form, the themes that have emerged from our inquiry into the interactional arenas of work and politics. The following additional propositions provide a summary of the interhuman logic of organizing:

Proposition #6: Under norms of an interhuman administrative logic, an organization will open the boundaries of its governance process and seek to create political structures that are increasingly catalytic.

Proposition #6.1: Members will discover more effective means of authentic consensus formation for building and mobilizing a dynamic group will.

Proposition #6.2: Members will develop processes of shared governance that eliminate formal hierarchical distinctions between the governing and the governed.

Proposition #6.3: Members will establish a system of group organization that is highly politicized, i.e., where publicly relevant governance decisions emerge through collegial group forums.

Proposition #6.4: The system of organizing will foster the learning of group and political skills; everyone will be viewed as an "executive" in the sense that all will be expected to help the organization become what it can potentially become.

Proposition #6.5: Members will develop a system of self-regulating rules or sanctions. It will become a system where nobody is exempt from the authority of common consent.

Proposition #7: Under norms of an interhuman administrative logic, an organization will construct work arenas that catalyze cooperative group action.

Proposition #7.1: Members will define their mission in open-ended terms and support a system where the work frontier is pursued by participants in all jobs.

Proposition #7.2: Members will build a system of increasingly intensive task-based interdependence.

Proposition #7.3: The organization will seek to link members promotively to one another through the use of systemic rewards and peer appraisal or feedback mechanisms.

Proposition #7.4: As the work advances technically, there will be corresponding developments in its moral significance as a normatively synthesizing force.

Proposition #7.5: Members will continuously seek to establish an inclusive design process where the discretionary elements of work are actively constituted through their own direct and active involvement.

III. The Predominant Social Paradigms

In the preceding sections, we have presented an appreciative analysis of both the ideological spirit and set of political and work arrangements that heighten the potential of a work organization as an open, egalitarian system. The egalitarian organization emerges, we have argued, as a result of spirited commitment to a group-based organization of inclusion, consent and excellence that by its very nature, focuses member attention on the nature and quality of interaction between participants in a shared social life world. It is this level of consciousness which, in turn, gives rise to what has been called an interhuman logic of administration; a system of sociological thought that places the participatory process and elements of the ideal membership situation at the fore of most any consideration having to do with the creation, maintenance or transformation of the organization itself. We now move to our final thematic discussion, which is introduced in the following additional proposition:

> *Proposition #8:* Direct experience in catalytic structures of interaction will reinforce the egalitarian spirit by having an educative effect on members (Pateman, 1970; Elden, 1983; Torbert, 1983). It socializes members in the direction of a cultural paradigm that is characterized by: (1) an "open" view concerning the nature of organizational reality, and (2) a "semi-autonomous" ontological relational stance between self and other. The potential of an *open participatory* system is largely a function of these two paradigmatic dimensions (see Figure V-2).

This final proposition is grounded in a set of themes that have been infused throughout the chapter. Any sense of repetition that may exist reflects the profuse difficulty in analytically separating factors that in practice are complexly interwoven.

By cultural or social paradigm:

> ...we refer to those sets of assumptions usually implicit, about what sorts of things make up the social world, how they act, how they hang together, and how they may be known (Brown, 1978, p. 373; Schein, 1983, p.16).

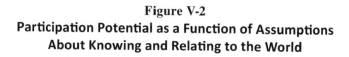

Figure V-2
Participation Potential as a Function of Assumptions
About Knowing and Relating to the World

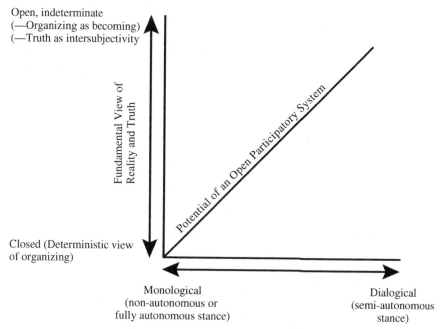

As a powerful set of presuppositions used to guide inquiry and action in organized social settings, a social paradigm represents a product of socialization built deeply into one's character structure. It can be argued that *organizations* develop and encourage distinctive social paradigms (Brown, 1978) that then become the taken-for-granted foundation on which sustained collective action is made possible.

Two conceptual dimensions of an organization's social paradigm have surfaced in our study as most important: (a) participant's view of organizational reality, the epistemic structure, and (b) the underlying participatory schema or "ontological relational stance" (Baxter, 1982) informing members' interactions with one another, the relational structure.

The *epistemic* structure of the egalitarian system is thematically summarized as *co-inquiry-in-action*.[20] As a way of knowing, co-inquiry is based on an "open" non-deterministic view of an organizational reality that is forever perceived in a dynamic state of flux. And, while change is apparent, it is viewed as a certain type of change. In the egalitarian system, organizational change is conceived largely as a social construction based on participant agreement. Co-inquiry, therefore, fuels a strong faith in, and belief in the need for, an intellectually demanding *inquiry in-action* that is public in nature, open to the scrutiny of the group. As such, the stance of co-inquiry assumes that for most problems of organizing, the guarantors of valid information are the members themselves. What is valid, true, or right for the organization emerges through a collegial inquiry process resulting in intersubject agreement. People "know" through consensual validation.

Is this the same as pointing out, more simply, that the organization relies on *consensus* as the primary mode of decision making? We don't think so. This section is intended to highlight something more.

What our data imply is that the consensus mode itself depends on a set of deeply structured background assumptions for its effective operation. It depends on an epistemology that is crudely portrayed by the following sub-themes of co-inquiry (along with sample corresponding quotes):

1. *Reality is always changing; it is a verb.*
   Our mission is changing. The whole ballgame is changing; the things that are going to happen in the next 20 years are going to boggle the mind.

   ...It is through areas of uncertainty that opportunities arise. They should not be erased. The alternative is a very rigid system.

2. *Truth is intersubjectivity.*
   If problems of human beings are to be solved, the solutions must originate with people.

---

20 For brevity we will refer simply to co-inquiry from now on.

Knowledge is for everyone to share. The physician is trained to share not only locally but worldwide. This is their reason for being...If we find an answer to something, we broadcast it.

3. *Need for experimentation-in-action.*
   Excellence is so strongly expected that, from the moment you join the organization, you are continuously questioning, seeking to find better ways.

   I found that management builds on the training we get in professional fields. You live in an assessment mode all day in the world of medicine.

4. *Creator-of-history attitude.*
   You must create your own way and not become reactionary. To be successful here, you to set the expectations.

   ...most people want to be involved in building and determining their future. In fact, that is why many people come here.

The life of the Cleveland Clinic revolves around its capacity to reproduce a collective belief system supportive of co-inquiry-in-action. Without an open view of reality—and without a questioning, learning, experimenting membership willing to enter into relationships of *joint* inquiry—the Cleveland Clinic would likely lose the self-generative capacity essential for sustaining its form.

While this is a possibility, we don't view it as very likely. For centuries, the physician has been the working model of the pragmatic scientist. As Plato saw it, medicine was the embodiment of a profession founded upon a code rigorous enough to be held up as an ideal type image of the competent relation between knowledge and its use in practical affairs; a system of inquiry-in-action devoted to enhancing the quality of human life (Ford, *et al.*, 1967). Bound by a system of high ethics, the best-known antidote to incomplete knowledge for physicians has been an experimental and systematic approach to inquiry while in the act of doing. The simultaneity of thought and action and reflection and experimentation so critical to a holistic form of learning (Kolb, 1983; Dewey, 1939) has never been institutionalized anywhere quite so profoundly as in the world of medicine. Physicians have shown that when the need for answers is demanded—yet the world in question will not stand still—the best known response continues to be an open, intellectually thorough stance of inquiry in the course of direct treatment of problems. Interestingly, Weick (1983) has recently written about the importance of this orientation as the essence of the executive mind.

In many respects, this study can be conceived of as a look into what happens when the epistemology of the physician is translated into the day-to-day affairs of managing an organization. Through the political system of shared governance, CC physicians, as worker-managers, have made their viewpoint on the nature of organizational reality felt.

The importance of this cannot be overstated. In contrast to the orientation of co-inquiry stands the epistemic mentality of "scientific management." Introduced in the 1920s, the Taylorist philosophy has become firmly entrenched in the minds, structures and operations of the bureaucratic organizational world. The scientific management approach promulgated the positivist belief that there is one ultimate reality to be found "out there" (one best solution to production problems); that the best way to understand something or generate knowledge is to separate thinking (conception) from doing (execution); that unilateral measurement technique should override personal experience as the source of valid data; and that the worker should bow obediently to hierarchically positioned sources of "true" knowledge (see Braverman, 1974; Jenkins, 1973; Clegg and Dunkerly, 1980). As we have described, co-inquiry is based on an alternative set of assumptions that link thinking and acting and thereby link executives and workers. In the egalitarian system all members, by definition, are called to function as executives. All executives are called upon as workers. And, in terms of significant planning and decision making, *the consensual mode is the only logical extension of the beliefs embedded in co-inquiry*. While the scientific management paradigm exhibits a strong ideological affinity to bureaucratic hierarchy, co-inquiry is uniquely suited for that form of organization committed to the ideals of inclusion, consent, and excellence.

The final theme of our study is largely a summarizing one. Throughout this appreciative assessment, one factor has stood out among all others: The egalitarian organization is one that rationally fuels and depends on the quality of cooperative interhuman experience. To single out the last paradigmatic dimension as the organization's basic *relational structure* may then appear unnecessary, but there are a couple of things that need to be said, especially as it relates to possible ways of understanding the participatory transformations taking place in the modern workplace.

The relational structure of the Cleveland Clinic is thematically characterized by what we will call the community of competence. This theme refers first of all to a profound faith in all those accepted into the organization: a belief that people can find within their organization the support, competence, affirmation, challenge, and diversity of talent required for the continuing discovery and achievement of selected values. The foundation of the community-of-competence was shown to be a commitment to a *semi-autonomous* world view where Self and Other are oriented together reciprocally; where actions are jointly attempted based on collegial respect, trust and/or friendship. Elaborations on this theme together with descriptive data are presented in Figure V-3.

Figure V-3
Ontological Stance in the Egalitarian Organization (Relational Structure)

PRIMARY THEME

Community of Competence: This refers first of all to a profound faith in others; a belief that members in the organization can find within the setting the support, affirmation, challenge and diverse talent required for setting in motion productive interactions leading to the ongoing discovery and achievement of selected values. Its foundation rests on a semi-autonomous world view where Self and Other are oriented toward one another reciprocally, where actions are jointly attempted based on collegial respect, trust and/or friendship.

SUB-THEMES AND DESCRIPTIVE COMMENTS

Sub-Theme #1: Semi-Autonomous Relational Stance

"You can't be an individual and not care about the group at all. So long as you can see what is going on from the group mentality then you can work from it."

"We are a federation of semi-independent states."

"I manage my interdependence and achieve a certain amount of independence. You have to cooperate with others but there is a lot of room for negotiation."

"I rule by consensus."

Sub-Theme #2: Basic Assumption Respect of Trust

"Even if I haven't worked with them yet, I know they are good because they are a part of the CC."

"This is not a normal group of people. Most everyone in this group is competent and interested in doing a good job."

"…working with a group like this you have confidence in group decisions."

"The CC, as it is set up now, is a remarkable collection of human beings."

Sub-Theme #3: The Group as Vehicle for Achievement

"To be successful, we need to find people who want to work together, who realize the strength of putting groups together, and realize that a number of minds are better than individual efforts."

Sub-Theme #4: Learning and Discovery Through Colleagueship

"To be successful here you must have the ability to give and take with other professional colleagues and to join up, teach and investigate with others.

(con't.)

Sub-Theme #3: The Group as Vehicle for Achievement

"The concept of group practice revolves around the concept of working with one another. We build and maintain the CCF through our support of one another."

"Our strength comes from belonging to a group."

"...somebody has to decide how we are going to make allocations of physical space—and this is best done through discussion and negotiation among colleagues."

(con't.)

Sub-Theme #4: Learning and Discovery Through Colleagueship

"Recognizing my weaknesses (as a new manager), I formed an advisory group of colleagues...that would toss ideas off me. It was a challenge because we were all changing. I'm still learning."

The theoretical importance of this theme has been spelled out brilliantly in the recent work of Brian Baxter (1982). In this scholarly work, Baxter proposes a model of "forms of ontological life" (see Figure V-4). It is a framework addressing the questions of a person's (the "Self") "being-in-the-world" in relation to all non-self factors (the "Other"). Accordingly, there are three basic forms the Self-Other relationship can take: the non-autonomous, semi-autonomous, and fully autonomous modes of related-ness. Viewing God as the most complex Other, Baxter builds a description of the three archetypal forms of ontological life. The key point is that the Other—"Whether it is as venerable as Horus the Egyptian god of heaven or as modern as capitalism"—confronts each person as a living presence that is coextensive to the Self. Thus, the ontological choice of how one relates to the Other permeates all of one's belief and actions in the world of work.

Figure V-4
Forms of Ontological Life

Category	Nature of Activity	Relationship to the Other
1. The Self in *non-autonomous* existence with the Other.	Actions are Other directed	Adoration
2. The Self in *semi-autonomous* existence with the Other.	Actions are jointly attempted or Other supported	Respect or love
3. The Self in *full autonomous* existence of the Other.	Actions are for the Self's own ends and/or "playful"	Indifference or hostility

Source: Baxter, 1982.

Possible choices are raised in reference to the work context such as: Do people relate to the workplace as an all-powerful Other, providing ultimate direction and strength to one's life, a non-autonomous stance? Or is it perceived as a supportive presence in which people enter into reciprocal relationships where actions are jointly attempted based on respect or love, a semi-autonomous stance? Or is it conceived as a barrier to one's full existence, an ever-present obstacle that must be defiantly overcome, a fully autonomous stance?

The tacit theme in the conclusion of Baxter's important work is that we are at a crossroad in the evolution of organizational theory. Today, as we enter the post-industrial era we, as scientists, need to acknowledge the fact that *we literally have no more idea of what kind of organization is possible than did the earliest capitalists paving the way for the Industrial Revolution* (Srivastva and Cooperrider, 1983). Seemingly immutable ideas about people and organizations are being directly challenged and transformed on an unprecedented scale. Social inventions as wide-ranging as the Mondragon industrial system in Spain (Whyte, 1982), to the emerging egalitarian partnership found in professional organizations such as the

Cleveland Clinic, represent a glimpse of the possibilities at hand. Other significant developments include the global workplace democracy movement, new understandings of Japanese management and organizational excellence, and thousands of dispersed quality of work life and organization development experiments designed to transform the quality of participatory processes in organizations of all types. Developments as broad as these are important, not only because they encourage an overdue involvement of the worker in traditionally isolated management areas, but because they represent the possibility of a paradigmatic shift in the ontological relationship of the Self to the organizational Other (Baxter, 1982). A spiritual and cultural shift from a largely non-autonomous perspective (hierarchical) to a reciprocal semi-autonomous (egalitarian) world view may indeed usher in a new era in organizational theory, an era where students of organizational life not only seek to understand such trends, but also, through their inquiry, seek to advance the possibilities inherent in the more cooperative forms of organizing.

What we have found at the Cleveland Clinic is a system that we believe is successfully responding to a shift from a largely non-autonomous perspective (hierarchical) to a reciprocal semi-autonomous (egalitarian) world view, on an organization-wide basis. Its success stems largely from its capacity to create and re-create structures of interaction that continue to catalyze a cooperative approach to organizational action. As a post-industrial social invention, the CC might well be a prototype of the knowledge-based professional organization of our future. But this is only speculation. At the very least this case presents important considerations for all those interested in more cooperative organizational forms. It is hoped that the theory generated from the case helps widen the scope of what we consider to be within the realm of possibility.

Epilogue

In February of 1985, one of the physicians whom I had worked with during the initial survey project set up an appointment to see me at the university: "Urgent," he said. The physician had been on the elected division council when I first met him. We hadn't spoken for about a year until the day of our meeting when he came to my office and asserted:

> I just got hold of your paper on "The Emergence of the Egalitarian Organization" and found myself sky-high after reading it while on a flight to a recent medical meeting—no pun intended! But then I became concerned. You see, so many things are happening to us right now—federal cost control programs, corporate competition in health care, DRG and TEFRA payment plans, and our own tremendous growth in size—all these things seem to be driving us toward more of a business mentality and away from the mentality of equal partnership you talk about so well in the paper. The group sentiment is one of concern and anxiety regarding these combined changes. I think you and Suresh Srivastva should come address the staff and discuss and reinforce the management approach presented in this paper. I don't know if you can say we're really living up to these things anymore, and there are many of us growing increasingly concerned.

At the time of our meeting, this physician was involved in a graduate program in business administration at our university and was working on an independent study course. After our talk we came up with the idea of a kind of re-enactment of the initial study in 1981 leading to the "emergent themes." Only this time the physician would do the study. The purpose is described in his own words:

> In June of 1981, publication of "The Transfer of Professional Instincts to Organizational Activities: A Listing of Emergent Themes Describing a Unique Organizational Form" gave the Cleveland Clinic new insight into the critical essence of the organization. A summary of the above publication is the list of 26 Emergent Themes (called by some ET) which were, from a

behavioral science point of view, an interpretation of the driving forces within the institution...The Emergent Themes were evaluated as to whether they represented the espoused ideals of the members of...the institution and then were evaluated as to how the themes were actually being practiced...The purpose of this paper is not to test the themes again, but to take the themes as an ideological and operative given for 1981. Since that time, there have been changes with the internal and external environment of the Cleveland Clinic. The changes have taken a variety of shapes and forms...realities of 1985 are so different that no one could have or did perceive their possible existence in 1981. The purpose of this project is to evaluate the Emergent Themes in the environment of the healthcare industry and the Cleveland Clinic in the spring of 1985. Are the Emergent Themes still viable in/for the Cleveland Clinic at this time? Are the Emergent Themes still the driving forces that the Cleveland Clinic needs to have for its future to meet its mission, patient care in the setting of research and education (Ruschhaupt, 1985, pp. 1-3)?

According to socio-rationalist assumptions, knowledge of the human group is never complete. The quest for trans-historical laws, for certainty and for ultimate truth is an illusive if not impossible quest. Because patterns of social-organizational action are not fixed by nature in any direct biological or physical way and because of our capacity for symbolic interaction, the vast share of social conduct is recognized as virtually stimulus free, capable of infinite conceptual variation. How then is rational action in the social realm made possible? Is there anything that resembles rationality when it comes to the social world? Here, it becomes clear that truth is not something "out there" just waiting to be discovered. What rationality exists in the social world is wrapped up not in some technical context or trans-historical law, but in the social *process* of making or creating meaning. As in all human construction, "rationality" is made possible and perhaps even equals *dialogue*. It is only through dialogue that thought, ideas, or theory can become creative of the social future. Thus, as Habermas (1970) posits, the only direct way of achieving a rational social order is to work toward creating egalitarian conditions where people are free to enter into dialogue, free from systematic distortion or constraint, whereby together the social world can be constructed in ways that match and respond to the values of those that make up the social whole.

In the conclusion to his revisitation of the egalitarian theory at the CC, the physician comes to a similar point of view. His recommendation to the institution was that "the Emergent Themes need wider exposure." He then described what this means by quoting from one of the participants in his study. The quote underscores the importance of *normative dialogue* among *all* those that make up the social whole:

> ...It isn't just what the physicians believe that makes this place and the people within it what it is, it is what everybody believes and ascribes to. You have to look at it from a total system framework, that there are different people within the system that have perhaps different values and levels of contribution. Nevertheless, we are a whole and what we need to do is to get this articulation of these ideals or values more easily and readily understood and have or encourage people to continue the dialogue around them (quotes in Ruschhaupt, 1985).

Hence, the inquiry is not over and perhaps has just begun.

This dissertation has presented a conceptual refiguration of action-research. It has argued both through logic and in case study for an enriched multi-dimensional view of action-research that seeks to be theoretically generative and active in a humanly significant way. Specifically, it has argued for ways to ignite the creative spirit of action-research and that to do this we need a fundamentally different perspective toward our life world, one that admits to its unexplicable, miraculous nature. An appreciative way of knowing, it has been suggested, is a form of inquiry distinct from a problem-solving mode and represents a dynamic process that is put in motion through a stance toward life that recognizes the unfathomable, that is, that at its core, social existence is indeed a creative miracle that can never be fully known. It was this simple recognition that inspired every phase in the emergence of the egalitarian theory.

But now it must be admitted, with a certain sense of limited capability and failure, that the viewpoint articulated here is simply not possible to operationally define and is very difficult to speak of in terms of practical, standardized steps. From the perspective of techno-rational thought, the miraculous is impossible. From that of problem solving, it is nonsense. And from that of empirical science, it is categorically denied (Reeves, 1984). Just as we cannot prove the proposition that organizing is a problem to be solved, so, too, we cannot prove in any rational, analytic, or empirical way that organizing is a miracle to be embraced.[21] Each stance represents a commitment—a core conviction so to speak—that is given only as a choice. It is felt, however, that through discipline and training we can educate the appreciative eye to see ordinary magic, beauty, and real possibility in organizational life; but I'm not so sure we can so easily transform our central convictions.

There are a number of principles and/or propositions about the appreciative mode that now can be stated. Not only do they further summarize the learnings from the study but, more importantly, represent questions that may, perhaps, usefully inform future research and social experimentation.

Proposition #1: Conscious cultural evolution is a viable human option for social-organizational systems as large as global society or as small as a two-person group.

Proposition #2: Whether intended or not, all social theory and theorizing contributes to cultural evolution. It does so through the creation and reproduction of language, by establishing perceptual cues and frames, by transmitting subtle values, by providing presumptions of logic, and by extending visions of possibility or constraint.

---

21 In fact, the very first time I presented these ideas in public at the 1984 National Academy of Management Meeting in Boston, the first time I used the word "miracle" in reference to organizational life, I was responded to with laughter. After recovering from my own startled reaction to this response, I completed the speech and found the discussion afterward to be rich and worthwhile in terms of lively debate.

Proposition #3: All social inquiry is an *interruption* in the ongoing flow of the social process. In this sense, it is because of the reactive and reflexive character of social inquiry that scientific work should be evaluated on the basis of its generative or non-generative enlightenment effect. Good theory may be one of the most powerful means human beings have for contributing to positive development (i.e., toward social system effectiveness) in the groups and organizations that make up our post-industrial world.

Proposition #4: The appreciative mode develops a context for inquiry that is uniquely suited for generative theorizing leading to social innovation.

Proposition #4.1: The appreciative mode engenders a reverence for life that draws the student of the social world to inquire beyond superficial appearances to the life-generating essentials and potentials of social existence.

Proposition #4.2: Through affirmation of the best of "what is," the appreciative mode ignites intuition of the possible, leading to theoretical articulations that are both grounded in and yet depart from reality as given to the senses. Theory is, therefore, generative to the extent to which it synthesizes both empirical and intuitive forms of knowing.

Proposition #4.3: In terms of its content and form, the generative potential of theory is positively associated with its vision, passion, and integrity.

Proposition #4.4: The generative potential of inquiry depends not only on the content of theory, but also on the *process* of inquiry. The process of *co-appreciative* inquiry will heighten the generative potential of science. The generative potential of knowledge is directly related to processes of normative dialogue and collective experimentation in the construction of new social arrangements.

Proposition #4.5: A co-appreciative inquiry process creates a research environment—a holding environment—that fosters empathy, hope, and a social bonding among people around desired values. As a deliberately supportive environment, appreciation inspires the collective imagination and thereby opens the status quo to social innovation.

Proposition #5: If taken deeply enough, appreciative inquiry arrives at a dynamic human ideal. It arrives at knowledge that enlarges our sense of solidarity with other human beings and provides an ever-expanding universe of theory concerning the possibilities for a more egalitarian social-organizational future.

The position that has been developed here is that for action-research to reach its potential as a vehicle for social innovation, it needs to begin advancing theoretical knowledge of consequence; that good theory may be one of the best means human beings have for producing change in a post-industrial world; that the discipline's steadfast commitment to a problem-solving view of the world is a primary restraint on its imagination and passionate contribution; that appreciative inquiry represents a viable complement to conventional forms of action-research; and that, through our assumptions and choice of method, we largely create the world we later discover.

In sum, this dissertation is a call for a humanly significant process of social-organizational inquiry, an inquiry that is based on co-appreciative modes of questioning, valuing, knowing, choosing and experimenting. As a holistic and collaborative form of knowing, appreciative inquiry represents a challenge to social systems to reach toward their noblest aspirations and to enact their ideals through innovations in social-organizational arrange-ments. We are infants when it comes to our understanding of appreciative processes of knowing and social construction. Yet we are beginning to see that the power of appreciation rests with its self-reinforcing and self-generative capacity. Through appreciation, the student of organizational life learns to affirm not only the topic of inquiry but also learns to affirm him or herself. As new potentials for inquiry are revealed and experi-enced within the student, new insights are made available that are shared with those in organization. As sharing occurs, the inquiry becomes a joint process of knowing—others are invited to explore and question their own ideals. Through dialogue, new knowledge is then continually made available. And, while such knowledge is always felt as an interruption in the social process, it is valued and made useful because it represents a joint creation of a world that matches the creators' present conception of human and social possibility.

Bibliography

Abrams, M.H. (1953). *The mirror and the lamp.* New York: W.W. Norton.

Ansoff, I., et al. (1976). *From strategic planning to strategic management.* New York: John Wiley.

Antonio, Robert J. (1979). The contradiction of domination and production in bureaucracy: The contribution of organizational efficiency to the decline of the Roman Empire. *American Sociological Review, 44,* pp. 895-212.

Argyris, Chris (1983). Action science and intervention. *The Journal of Applied Behavioral Science, 19,* pp. ll5-140.

Argyris, Chris (1970). *Intervention theory and methods.* Reading, MA: Addison-Wesley.

Argyris, C. and Schon, D. (1978). *Organizational learning: A Theory of action perspective.* Reading, MA: Addison-Wesley.

Barnard, Chester (1938). *The functions of the executive.* Cambridge, MA: Harvard University Press.

Bartunek, Jean (1983). How organization development can develop organizational theory. *Group and Organization Studies, 8,* pp. 303-318.

Bartunek, Jean (1984). Changing interpretive schemes and organizational restructuring: The example of a religious order. *Administrative Science Quarterly, 27,* pp. 355-372.

Baxter, Brian (1982). *Alienation and authenticity.* London: Tavistock Publications.

Bell, D. (1973). *The coming of the post-industrial society.* New York: Basic Books.

Bennis, Warren and Slater, Phillip (1968). *The temporary society.* New York: Harper and Row.

Berelson, Bernard (1954). Content analysis. In G. Lindzey (Ed.), *Handbook of social psychology.* Reading, MA: Addison-Wesley.

Berger, P.L. and Luckman, T.L. (1967). *The social construction of reality.* New York: Anchor Books.

Berman, Morris (1981). *The re-enchantment of the world.* Ithaca: Cornell University Press.

Beyer, Janice (1981). Ideologies, values and decision making in organizations. In Nystrom and Starbuck (Eds.), *Handbook of organizational design: Volume 2.* Oxford: Oxford University Press.

Beyer, J. and Trice, H. (1982). Utilization process: Conceptual framework and synthesis of findings. *Administrative Science Quarterly, 22,* pp. 591-622.

Bion, W.R. (1961). *Experiences in groups.* New York: Basic Books.

Black, May (1962). *Models and metaphors.* New York: Cornell University Press.

Blake, R. and Mouton, J. (1976). *Consultation.* Reading, MA: Addison-Wesley.

Blankenship, Ralph L. (Ed.) (1977). *Colleagues in organizations: The social construction of professional work.* New York: Wiley

Blau, Judith and Alba, Richard (1982). Empowering nets of participation. *Administrative Science Quarterly, 27,* pp. 363-379.

Bohr, Niels (1958). *Atomic Theory and Human Knowledge.* New York: John Wiley.

Bowles, Samuel and Gintis, Herbert (1981). Education as a site of contradictions in the reproduction of the capital-labor relationship. *Economic and Industrial Democracy, 2,* pp. 223-242.

Bradford, L.P., Gibb, J.R. and Benne, K. (1964). *T-group theory and laboratory method.* New York: John Wiley.

Braverman: Harry (1974). *Labor and monopoly capital.* New York: Monthly Review Press.

Brimm, M. (1972). When is change not a change? *Journal of Applied Behavioral Science, 1,* pp. 102-107.

Brown, Richard H. (1978). Bureaucracy as praxis: Toward a political phenomenology of formal organizations. *Administrative Science Quarterly, 23,* pp. 365-382.

246

Burns, James M. (1978). *Leadership*. New York: Harper and Row.

Chiles, Chester (1983). Comments on "design guidelines for social problem-solving interventions." *The Journal of Applied Behavioral Science, 19,* pp. 189-191.

Clegg, S. and Dunkerley, D. (1980). *Organization, class, and control.* Boston: Routledge and Kegan Paul.

Cohen, Allen, et al. (1984). *Effective behavior in organizations.* Homewood, IL: Irwin.

Collins, R. and Makowsky, M. (1978). *The discovery of society (2nd edition).* New York: Random House.

Cooper, Robert (1983). Some remarks on theoretical individualism, alienation and work. *Human Relations, 36,* pp. 717-724.

Cousins, Norman (1981). *Human options.* New York: Berkley Book.

Crile and Bunts (1971). *To act as a unit: The story of the Cleveland Clinic Foundation.* Cleveland, OH: Cleveland Clinic Foundation.

Dachler, Peter H. and Wilpert, B. (1978). Conceptual dimensions and boundaries of participation in organizations: A critical evaluation. *Administrative Science Quarterly, 23,* pp. 1-39.

Deal, T.E. and Kennedy, A.A. (1982). *Corporate cultures.* Reading, MA: Addison-Wesley.

Dewey, J. (1916). *Democracy and education.* New York: Macmillan.

Dewey, J. (1939). *Freedom and culture.* New York: Capricorn Books.

Diesing, P. (1971). *Patterns of discovery in the social sciences.* Chicago: Aldine.

Dubin, R. (1978). *Theory building.* New York: The Free Press.

Durkheim, Emile (1964). *The division of labor in modern society.* New York: Free Press.

Elden, Maxwell (1983). *Democracy at work for a more participatory politics.* Ann Arbor, MI: University Microfilms International.

Ellwood, Charles (1938). *A history of social philosophy.* New York: Prentice-Hall.

Emery, Fred E. and Trist, Eric (1973). *Social ecology: Contextual appreciations of the future in the present.* New York: Plenum Press.

Faucheux, Claude (1985). Leadership, power and influence within social systems. Paper delivered at the symposium on the *Functioning of Executive Power,* Cleveland, Ohio: Case Western Reserve University.

Festinger, L. (1957). *A theory of cognitive dissonance.* Stanford, CA: Stanford University Press.

Forester, John (1983). Critical theory and organizational analysis. In G. Morgan (Ed.), *Beyond method.* Beverly Hills: Sage Publications.

French, W. (1969). Organization development: Objectives, assumptions, and strategies. *California Management Review, 12,* pp. 23-34.

Friedlander, Frank (1984). Producing useful knowledge for organizations. *Administrative Science Quarterly* (book review), *29,* pp. 646-648.

Friedlander, Frank (1977). Alternative modes of inquiry. Presented at APA Conference, San Francisco.

Friedlander, Frank and Brown, L. David (1974). Organization development. *Annual Review of Psychology, 25,* pp. 313-341.

Frohman, M., Sashkin, M., and Kavanaugh, M. (1976). Action-research as applied to organization development. *Organization and Administrative Sciences, 1,* pp. 129-161.

Geertz, Clifford (1980). Blurred genres: The refiguration of social thought. *American Scholar, 49,* pp. 165-179.

Gergen, Kenneth (1982). *Toward transformation in social knowledge.* New York: Springer-Verlag.

Gergen, Kenneth J. (1978). Toward generative theory. *Journal of Personality and Social Psychology, 36,* pp. 1344-1360.

Gandhi, M. (1958). *All men are brothers.* New York: Columbia University Press.

Giddens, Anthony (1979). *Central problems in social theory.* Berkeley, CA: University of California Press.

Glaser, Barney G. and Strauss, Anslem L. (1967). *The discovery of grounded theory.* Chicago: Aldine.

Gorz, Andre (1973). Workers' control is more than just that. In Hunnius, Garson, and Case (Eds.), *Workers Control*. New York: Vintage Books.

Gould, Stephen Jay (1981). *The mismeasure of man*. New York: Norton and Company.

Gouldner, Alvin (1955). Metaphysical pathos and the theory of bureaucracy. *American Political Science Review, 49,* pp. 496-507.

Gouldner, Alvin (1976). *The dialectic of ideology and technology: The origins, grammar, and future of ideology*. New York: Seabury Press.

Gouldner, Alvin (1970). *The coming crisis of Western sociology*. New York: Basic Books.

Habermas, Jurgen (1970). *Toward a rational society*. Boston: Beacon Press.

Habermas, Jurgen (1971). *Knowledge and human interests*. Boston: Beacon Press.

Hare, P.H. (1976). *Handbook of small group research*. New York: The Free Press.

Harrison, Roger (1982). *Conscious evolution: Leadership strategies for a new age*.

Hartwell, Shattuck (1985). *To act as a unit: The story of the Cleveland Clinic*. Philadelphia: W.B. Saunders.

Hausser, Pecorella, and Wissler (1977). *Survey-guided development II*. LaJolla, CA: University Associates.

Hayward, Jeremy (1984). *Perceiving ordinary magic*. Bouldner: New Science Library.

Hearn, Francis (1978). Rationality and bureaucracy: Maoist contributions to a Marxist theory of bureaucracy. *The Sociological Quarterly, 19,* pp. 37-54.

Heider, Fritz (1944). *The psychology of interpersonal relationships*. New York: John Wiley.

Henshel, Richard (1975). Effects of disciplinary prestige on predictive accuracy. *Futures, 7,* pp. 92-106.

Hoffstede, Geert (1980). Motivation, leadership and organization: Do American theories apply abroad? *Organizational Dynamics, 4,* pp. 42-63.

Huizinga, Johan (1949). *Homo-ludens: A study of the play-element in culture.* London: Routledge and Kegan Paul.

Jenkins, W. (1973). *Job power: Toward blue and white collar democracy.* New York: Doubleday.

Jensen, Alan (1982). Professional approaches to organizational life. Unpublished doctoral dissertation. Cleveland, OH: Case Western Reserve University.

Jones, Gareth R. (1983). Transaction costs, property rights and organizational culture: An exchange perspective. *Administrative Science Quarterly, 28,* pp. 454-467.

Jung, Carl (1933). *Modern man in search of a soul.* New York: Harcourt Brace and Co.

Kanter, Rosabeth (1968). Commitment and social organization: A study of commitment mechanisms in utopian communities. *American Sociological Review, 33,* pp. 499-517

Kanter, Rosabeth and Zurcher, Louis, Jr. (1973). Editorial introduction: Alternative institutions. *The Journal of Applied Behavioral Science, 9,* pp. 137-143.

Keeley, M. (1980). Organizational analogy: Comparison of organismic and social contract models. *Administrative Science Quarterly, 25,* pp. 337-362.

Keen, Sam (1983). *The passionate life: Stages of loving.* New York: Harper and Row.

Kepner-Tregoe (1973). *Executive problem analysis and decision making.* Princeton, N.J.

Kierkegaard, Søren (1954). *The sickness unto death.* New York: Anchor Books. Translated by Walter Lowrie.

Kilmann, R. (1979). Problem management: A behavioral science approach. In G. Zaltman (Ed.), *Management principles for non-profit agencies and organizations.* New York: American Management Association.

Koch, Sigmund (1981). The nature and limits of psychological knowledge. *American Psychologist, 36,* pp. 257-269.

Kohlberg, L. (1964). Development of moral character and ideology. *Review of Child Development Research.* New York: Russell Sage.

Kolb, David A. (1984). *Experiential learning.* Englewood Cliffs, NJ: Prentice-Hall.

Kolb, David A. (1983). Problem management: Learning from experience. In S. Srivastva (Ed.), *The executive mind.* San Francisco: Jossey-Bass.

Levinson, Harry (1972). *Organizational diagnosis.* Cambridge, MA: Harvard University Press.

Lewin, Kurt (1952). Frontiers in group dynamics. In D. Cartwright (Ed.) *Field theory in social science.* London: Tavistock and Routledge and Kegan Paul.

Lewin, Kurt (1948). Action research and minority problems. In G.W. Lewin (Ed.), *Resolving social conflicts.* New York: Harper and Row.

Lewin, M. (1977). Kurt Lewin's view of social psychology: The crisis of 1977 and the crisis of 1927. *Personality and Social Psychology Bulletin, 3,* pp. 159-172.

Lukes, Steven (1974). *Power: A radical view.* London: Macmillan.

Lyles, Marjorie and Mitroff, Ian (1980). Organizational problem formulation: An empirical study. *Administrative Science Quarterly, 25,* pp. 102-119.

Mannheim, Karl (1936). *Ideology and utopia.* New York: Harcourt, Brace & World.

Marcel, Gabriel (1963). *The existential background of human dignity.* Cambridge: Harvard University Press.

Margulies, N. and Raia, A.P. (1972). *Organization development: Values, process and technology.* New York: McGraw Hill.

Marrow, Alfred (1968). *The practical theorist.* New York: Basic Books.

Maslow, Abraham (1968). *Toward a psychology of being.* New York: Van Nostrand Reinhold Co.

Matlin, Margaret and Stang, David (1979). *The pollyanna principle.* Cambridge: Schenkman Publishing.

May, Rollo (1969). *Love and will.* New York: W.W. Norton.

McHugh, Peter (1970). On the failure of positivism. In J. Douglas (Ed.), *Understanding everyday life.* Chicago: Aldine.

McCluskey, John (1976). Beyond the carrot and the stick. In Bennis, et al. (Eds.), *The planning of change.* New York: Holt, Rinehart and Winston.

Mitroff, Ian (1980). Reality as a scientific strategy: Revising our concepts of science. *Academy of Management Review, 5,* pp. 513-515.

Mitroff, I. and Kilmann, R. (1978). *Methodological approaches to social sciences.* San Francisco: Jossey-Bass.

Morgan, Gareth (1983). *Beyond method.* Beverly Hills: Sage Publications.

Morgan, Gareth (1980). Paradigms, metaphors, and puzzle solving in organization theory. *Administrative Science Quarterly, 24,* pp. 605-622.

Neilsen, Eric (1984). *Becoming an OD practitioner.* Englewood Cliffs, NJ: Prentice-Hall.

Ortony, Andrew (Ed.) (1979). *Metaphor and thought.* Cambridge: Cambridge University Press.

Ouchi, William G. and Johnson, Jerry B. (1978). Types of organizational control and their relationship to emotional well-being. *Administrative Science Quarterly, 23,* pp. 293-317.

Pasmore, William, et al. (1983). Introducing managers to performance development. In *The ecology of work,* Proceedings of the Sixth NTL Ecology of Work Conference, Cleveland, OH.

Pasmore, William and Friedlander, Frank (1982). An action-research program for increasing employee involvement in problem solving. *Administrative Science Quarterly, 27,* pp. 343-362.

Pasmore, William and Sherwood, Jack (1978). *Sociotechnical systems: A sourcebook.* LaJolla, CA: University Associates.

Pateman, C. (1970). *Participation and democratic theory*. New York: Cambridge University Press.

Pepper, S.C. (1942). *World hypothesis*. Berkeley: University of California Press.

Peters, Thomas J. and Waterman, Robert B. (1982). *In search of excellence*. New York: Harper and Row.

Peters, M. and Robinson, V. (1984). The origins and status of action-research. *Journal of Applied Behavioral Science, 20,* pp. 113-124.

Pfeffer, Jeffrey (1978). *Organizational design*. Arlington Heights, IL: AHAM.

Polanyi, M. (1958). *Personal knowledge*. Chicago: University of Chicago Press.

Quinney, Richard (1982). *Social existence: Metaphysics, Marxism, and the social sciences*. Beverly Hills: Sage Publications.

Reeves, Gene (1984). The idea of mystery in the philosophy of Gabriel Marcel. In Schlipp and Hahn (Eds.), *The philosophy of Gabriel Marcel*. LaSalle, IL: Open Court.

Rothschild-Whitt, Joyce (1979). The collectivist organization: An alternative to rational-bureaucratic models. *American Sociological Review, 44,* pp. 509-527.

Ruschhaupt, William (1985). The emergent themes in 1985. Unpublished paper for Policy 601, Case Western Reserve University, Cleveland, OH.

Sargent, Lyman Tower (1982). Authority and utopia: Utopianisms in political thought. *Polity, 4,* pp. 565–584.

Sathe, Vijay (1983). Implications of corporate culture. *Organizational Dynamics, 12,* pp. 5-23.

Schein, Edgar (1983). The role of the founder in creating organizational culture. *Organizational Dynamics,* pp. 12-28.

Schweitzer, Albert (1969). *The teaching of reverence for life*. New York: Holt, Rinehart and Winston.

Slater, P.E. and Bennis, W.G. (1964). Democracy is inevitable. *Harvard Business Review*.

Small, Albion (1905). *General sociology: An exposition of the main development in sociological theory from Spencer to Ratzenhofer.* Chicago: University of Chicago Press.

Smirchich, Linda (1983). Studying organizations as cultures. In G. Morgan (Ed.), *Beyond method.* Beverly Hills: Sage Publications.

Sproull, Lee S. (1981). Beliefs in organizations. In Paul C. Nystrom and William H. Starbuck (Eds.), *Handbook of organizational design (Vol. II).* New York: Oxford University Press.

Srivastva, Suresh (1985). *Executive power.* San Francisco: Jossey-Bass Publishers.

Srivastva, Suresh (1983). *The executive mind.* San Francisco: Jossey-Bass Publishers.

Srivastva, Suresh and Cooperrider, David (1983). Transcending the question of alienation. *Contemporary Psychology, 28*(3).

Srivastva, Suresh, Jensen, Alan, and Cooperrider, David (1981). The transfer of professional instincts into organizational activities. Technical report, Cleveland Clinic Foundation.

Srivastva, Suresh, Obert, Steve, and Neilsen, Eric (1977). Organizational analysis through group process: A theoretical perspective for organization development. In C. Cooper (Ed.) *Organization development in the U.K. and U.S.A.* New York: The Macmillan Press.

Staw, Barry (1984). Organizational behavior: A review and reformulation of the field's outcome variables. *Annual Review of Psychology, 35,* pp. 626-666.

Susman, Gerald and Evered, Roger (1978). An assessment of the scientific merits of action-research. *Administrative Science Quarterly, 23,* pp. 582-603.

Thayer, Frederick C. (1981). *An end to hierarchy and competition: Administration in a post-affluent world.* New York: New Viewpoints.

Thelen, Herb (1954). *Dynamics of groups at work.* Chicago: University of Chicago Press.

Thompson, James D. (1967). *Organizations in action.* New York: McGraw-Hill.

Tocqueville, Alexis de (1969). *Democracy in America*. Trans. by George Lawrence. New York: Anchor Books

Torbert, William (1983). Initiating collaborative inquiry. In G. Morgan (Ed.), *Beyond method*. Beverly Hills: Sage Publications.

Torbert, William C. and Rogers, Malcolm (1972). *Being for the most part puppets*. Cambridge, MA: Schenkman Publishing.

Vanek, Jaroslav (1971). *The participation economy*. Ithaca, NY: Cornell University Press.

Van Maanen, J. et al. (1982). *Varieties of qualitative research*. Beverly Hills: Sage Publications.

Vickers, Geoffrey (1970). *Value systems and social processes*. Middlesex, England: Penguin Books.

Watzlawick, et al. (1974). *Change: Principles of problem formations and problem resolution*. New York: Horton.

Weber, Max (1968). *Economy and society: An outline of interpretive sociology (3 vols.)*. Edited by G. Roth and C. Wittick. New York: Bedminister Press.

Weick, Karl E. (1977). Organization design: Organizations as self-designing systems. *Organizational Dynamics, 2,* pp. 293-317.

Weick, Karl E. (1979). *The social psychology of organizing*. Reading, MA: Addison-Wesley.

Weick, Karl E. (1983). Managerial thought in the context of action. In S. Srivastva (Ed.), *The executive mind*. San Francisco: Jossey Bass.

Weiss, C.H. and Bucuvalas, M. (1980). The challenge of social research to decision making. In C.H. Weiss (Ed.), *Using social research in public policy making*. Lexington, MA: Lexington Books.

Winnicott, D.W. (1965). *The maturational process and the facilitating environment*. New York: International University Press.

Wiesbord, Marv (1976). Organization diagnosis: Six places to look for trouble with or without a theory. *Group and Organizational Dynamics*.

Whitehead, A.N. (1929). *The function of reason*. Boston: Beacon Press.

Whyte, William F. (1982). Social inventions for solving human problems. *American Sociological Review, 47,* pp. 1-13.

Wilkinson, G.S. (1974). Social psychological dimensions of resistance to psychiatric innovations. *Psychological Reports, 34,* pp. 1083-1085.

Wilson, James (1982). *The romantic heroic ideal.* Baton Rouge: Louisiana State University Press.

Appendices

Appendix A

Introduction

LISTED ON THE FOLLOWING PAGES are the original 26 themes that served as the basis for building the survey of "Group Practice Ideology." The themes were identified after reviewing more than 300 pages of typed interview material. This material was analyzed quite *selectively*, looking only for quotes and examples that seemed to bear some relation to factors making up the ideal membership situation, i.e., commitment, critical control/ownership, normative consciousness, and community of competence. For example, the following quote was judged to portray material that helps explain a process of decision making that heightens the idea membership situation:

> (Quote) "I don't think the committee system is always the ideal way to do things and certainly it is often cumbersome. But what it does do is bring together people who feel a responsibility to the institution. Through discussions, they all become aware of the problems. They, then, feel a part of the process and they aren't being dictated to. And, being part of the process, they also learn more about the process and it leads to a higher level of intelligent action among all who work here."

This quote, then, became used (along with some other quotes) to create the following theme:

> (Theme #5) Members of the organization have the opportunity to acquire political skills (i.e., areas subject to discussion, debate, and choice) through participation on various groups and committees and by working through the informal system.

Each of the 26 themes were developed in this manner (for the actual "raw" data, the author has a 30-page report available upon request). These themes became the basis of the survey and even later were used to support the actual theory building process as described in the section on the appreciative methodology.

Emergent Themes Summary

1. There is an intense identification with a common goal that unites the group.

2. As a "partnership" of physicians who govern themselves, there is a high degree of shared ownership, involvement, and shared responsibility for the success of the CC. Also, the ultimate basis of authority resides not in any one individual or office, but rather in the group as a whole. It is a collective authority structure.

3. Collaborative effort is initiated through the widely held assumption that those in the group practice are competent and hold critical resources that need to be shared. Thus, interaction is facilitated through faith in others and high mutual respect.

4. Mutual adjustment through face-to-face interaction is used as a primary means for achieving coordination. Similarly, consensus through discussion is a primary method for reaching decisions.

5. Members of the organization have the opportunity to acquire political skills (i.e., those skills needed in order to participate in dealing with areas subject to discussion, debate, and choice) through participation in various groups and on committees, and by working through the informal system.

6. Inefficiency (in terms of time) is perceived as one of the consequences of consensus and collaborative approaches.

7. Collaborative achievement is supported through the group practice's collective reward system: a system where individuals and

departments benefit through the elevation of the organization as a whole.

8. A consensus system as it exists here can be conceptualized as a "negotiated order" marked by a high degree of face-to-face interaction, political processes, and negotiated agreements. The organization is a meeting ground between thought and action.

9. The organization is marked by a high degree of technological or task-based required interdependence. It is this "required" inter-dependence that provides the foundation for collaborative social relations.

10. One of the unintended consequences of a highly cohesive group practice is the development of boundaries reducing the quality of contact with other groups within the organization.

11. A collaborative, jointly operated organization is not for every-one. At the CC, there will be problems for those with a non-cooperative orientation.

12. Uncertainty is translated into opportunity. There is a high toler-ance for uncertainty that opens the door for initiative and taking responsibility. Uncertainty also fosters co-inquiry.

13. Within the relatively homogeneous group (i.e., a collection of individuals with similar basic values and similar prior training and socialization), there is a high tolerance for diversity.

14. The process of idea creation is essential to innovation and success at CC and, for those with ideas, the opportunities are perceived as endless. There is more concern at the CC with the power of ideas versus the idea of power itself. Ideas are given consideration on their merit, regardless of source.

15. The organization takes time and builds in mechanisms for ongo-ing review and reflection. Because reflection is a crucial phase in the learning process, the organization strengthens its learning

capacity through such widespread self-assessments. An assumption that seems to be present is that all members can contribute and have some responsibility to help the CC become more aware of itself and direct its process of becoming.

16. The candid recognition of talent is viewed as a prerequisite for success.

17. The members of the organization are supported in their extra-organizational activities such as national committees, national meetings, presentation of courses, etc. In this way, all members of the organization can be viewed as potential "boundary spanners" providing a necessary linkage to the CC's various environments.

18. Organizing is a means for accomplishing some common mission; thus, organizing becomes an ongoing experiment to find better ways of accomplishing the primary tasks. The CC is structured for adaptability and rapid change and is predictably unstable—it is the process of becoming.

19. The CC is distinguishable from many institutions by its high emphasis on excellence and high achievement. It is this emphasis on excellence that provides a basis for open inquiry into the actual progress toward the accomplishment of objectives.

20. Membership into the group practice requires a commitment to ongoing learning, both personally and professionally. Learning through collegial interaction is modus operandi. Failure is something to be learned from—not denied.

21. Full acceptance into the group practice requires one to learn about the CC and internalize some basic values through an informal, yet complex, socialization process.

22. The CC is viewed as a transforming organization that is in a relatively constant state of evolution. It is also an organization viewed as a tool for the release of human potential.

23. The release of human capacities is enacted through the strong "facilitative" role of leadership.

24. One of the costs of membership in the organization is the high emotional and personal involvement. It is as if people here live to work as opposed to the more traditional assumption of working to live.

25. While most bureaucracies are laden with obstacles, the CC is viewed as having minimal constraints. The two largest constraints have been identified as space and time.

26. To understand the basic norms of an organization, one can ask members, "What does it take to be successful here?" Such ideals, or standards, at the CC have been described as "leading by example; working collaboratively; viewing people as individuals; having an ability to risk; listening and communicating well; being respected professionally and nationally; knowing the institution well; being ambitious and idealistic; setting goals high; having a devotion to quality; having high interpersonal competencies; having political skills; having a team philosophy; being organized and innovative; being able to learn and discover; working hard; having scientific curiosity; maintaining the dignity of people; developing others; having endurance and physical stamina; understanding groups and committees; taking responsibility, etc."

Appendix B

Emergent Themes (ET) Study: Survey of Group Practice Ideology

Purpose

THE PURPOSE OF THIS SURVEY is to help staff members examine some of the important ideals of the organization (as espoused by organizational leaders) and to inquire into the extent to which the ideals are currently reflected in practice. Assuming that all organizations are shaped by the beliefs and visions of their members, then it becomes important to challenge them in a way that provides a springboard to the kind of future members' collectively desire to create. With this is mind, this survey has been designed as a catalyst for discovery and dialogue into some of the guiding ideals of this organization.[1]

Procedure

Given below are a series of descriptive statements related to the *physician group practice* of the Cleveland Clinic Foundation. For each statement, you will be asked to consider two ratings:

I. To what extent do you feel the statement *is important as an ideal* to be pursued by the organization?

P. To what extent is the statement actually *reflected in practice*?

1. As used here, an organizational ideology is a set of appreciative and provocative ideas, beliefs and assumptions that signify important ideals members feel their organization ought to live up to and be evolving toward. The ideological statements listed here have been drawn directly from studies with the leaders (i.e., Board of Governors and Division and Department Chairpersons) of the Cleveland Clinic Foundation. For more information on the methodology or content of these studies see: (1) the 1981 document on "Emergent Themes" and/or (2) the 1982 document on "The Transfer of Professional Instincts into Organizational Activities."

Each rating will be on a 7-point scale that will look like this:

1	2	3	4	5	6	7

To a *very little extent*   To a *very great extent*

Circle the number that best represents the extent of the characteristic being rated. Then, at the end of the survey, please add any explanatory or descriptive information that might be used to stimulate future discussions and understandings. It is realized that many of the statements are abstract and open to multiple interpretations, thus your added viewpoints and comments are especially important.

Special Note: While each statement may relate to the group practice as a whole, please respond to the items only as they pertain to your perceptions of *xxxx Division.*

Survey of Group Practice Ideology

I. To what extent do you feel the statement *is important as an ideal?*

P. To what extent is the statement actually *reflected in practice?*

In this group practice...

1. Members continuously work toward the clarification and regeneration of a meaningful purpose that unites the group.

I.	1	2	3	4	5	6	7
	very little					very great	

P.	1	2	3	4	5	6	7
	very little					very great	

2. There is a high degree of shared ownership, involvement, and shared responsibility for the success of the organization.

I.	1	2	3	4	5	6	7
	very little					very great	

P.	1	2	3	4	5	6	7
	very little					very great	

I. To what extent do you feel the statement *is important as an ideal?*

P. To what extent is the statement actually *reflected in practice?*

---

3. The ultimate basis of authority does not rest with any one individual (or set of individuals) based on position, title or expertise; rather, it is based on the consent of members as a group (i.e., if the group were mobilized around a basic issue, it would have the final say.)

I.   1   2   3   4   5   6   7
    very little   very great

P.   1   2   3   4   5   6   7
    very little   very great

4. Face-to-face (or small group) interaction is used whenever possible as the primary means for sharing important information and solving important problems.

I.   1   2   3   4   5   6   7
    very little   very great

P.   1   2   3   4   5   6   7
    very little   very great

5. Building consensus through discussion is the primary method of arriving at legitimate decisions.

I.   1   2   3   4   5   6   7
    very little   very great

P.   1   2   3   4   5   6   7
    very little   very great

6. Organizational politics are based on a philosophy that politics are more a matter of the fulfillment of the whole rather than a competitive balance of interests or containment of different groups.

I.   1   2   3   4   5   6   7
    very little   very great

P.   1   2   3   4   5   6   7
    very little   very great

I. To what extent do you feel the statement *is important as an ideal*?

P. To what extent is the statement actually *reflected in practice*?

7. Future plans and directions of the organization are based on free and informed choices of the members.

I. 1   2   3   4   5   6   7
    very little   very great

P. 1   2   3   4   5   6   7
    very little   very great

8. Members are committed to ongoing learning and discovery.

I. 1   2   3   4   5   6   7
    very little   very great

P. 1   2   3   4   5   6   7
    very little   very great

9. There is a climate of interaction whereby members feel free to candidly debate all sides of important issues. There is a high tolerance for diversity here.

I. 1   2   3   4   5   6   7
    very little   very great

P. 1   2   3   4   5   6   7
    very little   very great

10. The type of work done here requires people to work well together; thus, collaborative work relations (between individuals, departments, divisions, etc.) are pursued over competitive work relations.

I. 1   2   3   4   5   6   7
    very little   very great

P. 1   2   3   4   5   6   7
    very little   very great

I. To what extent do you feel the statement *is important as an ideal*?

P. To what extent is the statement actually r*eflected in practice*?

11. There is a high tolerance for uncertainty that opens the door for people to take initiative and responsibility.

I.   1   2   3   4   5   6   7
    very little   very great

P.   1   2   3   4   5   6   7
    very little   very great

12. The organization values and rewards a diversity of activities that members may be involved in (i.e., patient care, organizational management, research, teaching, national activities, etc.)

I.   1   2   3   4   5   6   7
    very little   very great

P.   1   2   3   4   5   6   7
    very little   very great

13. The process of idea creation is viewed as essential to the success of the institution. Thus, ideas are given full consideration on their merit, regardless of source.

I.   1   2   3   4   5   6   7
    very little   very great

P.   1   2   3   4   5   6   7
    very little   very great

14. Important decisions and actions are treated as experiments to be tested, reflected on, and learned from.

I.   1   2   3   4   5   6   7
    very little   very great

P.   1   2   3   4   5   6   7
    very little   very great

I. To what extent do you feel the statement *is important as an ideal*?

P. To what extent is the statement actually *reflected in practice*?

15. All members have an equal opportunity to become involved in the affairs of the organization and to help it become what it can potentially become.

I.	1	2	3	4	5	6	7
	very little					very great	

P.	1	2	3	4	5	6	7
	very little					very great	

16. Collaborative effort is supported through a collective reward system, a system where individuals and departments benefit through the elevation of the organization as a whole.

I.	1	2	3	4	5	6	7
	very little					very great	

P.	1	2	3	4	5	6	7
	very little					very great	

17. Members have a great deal of trust and confidence in the competence of those accepted into the group practice.

I.	1	2	3	4	5	6	7
	very little					very great	

P.	1	2	3	4	5	6	7
	very little					very great	

18. The organization has the capability "to ride the crest of the wave" and is constantly open to the newer and better things that come along. It is an experimental organization in a relatively endless state of formation and transformation.

I.	1	2	3	4	5	6	7
	very little					very great	

P.	1	2	3	4	5	6	7
	very little					very great	

I. To what extent do you feel the statement *is important as an ideal?*

P. To what extent is the statement actually r*eflected in practice?*

19. Members are ambitious and have a devotion to excellence.

    I. 1   2   3   4   5   6   7
        very little   very great

    P. 1   2   3   4   5   6   7
        very little   very great

    I. To what extent do you feel the statement is *important as an ideal?*

    P. To what extent is the statement actually *reflected in practice?*

20. The organization inspires the best in its members. It promotes the release rather than the constraint of member energies.

    I. 1   2   3   4   5   6   7
        very little   very great

    P. 1   2   3   4   5   6   7
        very little   very great

21. Members fulfill the responsibility of reviewing and regulating their own and others' work.

    I. 1   2   3   4   5   6   7
        very little   very great

    P. 1   2   3   4   5   6   7
        very little   very great

22. The leadership is more concerned with the development of others than the control of others. Thus, the leadership process is essentially an educative process.

    I. 1   2   3   4   5   6   7
        very little   very great

    P. 1   2   3   4   5   6   7
        very little   very great

I. To what extent do you feel the statement *is important as an ideal*?

P. To what extent is the statement actually *reflected in practice*?

23. There are minimal bureaucratic constraints because members are able to initiate changes when formal rules, procedures, or structures are no longer useful or relevant. There is nothing sacred or fixed about any organizational arrangement that shouldn't be questioned or changed once it has lost its usefulness.

I.   1   2   3   4   5   6   7
    very little   very great

P.   1   2   3   4   5   6   7
    very little   very great

24. The organization is a "partnership" of members who govern themselves through highly democratic processes.

I.   1   2   3   4   5   6   7
    very little   very great

P.   1   2   3   4   5   6   7
    very little   very great

25. Members realize that there are many organizational problems that have no permanent solutions. Thus, the quest for permanent dialogue among members has become more important than the search for permanent solutions.

I.   1   2   3   4   5   6   7
    very little   very great

P.   1   2   3   4   5   6   7
    very little   very great

26. Members are highly committed and feel convinced that their work in the organization is socially significant and meaningful.

I.   1   2   3   4   5   6   7
    very little   very great

P.   1   2   3   4   5   6   7
    very little   very great

I. To what extent do you feel the statement *is important as an ideal*?

P. To what extent is the statement actually *reflected in practice*?

---

27. Members make things happen through ongoing interaction and dialogue with their colleagues. Members do not need to be given "formal" authority in order *to begin* the process of proposing new plans or organizational changes.

I.   1   2   3   4   5   6   7
     very little   very great

P.   1   2   3   4   5   6   7
     very little   very great

28. The relations among members are marked by growth and development. Members realize that, by joining with colleagues here, they can become more than they would have had they chosen to work in isolation.

I.   1   2   3   4   5   6   7
     very little   very great

P.   1   2   3   4   5   6   7
     very little   very great

29. Information about what is happening is openly shared, leading to a widespread level of awareness among members.

I.   1   2   3   4   5   6   7
     very little   very great

P.   1   2   3   4   5   6   7
     very little   very great

30. The leaders have learned that, instead of dictating to the group, they need to listen to the group and work toward decisions that are sanctioned by the members.

I.   1   2   3   4   5   6   7
     very little   very great

P.   1   2   3   4   5   6   7
     very little   very great

31. Final Information:

    A. What department are you part of?

    B. How many years have you been with the Clinic (check one)?

        1. Less than one year ____

        2. One to three years ____

        3. Four to eight years ____

        4. Nine or more years ____

Additional Comments

1. Are there items from the survey you wish to elaborate on? List item number and additional comments below.

2. Do you have suggestions of other "ideals" that should be added to this survey?

3. What concerns you most about the ideals and practices as evidenced in this organization?

Appendix C

Contemporary (2020) use of:
Appreciative Inquiry: A Methodology for Understanding
and Enhancing Organizational Innovation

ORBH 513
Seminar on Prospective Theory
The Art and Science of Appreciative Inquiry as World Making

Spring, 2020
PhD Modules

Professor: David L. Cooperrider, PhD
Distinguished University Professor
&
Char and Chuck Fowler, Professor for
Business as an Agent of World Benefit

Covia-David L. Cooperrider Professor of Appreciative Inquiry
Department of Organizational Behavior
Weatherhead School of Management
Case Western Reserve University

"The most beautiful thing we can experience is the mysterious. It is the source of all true art and science. He to whom the emotion is a stranger, who can no longer pause to wonder and stand wrapped in awe, is as good as dead—his eyes are closed."

—Albert Einstein

"Portraiture is a method of qualitative research that blurs the boundaries of aesthetics and empiricism in an effort to capture the complexity, dynamics and subtlety of human experience in organizational life....it seeks to illuminate the complex dimensions of goodness... It is a palpable form, highly textured—what Jerome Bruner has referred to as 'life writing'."

—Sara Lawrence-Lightfoot

Overview

THE SPIRIT UNDERLYING THIS DOCTORAL seminar on human science inquiry is this: that qualitative research and theory building in the social sciences is one of the greatest adventures and significant vocations life can present. The impact of good theory, no matter how tiny or vast, can instantly move across our intimate planet and affect every human and living system in this interwoven, relationally alive, and reverberating universe. Ideas change the world. They assert that the truth of human freedom must count, and count affirmatively, in the ways we understand ourselves and our worlds. Ideas can be about life and they can be *life-giving* in the sense that they can inspire, open us to new horizons, and new depths. A new idea, especially the idea whose time has come in a prospective and betterment sense, does more than inform; it transforms. We've all experienced it. A single new understanding can change us deeply.

Through thrilling, creative human science inquiry, we are lured into life's compelling mysteries and, with that special "spirit of inquiry," we are often gifted, when least expected, with fresh questions that startle, interrupt, evoke. And, for those who allow themselves to "dare in scholarship," there seems always to be changes—transformed conceptions of life's potentials, surprising turns in relationships, decisive shifts in perspective, and articulations of generative knowledge in the service of building a better world. But the true gift of theory—indeed any good methodology of inquiry—is that it can tap into the adventure of ideas, empirical discovery, and the moral imagination to build better.

This course is about the craft of grounded and future-forming theory construction, of a way of doing research in the human sciences that exists, in William James' contrast, "not as a dull habit but as an acute fever." It is about what leading scholars, many of them inspired by appreciative inquiry, are now calling *research-method alive* (see Carlson and Dutton, 2011.)

The subtitle for this seminar on "The Art and Science of Appreciative Inquiry as World Making" grows out of a fusion of three exciting movements sweeping the social sciences. The first is constructionism's social epistemology, especially a second generation collaborative constructionism that is creating an era of radically new possibilities for dialogue across previously polarized paradigms, for example, the bringing together of qualitative and quantitative methods, dialogues between objectivist and interpretive practices, inquiries that are human-focused and ecologically attuned, and honoring the significant dialogues between frontiers in science and understandings from aesthetic, contemplative, indigenous, and spiritual traditions. In the sessions to follow, much will be said about constructionism's unique relational and polyphonic capacity—its profound respect for multiple voices—to bring out and connect the best across diverse paradigms.

But, for present purposes, here right now, there is a need to mention one contribution of even more significant dimension.

In a word it is the idea of "generative theory"—something that the prolific Kenneth Gergen proposed and first articulated in a classic article in 1978 in the *Journal of Personality and Social Psychology*, and which has subsequently been enriched in many writings, most notably in a major work, *Realities and Relationships,* published by Harvard University Press. Generative theory unites and eclipses, perhaps in the most inviting way ever, the artificial dualism separating theory from practice, something that heretofore has weakened the human sciences, keeping it from its full potential in terms of relevance, and on the periphery of society's great upheavals and imaginative opportunities.

What is the advance? In my view, it is the complete re-working of the concept of what it means to do good theory. Historically, the invitation to generative theory will be marked as a call that paves the way for elevating the craft of theory construction beyond the margins to the core of human science work. Hopefully, it will be recognized, not as a threat, but as an inspiring challenge toward more daring, purposeful, multi-paradigmatic and speculative writing. Hopefully, it will lead to methods courses that see and nourish each student's unique voice and his or her imagination and mind. Generative theory, as many are now realizing, has the broad potential to be an antidote to the inert, the secure, and the trivial in our fields. Good theory, in this view, is not just backward-looking, trying to standardize and simplify life or yesterday's patterns by stressing conformity to what we find. Instead, it is viewed as a rich cultural resource for creating, elevating, and shaping the world in a future-forming way to our most imaginative ideals and purposes. And, it takes the idea of interconnection and relatedness to heart in a serious, epistemological way. Instead of "cogito ergo sum," there is the invitation to *"communicamus ergo sum"*: "I communicate; therefore, I am." It is a way of saying, in a resounding way, that there is no longer room for excluding voices from our theory-building/world-making tasks. In the beginning, argued Martin Buber, is the relationship. Likewise, we are all theorists and, when judged against the call of our times, we need to draw on the entire universe of our collaborative and imaginative strengths. Especially for those intrigued with "engaged scholarship," we are invited to transfer our conception of the individual as center of human knowledge, to an understanding that centralizes social relationships carried out in language, dialogue, and conjoint discovery.

The generative theory perspective, as we shall see, is releasing extraordinary benefits in scholarship and practice. The key, especially for future scholars, will be in coming to grips with all the implications, opportunities, and new horizons of a decisive shift from a "correspondence theory" of truth to an entirely new standard that aims even higher. Good theory, if it is to really matter, is that which should be judged, not by its mirroring capacity, but by its overall anticipatory, expressive, and generative capacity.

> "*Generative theory* is that which has capacity to challenge the guiding assumption of the culture, to raise fundamental questions regarding contemporary social life, to foster reconsideration of that which is "taken for granted," and thereby furnish new alternatives for social actions."

The emerging story of generative theory from a philosophical point of view is neither simple nor is it complete. The "intelligibility nuclei" or its cross-paradigmatic stance deserves, in many places throughout this seminar, greater explanation than time allows. To be sure, the overarching purpose of this course is, in fact, more methodological; it is about the practices for constructing theory as future-forming and world-making.

The major strategy that we shall put forward for furthering the construction of generative theory emerges from a merger of two other stand-out approaches to knowledge, Glaser and Strauss's *Grounded Theory* method, and appreciative ways of knowing that are best articulated in our own work on appreciative inquiry and art and science of portraiture, is a grounded theory approach that blends empirical illumination with aesthetic expression. What emerges from the synthesis is the pragmatic core of our approach. This bringing together and interweaving—of appreciative ways of knowing, grounded portraiture, and generative theory—is, as we shall see, long overdue. If we succeed in bringing these together in a practical way, this alone will comprise the largest value of this seminar.

Readings for Our Course: From Grounded Buildup to Generative Breakthrough

This course is designed as a methodological practicum in future-forming theory building through qualitative methods. The process of good theory construction is portrayed as the discovery of theory from data in the real world of life (the grounded experience in human systems) resulting in the co-construction meaning, vision, of knowledge of consequence. The course asserts, in Lewinian fashion, that "there is nothing so practical as good theory"—it then focuses on the methods, personal disciplines, and empirical, aesthetic, and imaginative perspectives needed to bring this dictum alive.

Figure one is a framework of concepts and is offered below as a preview of what's to come in the course, building on the flywheel metaphor made popular by Jim Collins (2001) in his research study *Good to Great*. The future-forming or overall "prospective theory" building model below illustrates the journey's big components from *appreciative inquiry* and the *grounded portraiture buildup* all the way to the *generative breakthrough*. What the circle or flywheel means is that, no matter how dramatic the end result, generative outcomes (in this case, truly generative theories) never happen in one fell swoop. In building from grounded research, through weeks and months in the field and reams of data, emergent themes, early codes, and theoretical articulations, there is no single defining action, no solitary lucky break, or miracle moment. Rather, the iterative, grounded and then speculative theory-building process, being totally circular and iterative, resembles relentlessly pushing a giant, heavy flywheel, turn upon turn, at first totally strenuous and then building up to an interdependent momentum until a point of breakthrough. Edison famously said, "Genius is one per cent inspiration, ninety-nine per cent perspiration" and so, too, is theory-building: it's the result of hard work, disciplined and rigorous methods, as well as inspiration. With a flywheel in mind, here are six elements we shall explore in relation to the course's core question: "How might we elevate, enrich, and empower the disciplines and imaginative processes of future-forming theory?"

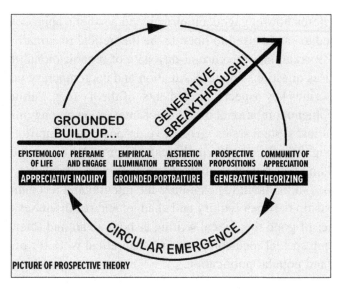

Prospective theory, as I define it through an appreciative paradigm of scholarship, is:

1. Theory inspired by life, it is designed to apprehend the best in all of life's fullest and best future possibilities while being grounded in the midst of the *extraordinary*, the *ordinary*, as well as the *tragic*;

2. Has the enlivenment and generative capacity to challenge the status quo and *open the world to new better possibilities* for life and living;

3. Articulates a future story of prospective possibility. It involves a proleptic merging of the ideal conditioned in the texture of the actual—e.g., vivid utopias that are right there in front of us— informing our future story for establishing the new and eclipsing the old. And all of this in the service of *advancing of a world of full spectrum flourishing*…a world where human organizations can excel, all people can thrive, and our living biosphere can flourish, now and across generations.

As a hands-on and practical guide to the craft of theory construction, the course:

(1) explores how engaged, empirical, and aesthetic approaches to knowledge can be used to liberate the theoretical imagination and mind; (2) examines the current-day state of organizational theory and raises questions about its situation and contemporary task; (3) describes key aspects, or elements, of theory (e.g., "units" of a phenomenon, relational direction of interaction among units, boundaries, system states, generative propositions, empirical and vivifying indicators and hypotheses); (4) provides a practicum in building theory that is qualitatively inductive, abductive, and grounded in the field; (5) examines the integral and resonant relationship between inquiry and change; and (6) discusses the qualities of good theoretical writing as both an art and science, including special focus on preparing theoretical work for professional and popular publication.

The course is filled with rich readings, a pilot project, and collaborative engagement—and depends on all of us as co-inquirers, colleagues, and makers of a generous learning community. The seminar is intensive. It requires careful reading of major works (plentiful readings) that deal with qualitative methods. Participants are expected to connect the issues raised in the seminar discussions to their own research interests through a semester-long project. In the project, each participant will select one significant (seminal or turning point) piece of qualitative research from his/her area of interest, and will systematically subject it to analysis in light of the course materials; e.g., uncovering its unstated assumptions, appreciating its beauty and originality, challenging its operant logic, and highlighting its strengths and weaknesses.

This course is designed as a methodological practicum in future-forming or prospective theory-building through grounded methods, both qualitative and quantitative. The process of good theory construction is portrayed as the discovery of theory from data in the real world of life (the grounded experience in human systems) resulting in the co-construction of knowledge of consequence. The course asserts, in Lewinian fashion, that "there is nothing so practical as good theory"—it then focuses on the methods, personal disciplines, and perspectives needed to bring this dictum alive. In this course, we will explore pertinent issues in qualitative research methodology and typical and leading methods of qualitative research applied in organization theory. Knowledge and skills associated with these methods will help you conduct rigorous and insightful qualitative research.

Course Readings

Note: the books with 3 stars*** are the core texts everyone will read.

1. Cooperrider, D. (2020). *Prospective Theory: Appreciative Inquiry—Toward a Methodology for Understanding and Enhancing Organizational Innovation.* Fort Myers Beach, FL: NRD Publishing.***

2. Creswell, J. (2017). *Qualitative Inquiry and Research Design. 4th edition.* Beverly Hills: Sage Publications.***

3. Carlsen, A. and Dutton, J.E., Eds. (2011). *Research Alive: Exploring Generative Moments in Doing Qualitative Research.* Sweden: Liber AB.***

4. Carlsen, A. and Sandelands, L. (2014). *First Passion: Wonder in Organizational Inquiry*, pp. 1-8. Beverly Hills: Sage Publications. https://journals.sagepub.com/doi/pdf/10.1177/1350507614533756

5. Cameron, K. and Spreitzer, G. (2011). *Oxford Handbook of Positive Organizational Scholarship.* Oxford: Oxford University Press.***

6. Cameron, K., Dutton, J., and Quinn, R.E. (2003). *Positive Organizational Scholarship.* San Francisco: Berrett-Koehler Publishers, Inc.

7. Collins, J.C. (2009). *Good to Great.* New York, NY: Random House.

8. Cooperrider, D.L., Barrett, F., and Srivastva, S. (1995). *Social Construction and Appreciative Inquiry: A Journey in Organizational Theory.* In D. Hosking, P. Dachler, & K. Gergen (Eds.), *Management and Organization: Relational Alternatives to Individualism.* Aldershot, UK: Avebury Press.

9. Davis, M. (1971). *That's Interesting: Towards a Phenomenology of Sociology and Sociology of Phenomenology.* https://prosemi-narcrossnationalstudies.files.wordpress.com/2009/11/thatsinter-esting_1971.pdf

10. Dutton, Jane (2003). Breathing Life into Organizational Studies. *Journal of Management Inquiry, 12* (1), pp. 5-19.

11. Lawrence-Lightfoot, S., and Davis, J. H. (1997). *The Art and Science of Portraiture.* San Francisco: Jossey-Bass.***

12. Gergen, K. (1994). *Toward Transformation of Social Knowledge (2nd edition).* London: Sage Publications Ltd.***

13. Glaser, B. G., & Strauss, A. L. (2009). *The discovery of grounded theory: Strategies for qualitative research (4th edition).* New Brunswick, NJ: Aldine Transaction.***

14. Strauss and Corbin (2014). *Basics of Qualitative Research: Techniques for Developing Grounded Theory (4th edition).* Sage Publications.***

15. Corley, K. and Gioia, D. (2011). Building Theory About Theory Building: What Constitutes a Theoretical Contribution? *Academy of Management Review, Vol. 36, No. 1,* pp. 12-32.

16. Gioia, D. A., Corley, K. G., & Hamilton, A. L. (2013).Seeking qualitative rigor in inductive research: Notes on the Gioia meth-odology. *Organizational Research Methods, 16* (1): 15–31.

17. Byron, K. and Thatcher, S. (2016). What I Know Now That I Wish I Knew Then: Teaching Theory and Theory Building. *Academy of Management Review. Vol. 41 No. 1*, pp. 1-8.

18. Seligman, M., Railton, P., Baumeister, R., and Sripada, C. (2016). *Homo Prospectus.* New York NY: Oxford University Press.***

19. Tsai, C., Chai, C., Wong, Hong, H., Tan, S. (2013). Positioning Design Epistemology and its Applications in Education Technology. *Education Technology and Society,* 16 (2), pp. 81-90.

20. Weber, Andreas (2008). *Enlivenment: Toward a Poetics for the Anthropocene.* Cambridge, MA: The MIT Press***

21. Weick, K. E. (1989). Theory Construction as Disciplined Imagination. *The Academy of Management Review, 14* (4), p. 516

22. Bennis, W. and O'Toole, J. (2005). How Business Schools Lost Their Way. *Harvard Business Review*, May Issue, 2005.

23. Grudin, R. (1990). *The Grace of Great Things: Creativity and Innovation.* New York: Houghton Mifflin Company.

24. Van de Ven, Andrew (2007). *Engaged Scholarship: A Guide for Organizational and Social Research.* New York: Oxford University Press.***

25. In her Cambridge University book *Intellectual Shamans: Management Academics Making a Difference,* Sandra Waddock (2015) spotlights the work of 26 scholars and shows how the spirit of appreciative inquiry and something of an enlivenment paradigm is associated, in almost every instance, with generative scholarship that makes a high purpose difference in the field and for the greater good. I was honored to be featured in the volume, especially pages 246-278, and it is a volume that's now being brought into many research seminars.

Assignments

Learning Paper #1. This is a short paper which should address the question: What is generative theory and how—what approaches, tactics, processes, or strategies—can the theorist use to heighten the generative potential of their work? Two options for approaching this paper include:

1. An exemplar theory: select a theory you consider "generative." What makes it generative? Examples? What does the theorist do that increases the generative capacity of the work? OR

2. Draw from several great theories, and write a paper, "10 ways of increasing the generative potential of theory building."

Note: organizational researchers are primarily trained in data collection techniques and the latest analytic tools, not the nuances of theory building. And many young or early professors are often warned that their careers will be compromised if they do not follow the norms of research precision, verification, and the general cannons of "ivory tower scholarship." And yet when one looks at the landscape of "scholarship with impact," it is eye-opening to see the list of prospective and generative theorists. Peter Drucker's work, beginning with his qualitative research at General Motors, led to his future-forming theory of management; Abe Maslow's study of peak experience and theory of the hierarchy of needs led to endless impact in our field; Harvard's Rosabeth Moss Kanter's work has been prolific, always combining grounded discovery, appreciative analysis, and future-forming theory; C.K. Prahalad's research on eradicating world poverty through business, mostly case studies, was used to leverage the building of prospective theory and rocked the business world...the list goes on: Jane Dutton's studies of compassion; Sara Lawrence-Lightfoot's research into the good schools; Clayton Christenson's studies and theories of disruptive innovation, etc. Every one of these thinkers invites us to fire up the imagination. Every one of these thinkers built theory from illustrative rather than definitive data and through combinations of mixed methods.

Learning Assignment #2. Let's assume you may be launching a major study and you want to begin the earliest pre-framing of your topic. In groups of six, we want to you coach each other using the "ladder of inquiry" we will present and apply in our seminar—a ladder that elevates a topic—until it truly "sings" and "speaks to you."

Before our group exploration, please read: Carlsen, Arne and Dutton, Jane (2011). *Research Alive: Exploring Generative Moments in Doing Qualitative Research.* Sweden: Liber AB. As you read, we invite you to consider this quote and series of questions below:

> "Don't ask yourself what the world needs. Ask yourself what makes you come alive, and go do that, because what the world needs is people who have come alive." —Howard Thurman

1. Next, in conversation with your learning group, ask yourselves and share:

   - How might I answer Howard Thurman's question in relation to my life as a researcher?

   - How do you/we come alive in how we do our research?

   - What do you/we look for in organizational contexts to see life?

   - Have we ever seen or experienced, in any research methods course, how to breathe life into our own theory-building work and a first step in prospective theory work?

2. Finally, ask each person to explore and share from these two questions:

   - "If human systems become or tend to grow into the direction of what you/we most deeply, powerfully, and rigorously study, then the question is: what kind of world do you/we want to help create through the scientific construction of reality?"

   - Now, become a sensitive listener to our world—the voices of

future generations, the call of our times, and the future that
is wanting to happen and ask, in relation to your passions in
research: "What's the future that is wanting to be born?"

Everyone once again shares—inviting individual emerging topics—as well
as a group brainstorm on elevating topics.

Write a five-page paper: begin part one of your paper by reflecting on the
Howard Thurman quote; then share your views and insights related to #1
(sets of questions) and #2 (sets of questions.)

Assignment #3. Pilot Project—Building a "Mini Theory via Qualitative
Research." After identifying a topic you are excited to inquire into, you
will do a mini-data collection—either through five in-depth interviews or
two periods of field observation.

Your assignment is to transcribe the interviews or complete a written set of
field notes, and distribute them to members of the class one week before
a session where, together, we all will do some grounded theory building
with you based on your data. In order to make the session come alive, it is
really important to hand the material to colleagues one week ahead of time.
Our experience teaches this is key. If this is not possible—to have the data
handed out a week in advance so we will each be able to do our prep—we
will simply cancel that class session. It is the basis of the session.

Paper #2. Writing your Theory OR, Doing a Deeper Dive on Creating
a Portrait of a Generative Scholar. Using your grounded data, you will
create a series of propositions, a mini-theory, intended to be generative
and prospective or future-forming. The paper should be short, no more
than 12 pages. The last page should be a reflection on the key learning in
the semester and the significance of the course for you as a scholar and
world-maker. Or you may choose to do a deeper dive on Paper #1. To be
discussed in class.

Preview of Sessions

(Typically whole day interactive sessions)

Friday, January

Friday, February

Saturday, February

Friday, April

Saturday, April

January 9:00–4:00: What is Theory? Theory Building?

1. The Adventure of Ideas
   - The high point moment of my career?
   - Who are we? What are our interests?

2. Course Overview and Introductions to:
   - Toward Transformation in Social Knowledge
   - Appreciative Inquiry and Positive Organizational Scholarship
   - Grounded Theory
   - Dissertation Examples: see Cooperrider, D. (2020) Prospective Theory: Appreciative Inquiry—Toward a Methodology for Understanding and Enhancing Organizational Innovation.

3. The Learning Assignments
   - Exemplary scholar of your choice with generative impact
   - Your pilot project

Prep for next session: read your assigned book and prepare a two-hour seminar module on it.

In addition: select a scholar that, for you, represents a generative theorist. Come ready to discuss their scholarship: what are at least five qualities or approaches that makes their work generative?

February 9:00–4:00

- Lawrence-Lightfoot, S. and Davis, J. (1997). *The Art and Science of Portraiture.* John Wiley and Sons.

- Glaser, B.G. and Strauss, A.L. (2009). *The discovery of grounded theory: Strategies for qualitative research (4th edition).* New Brunswick, NJ: Aldine Transaction

- Gergen, K. (1994). *Toward Transformation of Social Knowledge (2nd edition).* London: Sage Publications Ltd.

- Strauss, J. and Corbin, A. (2004). *Basics of Qualitative Research: Techniques for Developing Grounded Theory, 4th edition.* Sage Publications, Inc.

- Gioia, D. A., Corley, K. G., and Hamilton, A. L. (2013). Seeking qualitative rigor in inductive research: Notes on the Gioia methodology. *Organizational Research Methods, 16* (1), pp. 15–31

- PhD Dissertation Examples

- Development of Your Pilot Project

- Abram, D. (1997). *The Spell of the Sensuous: Perception and Language in a More-Than-Human World.* Vintage.

- Grudin, R. (1990). *The Grace of Great Things: Creativity and Innovation.* Ticknor & Fields.

- Cooperrider, D. (2020). *Prospective Theory: Appreciative Inquiry—Toward a Methodology for Understanding and Enhancing Organizational Innovation.* NRD Publishing.

Prep for next session: (1) Doing your pilot project interviews and qualitative data gathering & transcription of interviews of or writing of field notes—then send to colleagues in the class ahead of time. (2) Read your colleagues' data and be ready to participate in grounded generative and prospective theory building—with them.

April 9:00–4:00

- Theory Building & Courage to Create
- Collaborative Theory Building
- Theoretical Sampling; Open Coding; Axial Coding
- Theory Building & Writing for Publication
- Inquiry & Reflexivity
- The Spirit of Inquiry: What Good is Curiosity?

Davis, M. (1971). *That's Interesting: Towards a Phenomenology of Sociology and Sociology of Phenomenology*

Other Resources

- Use of qualitative software such as Atlas.ti. Download Atlas.ti demo software https://atlasti.com/ and configure it to your system. Download the guided tour of using Atlas.ti and read it through so you understand the logic and ideas behind the software (or try it out separately).

- Coding: http://www.youtube.com/watch?v=TUZpXEySp1U

- Corley K., Gioia Dennis: "Identity Ambiguity and Change in the Wake of a Corporate Spin-Off Administrative Science Quarterly, Vol. 49, No. 2 (Jun., 2004) pp. 173-20; 8Stable URL: http://www.jstor.org/stable/4131471

- You might want to watch a short presentation on grounded theory by Kathy Charmaz (the presentation starts around 7.22 so you can skip the start if you want) http://www.youtube.com/watch?v=zY1h3387txo

About the Author

DAVID L. COOPERRIDER, IS BEST known for his founding theory and research giving birth to Appreciative Inquiry or "AI" as it is now known around the world. Today AI's approach to strengths-based and life-centric—instead of problematizing organization development and deficit-based change is being practiced everywhere: the corporate world; the world of public service, of economics, of education, of faith, of philanthropy, and social science scholarship—it is affecting them all. Cooperrider is a Distinguished University Professor with two endowed chairs, including the Covia—David L. Cooperrider Professorship for Appreciative Inquiry at Case Western Reserve University's Weatherhead School of Management. David serves as an advisor to heads of state, governors, mayors, UN Secretary Generals, and CEO's throughout the world, including projects with five Presidents and Nobel Laureates such as William Jefferson Clinton, His Holiness the Dalai Lama, Kofi Annan and others. The recipient of "The Lifetime Achievement Award" in the field of Organization Development, the Peter F. Drucker Distinguished Fellow Award, and named as one of the nation's top thought leaders by Trust Across America. Cooperrider is author of over 20 books, among them the five-volume series on Advances in Appreciative Inquiry. Jane Nelson, at Harvard's Kennedy School of Leadership recently wrote, "David Cooperrider is one of the outstanding scholar-practitioners of our generation" and, for the opening of the new David L. Cooperrider Center for Appreciative Inquiry at Champlain College, Marty Seligman wrote: "David Cooperrider is a giant: a giant of discovery, a giant of dissemination, and a giant of generosity."

Are You Interested in Learning More About Appreciative Inquiry?

FOR HUNDREDS OF CASE STUDIES, articles, tools, research studies on Appreciative Inquiry go to **The Appreciative Inquiry Commons** sponsored by the David L. Cooperrider Center for Appreciative Inquiry at the Stiller School of Business at Champlain College together with Case Western Reserve University's Weatherhead School of Management. The Appreciative Inquiry Commons is at https://appreciativeinquiry.champlain.edu/ and the **David L. Cooperrider Center for Appreciative Inquiry** including its many workshop and training opportunities can be entered through https://www.champlain.edu/appreciativeinquiry.

INTERESTED IN FULL CERTIFICATION? For the Foundations In Appreciative Inquiry as well as full certification in Appreciative Inquiry and Positive Business and Society Change please see the Executive Education Center at Case Western Reserve University: https://weatherhead.case.edu/executive-education/certificates/appreciative-inquiry. If you are interested in contacting David Cooperrider's office just email DLC6@case.edu.

Made in the USA
Middletown, DE
24 April 2022